DECODING ADVERTISEMENTS

When I'm drivin' in my car
And that man comes on the radio
And he's telling me more and more
About some useless information
Supposed to fire my imagination
        I can't get no
        Satisfaction

When I'm watchin' my TV
And that man comes on to tell me
How white my shirts can be
Well he can't be a man 'cause he doesn't smoke
The same cigarettes as me
        I can't get no
        Satisfaction
        I can't get me no
                Satisfaction....

Mick Jagger and Keith Richard
from '*I can't get no Satisfaction*'

'The reader who wishes to follow me
at all must resolve to climb from
the particular up to the general.'

Karl Marx
Critique of Political Economy

IDEAS IN PROGRESS

Judith Williamson

DECODING ADVERTISEMENTS

Ideology and Meaning in Advertising

LONDON
Marion Boyars
NEW YORK

Reprinted in Great Britain and the United States in 2002 by
MARION BOYARS PUBLISHERS LTD
24 Lacy Road, London SW15 1NL
237 East 39th Street, New York NY 10016

www.marionboyars.co.uk

Distributed in Australia and New Zealand by Peribo Pty Ltd, 58 Beaumont Road, Kuring-gai, NSW 2080

Reprinted 1978, 1981, 1983, 1985, 1987, 1988, 1990, 1991, 1993, 1994, 1995, 1998, 2000, 2002
This enlarged edition first published in 1995 by Marion Boyars, London

Reprinted in 2002
10 9 8 7 6 5 4 3 2 1

A CIP catalogue record for this book is available from the British Library.

A CIP catalog record for this book is available from the Library of Congress.

ISBN 0-7145-2615-0

Printed and bound in Great Britain by Bath Press, CPI Group

CONTENTS

PREFACE TO THE FIFTEENTH IMPRESSION

I started writing this book in 1976, in a world plastered with glossy images and ringing with catchy slogans: a world where advertising encouraged us to create our identities through consumer goods and relate to one another through the language of our possessions. Over twenty-five years later, I am writing the preface to its fifteenth impression in a world which is, in that respect at least, remarkably similar. The ads on the following pages may seem as 'retro' in style as any film or fashion-spread of the 1970s: a reminder of how rapidly cultural images shift and date. But the process I set out to analyse through them has changed only in its intensity and ubiquity – and the need to understand it and challenge it is more pressing than ever.

Certainly ads themselves change all the time, both in content and style: they reflect social developments (more women behind the wheel, more men in the kitchen) and also the subtler shifts in media self-consciousness that are often labelled 'postmodern'. An increasing number of ads either use self-denigrating images or play at undermining their role (for example, the soft drink ad that claims 'Image is nothing – Obey your thirst') and it has become commonplace to assume that this shows advertising has become more sophisticated, its audiences more knowing, over the past few decades. Of course, the 1970s ads seemed more sophisticated and knowing than those of the 1950s. Each era likes to think it has moved on, and this is built into the very structure of advertising: ads must always appear up to date, as new products must constantly appear to supersede old ones.

But while they may look different now from a quarter of a century ago, ads still perform the same function, and in fundamentally the same way. Where once they might have shown a 'sophisticated, knowing' consumer using a product, now they may incorporate the 'sophistication and knowingness' into their own imagery: a tactic developed especially with cigarette and drinks ads, where picturing consumption is limited by law (see Chapter Eight). However, this is just another way of doing basically the same thing. Advertisements' role is to attach meanings to products, to create identities for the goods (and service providers) they promote: a process today described as branding. The fact that this has become one of the hot issues of our time shows that while advertising's basic purpose has changed little since I wrote this book, the context in which it is understood and discussed has changed enormously.

A marker of this change is the success of Naomi Klein's powerful book *No Logo* (published in 2000). Klein speaks for a generation growing up in what she calls a 'new branded world', where advertising has penetrated beyond the media into schools, sports and public life: where the use of logos means that every product can be its own ad, the Nike swoosh on a garment turning it into corporate publicity simply by being worn. This is a world where some children suffer desperately if they go to school without the right symbol on their trainers, while thousands of miles away, other children suffer desperately making them. *No Logo* is a passionate indictment of this situation: it charts the 'rage' of young people in the First World, at a parasitic corporate culture that 'steals their cool', while, importantly, it also investigates some of the labour conditions in the Third World under which corporations manufacture those 'cool' goods in the first place.

No Logo grew out of the anti-capitalist movement, and anti-capitalism has grown in part as a response to developments within capitalism itself. Consumer culture has certainly intensified over the last twenty years: in 1980s Britain and North America the deliberate 'rolling back of the State' by right-wing governments encouraged capital to increase its hold in the public arena, and the marketplace became the model for public as well as corporate institutions. Branding and logos now seem to be everywhere, and business is increasingly global: companies operating across continents become harder to pin down under national legislation, and the trend towards subcontracted labour releases corporate employers from responsibility towards their workforce, which can be treated as expendable.

All this happens, and it is morally wrong; and the emergence of a movement that makes its voice heard around the world saying so is utterly welcome. Back in 1976, although Marxists talked about capitalism, hardly anyone else did: in Western societies it was generally taken as a given, the backdrop to our way of life. Today we have international debate about globalisation, branding, the impact of capitalism on the very future of our planet – there is a public language available for opposing this politically unjust, materially exploitative, spiritually crushing system which is neither a natural nor an inevitable mode of conducting human affairs.

And yet, sometimes just saying something is wrong – even though it is – isn't enough. We need to understand how the system works: which is where theory and analysis play a crucial part. Anti-capitalism hasn't made Marxism redundant – it has made it still more necessary, as a theoretical framework that analyses capitalism as a dynamic, and seeks to understand the way it works. A Marxist perspective enables us to see capitalism's 'excesses' as integral to its structure: how could it not exploit its workforce, and still make profits? And Marx's notion of commodity fetishism has never been more relevant, in a world where relations between people increasingly take the form of relations between things.

These concepts are as topical as ever, and can help us to understand what we now call globalisation and branding – which might once have been called economic imperialism and marketing. Fashions in words change, often more rapidly than the phenomena they refer to: this can often provide fresh ways of seeing the same things. However, it can sometimes give the impression that the world is changing faster than it really is. An example is the rise of the word 'postmodern': once it came into use, it suddenly seemed we were living in a newly postmodern world – but what that meant, let alone whether we really are, remains a mystery. Similarly, branding, though definitely a more widespread phenomenon than, say, thirty years ago, is not a new one, though recent debates may make it seem so. A hundred years before *No Logo* was published, H.G. Wells wrote the fascinating (and hilarious) novel *Tono Bungay*, which charts the fortunes of a patent-medicine manufacturer building brand-identification through remark-ably modern methods of advertising and niche marketing. And, of course, the ruthless exploitation of cheap labour is not new either: it is just that the industrial slums are now more likely to be in the Philippines or Indonesia than in Manchester or Detroit.

So while we look for the changing elements in the world around us, we can also learn from seeing the structural continuities. And this is another reason theory and analysis are so valuable: they are tools that can be used and reused, as it were – this is in the nature of conceptual, rather than descriptive, systems. Two plus two still makes four, whether you are adding two apples or two tanks: any analysis of a consistent structure will hold true even as the details of its appearance may shift.

Which brings me back to the project of this book. My aim in it was to analyse the way ads work – not merely to comment on their content. The 'decoding' process was intended as a sort of dismantling of their mechanisms, to show how they convey meanings to their products. And while those meanings change all the time, the mechanisms don't: which is why a structural analysis remains valid, it still 'works'. The semiotic and psychoanalytic theories I draw on for this analysis complement a Marxist perspective: together they make it possible to understand the way things mean within our culture – the very forms of meaning: which are also, at a deep level, the patterns of how we feel and think.

Ideology is a very unfashionable word: in today's intellectual climate it makes the user sound like a Stalinist dinosaur. But it is a term linked with a body of theory that addresses contradictions and complexity, and investigates the political dimensions of our senses of self. Its falling into disuse suggests an abandonment of the attempt to understand those struggles with the status quo that are internal, as well as external to us; a reluctance to acknowledge that what we think and feel is not always one hundred per cent within our control. Yet without such a framework, how can we explain why someone may want to be 'cool' even as they attack the logos that 'make' them so? Or the difficulties people have giving up parts of themselves which they know perfectly well to be bad either for them ('smoker') or the world at large ('motorist')? Ideology – whatever we call it – mediates what we know, how we feel, and the way we live. And I believe now, as I did in 1976, that grasping the tools for understanding ideology and meaning in advertising can form part of the wider struggle for change, for the liberating transformation of ourselves and the world.

August 2002

FOREWORD

I want to say how and why this book was written: to give it a context. The introductory section to follow gives a basic outline of its content, and explains its structure and subtitle.

I first submitted this as a project for a course in popular culture at the University of California, Berkeley. It consisted simply of advertisements and a formal analysis of each one. But in the course of my analysis conclusions emerged which formed the basis of the theory which I present here. The book in its present form has been entirely rewritten and re-structured in terms of that theory.

But the reasons for its being written at all go much further back. I arrived in Berkeley with a bulging file of advertisements collected over many years. I had been tearing them out of magazines, and keeping them with a vague hope of coming to terms with their effect on me. As a teenager, reading both Karl Marx and 'Honey' magazine, I couldn't reconcile what I knew with what I felt. This is the root of ideology, I believe. I knew I was being 'exploited', but it was a fact that I was attracted. Feelings (ideology), lag behind knowledge (science). We can learn from their clash. We move forward as the revolutionary becomes the obvious.

This process can be reversed, however. When I looked at advertisements and wrote my Berkeley project, my conclusions seemed obvious and clear to me; they explained, *although they did not explain away*, my reactions to advertisements. But when I read structuralist thinkers, indeed, some modern Marxist thinkers, I found my project placed in quite a new context. It seemed as if people were getting excited about, and taking as unusual, certain aspects of structure and relationships. These are essential, but they are not new. Of course relations between things are important: of course systems are important.

Thus it seems that recently, the very obvious (for example, structure) has become '*revolutionary*'. This is in fact retrograde. We should be trying to see *new* things both in society and in ourselves, our own feelings and reactions. I could not have written this, theoretical though it has turned out in its final version, without that battle throughout my teenage years, and still now, between the desire for magazine glamour and the knowledge that I will never achieve it, that it is a myth. So what made me want it? A real need—but falsely fulfilled: in fact, sustained by its perpetual unfulfilment.

This is personal, because much of my book is impersonal. I value a theory and formal structure of approach precisely because it can be shared. Yet it should also be material and practical. I like to think of the title of this book as suggesting 'dismantling cars' or something—a sort of handbook. I am impatient with any theory of ideology which is not tied to anything practical, to the material factors which influence our feelings, our lives, our images of ourselves.

The personal context for this book, which I have given here, does not fundamentally differ from the wider reasons I give below for studying advertisements. Politics is the intersection of public and private life. This book deals with a public form, but one which influences us privately: our own private relations to other people and to ourselves. The ideology of interpersonal relations (the supply and demand of love, for example) is the subject for quite another kind of work. But these areas are influenced by advertising, and it is in them that the struggle against false consciousness is at once most bitter, and most concealed. This struggle does not take place in theory, but is every day all around us; however, to form a *theory* of advertising (one which I have since found 'works' for other ideological forms, television, film, etc.), breaks through the isolation of individual struggle. It can help to put personal reaction on a scientific basis, and its very impersonality is what validates the particular.

Because, for this reason, I believe that structural analysis and a clear theory of popular media are crucial to a political understanding of media, I must acknowledge my debt to structuralist thinkers. But I have used other people's ideas only as *tools:* I have taken the tools which have been useful in 'decoding' advertisements and rejected the others. I believe Marxists cannot afford totally to reject structuralism: as the subtlety of capitalism's ideological processes increases, so does the need for subtlety in our understanding of them. We cannot afford to let any tool that might be useful slip through our hands. This is not being 'eclectic' but being practical.

Having attempted both to locate my own subjectivity in this work and to place it in relation to current intellectual trends, I must point out that in its rudimentary form it is already over a year old, and is in no way a final statement. It is, rather, an attempt to find a shareable method of dealing with the ideology with which we are bombarded.

I would like to thank Katherine Shonfield and Leslie Dick for helping me out with some of the typing: Janet Gray, who typed the whole of the final copy: Gerard Duveen for finding the last two advertisements in the book and sending them to me in America: and Chris Hale, whose arguments kept me mentally alert and whose encouragement gave me moral support throughout the time I was writing this.

Berkeley–Brighton
1976–7

INTRODUCTION: MEANING AND IDEOLOGY'

'The process, then, is simply this: The product becomes a commodity, i.e. a mere moment of exchange. The commodity is transformed into exchange value. In order to equate it with itself as an exchange value, it is exchanged for a symbol which represents it as exchange value as such. As such a symbolized exchange value, it can then in turn be exchanged in definite relations for every other commodity. Because the product becomes a commodity, and the commodity becomes an exchange value, it obtains, at first only in the head, a double existence. This doubling in the idea proceeds (and must proceed) to the point where the commodity appears double in real exchange: as a natural product on one side, as exchange value on the other.'

Karl Marx, *Grundrisse*

Advertisements are one of the most important cultural factors moulding and reflecting our life today. They are ubiquitous, an inevitable part of everyone's lives: even if you do not read a newspaper or watch television, the images posted over our urban surroundings are inescapable. Pervading all the media, but limited to none, advertising forms a vast superstructure with an apparently autonomous existence and an immense influence. It is not my purpose here to *measure* its influence. To do so would require sociological research and consumer data drawing on a far wider range of material than the advertisements themselves. I am simply analysing what can be *seen* in advertisements. Their very existence in more than one medium gives them a sort of independent reality that links them to our own lives; since both share a continuity they constitute a world constantly experienced as real. The ad 'world' becomes seemingly separate from the material medium—whether screen, page, etc.—which carries it. Analysing ads in their *material form* helps to avoid endowing them with a *false* materiality and letting the 'ad world' distort the real world around the screen and page.

It is this ubiquitous quality and its tenacity as a recognisable 'form' despite the fact that it functions within different technical media and despite different 'content' (that is, different messages about different products) that indicates the significance of advertising. Obviously it has a function, which is to sell things to us. But it has another function, which I believe in many ways replaces that traditionally fulfilled by art or religion. It creates structures of meaning.

For even the 'obvious' function of advertising—the definition above, 'to sell things to us'—involves a meaning process. Advertisements must take into account not only the inherent qualities and attributes of the products they are trying to sell, but also the way in which they can make those properties *mean something to us.*

In other words, advertisements have to translate statements from the world of things, for example, that a car will do so many miles per gallon, into a form that means something in terms of people. Suppose that the car did a high mpg: this could be translated into terms of thriftiness, the user being a 'clever' saver, in other words, *being a certain kind of person*. Or, if the mpg was low, the ad could appeal to the 'above money pettiness', daredevil kind of person who is too 'trendy' to be economising. Both the statements in question could be made on the purely factual level of a 'use-value' by the simple figures of '50 mpg' and '20 mpg'. The advertisement translates these 'thing' statements to us as human statements; they are given a humanly symbolic 'exchange-value'.

Thus advertising is not, as might superficially be supposed, a single 'language' in the sense that a language has particular, identifiable constituent parts and its words are predetermined. The components of advertisements are variable (as will be seen in Part II) and *not* necessarily all part of one 'language' or social discourse. Advertisements rather provide a structure which is capable of transforming the language of objects to that of people, and vice versa. The first part of this book attempts to analyse the way that structure functions. The second part looks at some of the actual systems and things that it transforms.

But it is too simple to say that advertising reduces people to the status of things, though clearly this is what happens when both are used symbolically. Certainly advertising sets up connections between certain types of consumers and certain products (as in the example above); and having made these links and created symbols of exchange it can use them as 'given', and so can we. For example: diamonds may be marketed by likening them to eternal love, creating a symbolism where the mineral means something not in its own terms, as a rock, but in human terms, as a sign. Thus a diamond comes to 'mean' love and endurance for us. Once the connection has been made, we begin to translate the other way and in fact to skip translating altogether: taking the sign for what it signifies, the thing for the feeling.

So in the connection of people and objects, the two do

become interchangeable, as can be seen very clearly in ads of two categories. There are those where objects are made to speak—like people: 'say it with flowers'; 'a little gold says it all', etc. Conversely there are the ads where people become identified with objects: 'the *Pepsi People*' and such like. (See below, chapters 1 and 2.) This aspect of advertising's system of meaning is shown in Mick Jagger's lines above. The classifications of advertisements rebound like a boomerang, as we receive them and come to use them. When 'the man' comes on in one advertisement, the TV watcher (who, it is interesting to note, sees all advertisements as one, or rather, sees their rules as applicable to one another and thus part of an interchangeable system) *uses* the classificatory speech from *another* advertisement and directs this speech back at the screen. 'Well he can't be a man 'cause he doesn't smoke/the same cigarettes as me'. Advertisements are selling us something else besides consumer goods: in providing us with a structure in which we, and those goods, are interchangeable, they are selling us ourselves.

And we need those selves. It is the materiality and historical context of this need which must be given as much attention as that equation of people with things. An attempt to differentiate amongst both people and products is part of the desire to classify, order, and understand the world, including one's own identity. But in our society, while the real distinctions between people are created by their role in the *process* of production, as workers, it is the *products* of their own work that are used, in the false categories invoked by advertising, to obscure the real structure of society by replacing class with the distinctions made by the consumption of particular goods. Thus instead of being identified by what they produce, people are made to identify themselves with what they consume. From this arises the false assumption that workers 'with two cars and a colour TV' are not part of the working class. We are made to feel that we can rise or fall in society through what we are able to buy, and this obscures the actual class basis which still underlies social position. The fundamental differences in our society are still class differences, but use of manufactured goods as means of *creating* classes or groups forms an overlay on them.

This overlay is ideology. Ideology is the meaning *made necessary* by the conditions of society while helping to *perpetuate* those conditions. We feel a need to belong, to have a social 'place'; it can be hard to find. Instead we may be given an imaginary one. All of us have a genuine need for a social being, a common culture. The mass media provide this to some extent and can (potentially) fulfil a positive function in our lives.

But advertising seems to have a life of its own; it exists in and out of other media, and speaks to us in a language we can recognise but a voice we can never identify. This is because advertising has no 'subject'. Obviously people invent and produce adverts, but apart from the fact that they are unknown and faceless, the ad in any case does not claim to speak from them, it is not their speech. Thus there is a space, a gap left where the speaker should be; and one of the peculiar features of advertising is that we are drawn in to fill that gap, so that we become both listener and speaker, subject and object. This works in practice as an anonymous speech, involving a set of connections and symbols directed at us; then on receiving it, we *use* this speech, as shown in the 'diamond' example, or in the use of 'a little gold' to 'say it all'. Ultimately advertising works in a circular movement which once set in motion is self-perpetuating. It 'works' because it feeds off a genuine 'use-value'; besides needing social meaning we obviously *do need* material goods. Advertising gives those goods a social meaning so that two needs are crossed, and neither is adequately fulfilled. Material things that we need are made to represent other, non-material things we need; the point of exchange between the two is where 'meaning' is created.

This outlines and necessarily anticipates ground covered step by step below. By examining the *ideological function* of advertisements' *way of meaning*, Part I, 'Advertising Work', seeks to understand the meaning process: this is where structuralism has been influential and helpful. Part II, 'Ideological Castles', examines the ideological context in which things and people are re-used in that process to create new symbolic systems. These systems are an ideological bric-à-brac of things, people, and people's need for things.

The need for relationship and human meaning appropriated by advertising is one that, if only it was not diverted, could radically change the society we live in.

PART I: 'ADVERTISING-WORK'

'The *work* which transforms the latent dream into the manifest one is called the *dream-work*. The work which proceeds in the opposite direction, which endeavours to arrive at the latent dream from the manifest one, is our *work of interpretation*. This work of interpretation seeks to undo the dream-work.

The dream-work . . . consists in transforming thoughts into visual images. . . . And so . . . does the dream work succeed in expressing some of the content of the latent dream-thoughts by peculiarities in the *form* of the manifest dream—by its clarity or obscurity, by its division into several pieces, and so on. Thus the form of dreams is far from being without significance and itself calls for interpretation. . . . One cannot give the name of "dream" to anything other than the product of the dream-work—that is to say, the *form* into which the latent thoughts have been translated by the dream-work.'

Freud, *Introductory Lectures on Psychoanalysis*

Signifier, Signified, Sign

A sign *is quite simply a thing—whether object, word, or picture—which has a particular meaning to a person or group of people. It is neither the thing nor the meaning alone, but the two together.*

The sign consists of the Signifier, *the material object, and the* Signified, *which is its meaning. These are only divided for analytical purposes: in practice a sign is always thing-plus-meaning.*

We can only understand what advertisements mean by finding out *how* they mean, and analysing the way in which they work. What an advertisement 'says' is merely what it *claims* to say; it is part of the deceptive mythology of advertising to believe that an advertisement is simply a transparent vehicle for a 'message' behind it. Certainly a large part of any advertisement *is* this 'message': we are told something about a product, and asked to buy it. The information that we are given is frequently untrue, and even when it is true, we are often being persuaded to buy products which are unnecessary; products manufactured at the cost of damaging the environment and sold to make a profit at the expense of the people who made them. A criticism of advertising on these grounds is valid, and I would support it. However, such a criticism is in many ways the greatest obstacle of all to a true understanding of the role of advertisements in our society, because it is based on the assumption that ads are merely the invisible conveyors of certain undesirable messages, and only sees meaning in the overt 'content' of the ad rather than its 'form'—in other words, ignoring the 'content' of the 'form'.

That a 'content' of 'form' should be such a paradoxical idea draws attention to the assumptions inherent in the use of these words. 'Form' is invisible: a set of relations, a scaffolding to be filled out by 'content', which is seen as substantial, with a solidity of meaning. These connotations make the terms 'form' and 'content' particularly unsuited for my argument, since it is based on the assumption that the conveyors of messages are things—and significant things—in themselves; and that it is messages which exist in the realm of the ideal. So having introduced it only to make this clear at the outset, I am now going to drop the terminology of 'form and content'. Although the *word* 'form' and the *word* 'content' may usefully be used singly, as a pair they constitute a conceptual attitude which I find unhelpful in any attempt to engage with meaning as a process, rather than as the end-result of a process.

The terminology which I will use in place of 'form and content' is that of 'signifier and signified'. This is not a simple replacement, an updating of terms, but involves a total reversal of emphasis. Signifiers are things, while form is invisible; signifieds are ideas, while content implies materiality. Furthermore, while form and content are usually seen as separable and their conceptual unity is one of opposition (form vs. content), signifier and signified are materially inseparable, since they are bound together in the *sign*, which is their totality. What is *meant* by a sign, the signified, may be talked about separately from what means it, the signifier; but an understanding of this terminology involves the realisation that the two are not *in fact* separated either in time or space: the signified is neither anterior nor exterior to the sign as a whole. Therefore my use of these words has in itself a very particular significance: it emphasises both the materiality and the meaning of the signifier in any communication.

The role played by the signifier in creating meaning is shown very clearly in the following advertisement for tyres:

A1: The ostensible meaning of this advertisement is that Goodyear Tyres have a very good braking performance. The written message states this: 'That set of Supersteels had already done thirty-six thousand miles when I drove onto a jetty at Bridport, Dorset for a test of braking performance. We set our marks only 66 feet apart, and from 50 mph, those Supersteels pulled me up in half the Highway Code stopping distance (125 feet). And on that same jetty they still held a clean, firm line through a slalom—even after 36,000 miles of motoring.'

This is a rational message: it describes actual tests and results and gives a logical argument to show that Goodyear tyres are safe and durable.

Now look at the picture. The jetty is supposedly here as a test of braking power; it provides an element of risk (will the car be able to stop before reaching the end?) in the experiment, a convenient and yet dramatic way of measuring the maximum braking distance. It has a place in a rational 'scientific' proof, and its function thus seems to arise merely from its place in the transmission of the 'signified' in the ad.

However, the significance of the jetty is actually the opposite of risk and danger and it works in a way that is not part of the rational narrative sequence of the verbal ad; it functions in its second role as signifier on a completely different axis from that of the signified and cuts vertically through it. The outside of the jetty resembles the outside of a tyre and the curve is suggestive of its shape: the whole jetty is one big tyre. In case we need a mental nudge to make the connection, there are actually some tyres attached to the outside of the jetty, on the right hand side of the picture. The jetty is tough and strong, it withstands water and erosion and does not wear down: because of the visual resemblance, we assume that this is true of the tyre as well. In the picture the jetty actually encloses the car, protectively surrounding it with solidity in the middle of dangerous water: similarly, the whole safety of the car and driver is wrapped up in the tyre, which stands up to the elements and supports the car. Thus what seemed to be merely a

A1

part of the apparatus for conveying a message about braking speed, turns out to be a message in itself, one that works not on the overt but almost on the unconscious level; and one which involves a connection being made, a correlation between two objects (tyre and jetty) not on a rational basis but by a leap made on the basis of appearance, juxtaposition and connotation.

This advertisement shows how the signifier of the overt meaning in an advertisement has a function of its own, a place in the process of creating another, less obvious meaning. It has already emerged that this 'latent' meaning, unlike the open 'manifest' message, does not simply lie completed in the words, for us to read as a finished statement. There are three crucial points here. In the first place this 'meaning of the signifier' involves a correlation of two things: the significance of one (the jetty) is transferred to the other (the tyre). This correlation is non-sequential; the two things are linked not by the line of an argument or a narrative but by their place in a picture, by its *formal structure*. In the second place this transference of significance does not exist as completed in the ad, but requires us to *make* the connection; it is nowhere stated that the tyre is as strong as the jetty, therefore this meaning does not exist until we complete the transference ourselves. In the third place, the transference is based on the fact that the first object (the jetty) *has* a significance to *be* transferred: the advertisement does not create meaning initially but invites us to make a transaction whereby it is passed from one thing to another. A system of meaning must already exist, in which jetties are seen as strong, and this system is exterior to the ad—which simply *refers* to it, using one of its components as a carrier of value (in the case of A1, strength, durability)—i.e. as a currency.

The systems which provide ads with this basic 'meaning' material—a grist of significance for the ad mill—are what I call '*Referent* Systems': the subject of Part II. They are clearly ideological systems and draw their significance from areas outside advertising. But the way in which this material is used and ordered inside advertisements, and is made to mean, is the subject of this half of the book; in the course of which I hope it will be made clear that this process of meaning, the work of the *signifiers*, is as much a part of ideology and social convention as the more obvious 'signifieds'.

Therefore I have used the term 'advertising-work' deliberately, because of Freud's crucial emphasis, in understanding dreams, on the 'dream-work' that is the *system* of creating meaning.

I intend to start with an investigation of signifiers and their systems in ads.

CHAPTER ONE
A CURRENCY OF SIGNS

'A sign is something which stands to somebody for something else, in some respect or capacity.'

C. S. Peirce[1]

'That which exists for me through the medium of *money*, that which I can pay for, i.e. which money can buy, that *am I*, the possessor of the money.'

Karl Marx, *Economic and Philosophical Manuscripts*

Referent

Saussure says that with the word H-O-R-S-E, where the concept of horse is what is signified, the referent *is what kicks you. Thus the referent always means the actual thing in the real world, to which a word or concept points. The referent is external to the sign, whereas the signified is part of the sign. (However, the external 'reality' referred to by the collection of signs in an advertisement is itself a mythological system, another set of signs. These mythologies I call Referent* Systems:*(cf. Part II.)*

In A1 we saw how two things—an object from the ordinary world (jetty) and a product (tyre)—were connected. The jetty stood for a certain quality (strength), and by making the object and the product interchangeable in terms of this quality, its value adheres to the product. The intermediary object, the jetty, in representing a value which becomes attached to the product, is thus a sort of currency. Currency is something which represents a value and in its interchangeability with other things, gives them their 'value' too. It thus provides a useful metaphor for the transference of meaning; especially as this meaning is so intimately connected with real money transactions.

As a preliminary to this chapter I want to start with a look at colour in visual advertising: it provides an introduction both to my method of analysis, to the way in which most visual adverts function, and to various aspects of the use to which this functioning can be put. Although the colour cannot be reproduced here it is described in the analyses. The next six examples all use colour in a slightly different way, but in each case it is the basis for a connection or connections unstated by the verbal part of the ad, and sometimes quite— apparently— irrelevant to it.

[1]From Collected Papers: quoted by Umberto Eco in 'Social Life as a Sign System' in *Structuralism: An Introduction*, Paladin Press, Oxford 1973.

Go where there's still room.
Enjoy a screwdriver made with white rum from Puerto Rico.

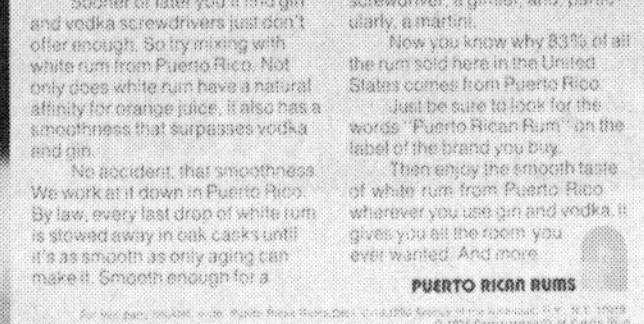

Sooner or later you'll find gin and vodka screwdrivers just don't offer enough. So try mixing with white rum from Puerto Rico. Not only does white rum have a natural affinity for orange juice, it also has a smoothness that surpasses vodka and gin.
No accident, that smoothness. We work at it down in Puerto Rico. By law, every last drop of white rum is stowed away in oak casks until it's as smooth as only aging can make it. Smooth enough for a screwdriver, a gimlet, and, particularly, a martini.
Now you know why 83% of all the rum sold here in the United States comes from Puerto Rico.
Just be sure to look for the words "Puerto Rican Rum" on the label of the brand you buy.
Then enjoy the smooth taste of white rum from Puerto Rico wherever you use gin and vodka. It gives you all the room you ever wanted. And more.
PUERTO RICAN RUMS
White rum screwdriver

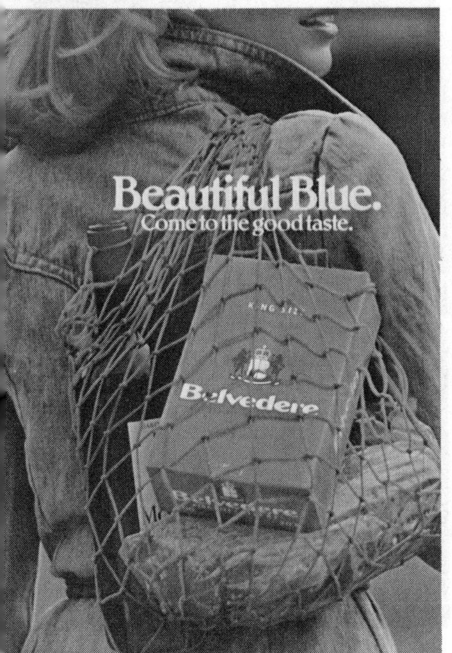

Beautiful Blue.
Come to the good taste.
Belvedere

A2 Colour tells a story: In this picture the colour 'axis' is the triangle of orange-gold, formed by the two glasses of screwdrivers and the sun behind the trees. This connection already suggests a warm, natural, pure, light quality in the drink, since it is linked to the sunlight. This gold colour is echoed in the golden corn which surrounds the couple, also suggesting something natural, ripe, mellow. The other colour connection in this picture is the white of the couple's clothes and of their bag. One would expect this white to be a reminder of the 'White Rum' but in fact it functions differently inside the picture. It helps tell a story, bridging time past and future. The white bag is already full of golden corn; this 'harvesting' is a piece of past consumption that hints at a similar action in the (at present undrunk) golden screwdrivers being placed inside, consumed by, the white couple. This hint is supported by the additional fact that the golden sun is just about to set, to 'go down' just as the drinks will. And so, as sure as the bag is already filled, and the sun is bound to set into the white sky, the drinks will, undoubtedly, end up inside the white people.

This 'story' gives a new meaning to the words beneath. The idea of there being 'still room' now refers less to the environment (although it obviously does this on a simple level—countryside, a field, is shown) than to the fact that there is room inside the people for the drinks. The theme is, in fact, *filling up*, like the corn in the bag—consumption rather than expansion. It is significant that the space shown—the 'room' in the 'intended' sense—is not particularly expansive and is almost entirely taken up with the three white, consuming figures (the man, the woman, and the bag).

In this way there is an almost total reversal of the meaning one might expect, just as it is the people who are white, the consumers, *not* the 'White Rum', which is in fact the thing that is 'going where there's still room'. A basic idea of space and extensiveness has been made to operate through the picture in a way that really '*means*' quite the opposite: enclosure, consumption.

A3 The oral connection: 'Beautiful Blue' is not, in fact, the most important colour in this ad. The blue cigarette packet merges into indistinctness in the blue of the denim, and the blue shopping bag. The colour that *does* stand out, poking through the string bag, is the deep red-purple of the bottle top, that exactly matches the colour of the girl's lips. Significantly, these are all that is shown of her face: nothing else in it matters, only the mouth, the means of oral consumption. The bottle and the mouth are joined by colour as clearly as if there were an arrow from one to the other. There is an obviously sexual suggestion here: however, the connection of bottle and mouth is a parallel for that of cigarette and mouth, which is the subject of the ad. The important word in the ad is 'taste': this is the theme of the *picture* and the crucial element in selling cigarettes.

A4

A4 Connecting an object with an object: This is perfectly simple: the colours of the cigarette packet are exactly those of the cup of coffee—white and maroon; and there is even a hint of gold on the rim of the packet's lid, matching the rim of the cup and saucer. The assumption here is that because the containers are the same (in terms of colour) the products have the same qualities: here, primarily mildness, though also a slight suggestion of richness. The cup of coffee acts as an 'objective correlative' (cf. section b) for the quality invoked.

A5 Connecting an object and a world: Here, the colours—black and white, with a touch of silver—and also the shapes—rectangular, streamlined—connect the cigarette packet to what the ad itself describes as a whole 'world': 'the world of Lambert and Butler'. The visual link between the packet and the world is exaggeratedly apparent: literally everything in the room is black and white and geometrical. However, as the two containers were compared in the last example, here also the correlated objects, packet and world, are in fact containers; the parallel of the cigarettes being, here, not coffee (in matching cup) but people (in matching room). The people are the contents of the room just as are the cigarettes of the packet. Thus the words can be read as relating directly to the people; they are obviously terms usually applied to people and *not* things, yet here, in using them *about* things, they are equating these with people: 'The first of a new generation of distinguished cigarettes [/people] . . . with a quality and style that sets them apart from other cigarettes [/people].' So here the colour correlation brings explicitly into focus a link between the people and the cigarettes that was implicit in the words chosen. There is, however, another sort of reversal here as the packet of cigarettes is, supposedly, an accessory to the distinguished, stylish world depicted, fitting into it visually by colour and style; yet, in naming the *world* after the *cigarettes* ('the world of Lambert and Butler'), and in greatly exaggerating the features of the cigarette box in this physical world, we see that the world and the people are actually an accessory of the product, and not the other way round. Instead of the product being created out of a need in the world, it creates its own world, an exaggerated reflection of itself.

A6 Connecting the object and a person: The product is a whole kitchen, yet here again, the person – a woman – has been made to match it. Her white clothes immediately link her to the slightly open cupboard, whose interior is the only other patch of white in the room. This gives a suggestion of availability. The woman's skin is precisely the same colour as the eggs. Her hair matches the cupboards. Again, we see that while the kitchen is meant to reflect *her*, she is in fact merely an object in the kitchen like one of the copper pans or the eggs or pieces of French bread. No wonder she looks so uncomfortable in it.

A5

A6

A7 The retinted world of the advertisement: Finally, a straightforward example just to illustrate the wide use and significance of colour correlations: the product and the world and the woman (the consumer) are all reduced to just two colours (gold and brown)—a typical manipulation or restatement of the world to link it to the two-dimensionality of advertising. This shows very clearly what has been seen in all these ads: a selecting of certain elements, things or people from the ordinary world, and then a rearranging and altering them in terms of a product's myth to create a new world, the world of the advertisement. This is the essence of all advertising: components of 'real' life, our life, are used to speak a new language, the advertisement's. Its language, its terms (here, gold and brown; the 'bronze lustre' message), *are* the myth; for as we have seen, they are too full of coincidence, of colour co-ordination, to be real. The very means of expression (as shown by colour, in this case) is the myth.

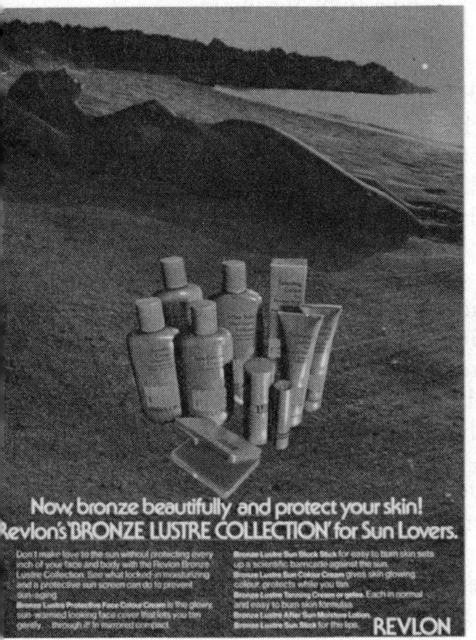

7

Use of colour is simply a *technique*, used primarily in pictorial advertising, to make correlations between a product and other things. Since this book is based on magazine advertisements which are more easily reproduced than those in the cinema or on TV, I have included analyses of ads A2–A7 simply to alert the reader to this technique. The use of colour is not significant in itself; it is the significance of the correlation it makes that forms the basis of my theory. It is important not to confuse the particular properties of the technological medium with the generic properties of advertisements. On the screen, for example, connections are made by cutting, by the reverse field technique (where facing fields of vision are shown alternately), and so on. There is an advertisement for chocolate in cinema intermissions where a girl jumps upwards into the air, and then there is a cut to a bar of chocolate leaping upwards—so that the *movement* is continuous, although the objects are different. The cutting here fills the same correlating function as colour in the preceding ads; what is important is that ads in all media make these connections, *through formal techniques*, not on the level of the overt signified but via the signifiers.

Having established with these examples that such connections are made, I now embark on my theory of *why* they are made, and the significance of *how* they are made.

(*a*) *Differentiation*

There is very little real difference between brands of product within any category, such as detergents, margarine, paper towels and so on. Therefore it is the first function of an advertisement to *create* a differentiation between one particular product and others in the same category. It does this by providing the product with an 'image'; this image only succeeds in differentiating between products in so far as *it* is part of a system of differences. The identity of anything depends more on what it is *not* than what it is, since boundaries are primarily distinctions: and there are no 'natural' distinctions between most products. This can be seen by the fact that a *group* of products will sometimes be marketed with the same 'image', in a set or 'range' (cf. All)—these usually have names, like 'Maybelline' or 'Spring Bouquet' etc.: the limits of identity are chosen arbitrarily, it is clear, because in other cases two identical products from the very same manufacturer will be given different names and different images. If two different bottles of cleansing milk can have the same name—'Outdoor girl' or suchlike, but a third, apparently similar, can appear with a different name and therefore with supposedly different properties, it immediately becomes apparent that there are no logical boundaries between most products. Surf and Daz essentially contain the same chemicals. Obviously there *are* products with special qualities or particular uses, but these do not usually need extensive advertising campaigns: the bulk of advertising covers exactly the areas where goods are the same: cigarettes, cornflakes, beer, soap.

I am taking a group of perfume advertisements—two of which come from the same manufacturer: these provide a good example of the creation of 'images' since perfumes *can* have no particular significance. This is a type of ad which can give no real information about the product (what information can be given about a smell?) so that the function of differentiation rests totally on making a connection with an image drawn from outside the ad world.

8

A8: Catherine Deneuve's face and the Chanel bottle are not linked by any narrative, simply by juxtaposition: but there is not supposed to be any *need* to link them directly, they are as it were in apposition in the grammar of the ad, placed together in terms of an *assumption* that they have the same meaning, although the connection is really a random one. For the face and the bottle are not inherently connected: there is no link between Catherine Deneuve *in herself* and Chanel No. 5: but the link is in terms of what Catherine Deneuve's face *means to us*, for this is what Chanel No. 5 is trying to mean to us, too. The advertisement presents this transference of meaning to us as a *fait accompli*, as though it were simply presenting two objects with the same meaning, but in fact it is only *in* the advertisement that this transference takes place. Chanel No. 5 only has the 'meaning' or image that it shares with Catherine Deneuve by having become associated with Catherine Deneuve through this very advertisement. So what Catherine Deneuve's face means to us in the world of magazines and films, Chanel No. 5 seeks to mean and comes to mean in the world of consumer goods. The ad is using another already existing mythological language or sign system, and appropriating a relationship that exists in that system between signifier (Catherine Deneuve) and signified (glamour, beauty) to speak of its product in terms of the same relationship; so that the perfume can be substituted for Catherine Deneuve's face and can also be made to signify glamour and beauty.

Using the structure of one system in order to give structure to another, or to translate the structure of another, is a process which must involve an intermediate structure, a system of systems or 'meta-system' at the point where the translation takes place: this is the advertisement. Advertisements are constantly translating between systems of meaning, and therefore constitute a vast meta-system where values from different areas of our lives are made interchangeable.

Thus the work of the advertisement is not to invent a meaning for No. 5, but to translate meaning for it by means of a sign system we already know. It is only because Catherine Deneuve has an 'image', a significance in one sign system, that she can be used to create a new system of significance relating to perfumes. If she were not a film star and famous for her chic type of French beauty, if she did not *mean* something to us, the link made between her face and the perfume would be meaningless. So it is not her face as such, but its position in a system of signs where it signifies flawless French beauty, which makes it useful as a piece of linguistic currency to sell Chanel.

The system of signs from which the product draws its image is a *referent system* in that the sign lifted out of it and placed in the ad (in this case, Catherine Deneuve's face) *refers back to it*. It is not enough simply to know who Catherine Deneuve is: this will not help you to understand the ad. Someone from another culture who knew that Catherine Deneuve was a model and film star would still not understand the significance of her image here, because they would not have access to the referent system as a whole. And it is only by referring back to this system as a system of *differences* that the sign can function: it is hollow of meaning in itself, its signified is only a distinction rather than a 'content'. Only the form and structure of the referent system are appropriated by the advertisement system; it is the relationship and distinction between parts, rather than the parts themselves, that make an already-structured external system so valuable to advertising. The links made between elements from a referent system and products arise from the *place* these elements have in the whole system rather than from their inherent qualities. Thus Catherine Deneuve has significance only in that she is not, for example, Margaux Hemingway.

A

The Fabulous
Babe
Introducing Babe,
a fragrance so fresh, so natural,
Faberge named it just for you.

A9 Babe: The 'image' of this ad derives its impact from the existence of precisely such ads as A8, as it is able to 'kick off' against the more sedate Catherine Deneuve image and others like it. This new perfume, 'Babe', has been launched in a campaign using the new 'discovery' Margaux Hemingway. The significance of her novelty, youth and 'Tomboy' style, which has value only *in relation* to the more typically 'feminine' style usually connected with modelling, is carried over to the perfume: which is thus signified as new and 'fresh', in relation to other established perfumes. There would be no significance at all in the fact that Margaux Hemingway is wearing a karate outfit and has her hair tied back to look almost like a man's, were it not that *other* perfume ads show women wearing pretty dresses and with elaborately styled hair. The meaning is not, however, generated *inside* the advertisement system: there is a meaning in terms of 'women's liberation' and 'breaking conventions' in a model's having a tough, 'liberated' image (in one TV ad for 'Babe', Margaux Hemingway mends the car while her boyfriend watches) rather than a passive, 'feminine' one. In the widest sphere of meaning which the ad draws on, even outside modelling and images, the meaning still depends on a contrast, since the very idea of women doing karate is only significant because most women do *not* and have not done anything of the sort. (See Chapter 8.)

So this advertisement uses the 'Margaux Hemingway' image, *which itself depends for its significance on not being Catherine Deneuve's image* to give 'Babe' a distinct place in the inventory of perfumes, emphasising its novelty (its *not being like* what has gone before) and its difference from all the others. It uses a contrast made in social terms, 'feminine' vs. 'liberated', as signified by two models, to make a contrast between products.

In the mythological system of fashion and publicity Catherine Deneuve and Margaux Hemingway are mutually differentiated and can only have value as signs in relation to each other: as Saussure says: 'in all cases, then, we discover not *ideas* given in advance but *values* emanating from the system. When we say that these values correspond to concepts, it is understood that these concepts are purely differential, not positively defined by their content but negatively defined by their relation with other terms of the system. Their most precise characteristic is that they are what the others are not.'[1] Thus with Catherine Deneuve and Margaux Hemingway it is the *difference* between their significances (taking them not as women but as signs, for this is what they are in this context) that makes them valuable in advertising. Advertisements appropriate the formal relations of pre-existing systems of differences. They use distinctions existing in social mythologies to create distinctions between products: this seems like the reverse of 'totemism', where *things* are used to differentiate groups of people: however the differentiating process in advertisements works in both directions simultaneously. I have only unravelled the elements of this process in order to make the discussion of them clearer, focusing here on the differentiating of products, while 'totemism', differentiating between people, is discussed in the next chapter.

[1]Saussure, *Course in General Linguistics*, quoted in *Saussure* by Jonathan Culler, Fontana, 1976, p. 26.

The basis of advertising's use of differences in other systems is a simple equation of parallel relations: Catherine Deneuve is to Margaux Hemingway as 'No. 5' is to 'Babe'. Thus the original pattern is like this:

$$\begin{array}{ccc} \text{C.D.} & \neq & \text{M.H.} \\ & \downarrow & \\ \text{No. 5} & \neq & \text{Babe} \end{array}$$

and the link is in the relationship, the 'is not' itself.

There is even an interesting subdivision within the Chanel range itself.

A10

A10: This image is half-way between Catherine Deneuve's and Margaux Hemingway's. The woman is 'witty, confident' (therefore the *product* is 'outspoken'—a typical piece of anthropomorphism) yet still 'devastatingly feminine'. It is important for Chanel to distinguish between No. 5 and No. 19; and the difference between the 'classical' feminine style of Catherine Deneuve and the outspoken yet 'feminine' (not into karate yet by a long way) model, creates this distinction. Yet at the same time, both Chanel products must be given a different aura from other manufacturers' products, and they are alike in having a 'feminine' very 'French' image, while Margaux Hemingway in the 'Babe' ad is younger, American, more 'way out'.

A further feature of the differentiation between products is that as already mentioned, they may be given an identity not only singly but in groups: Catherine Deneuve stands for a whole variety of products, all linked by the name 'No. 5' and her image.

A11: This is a perfect example of reversed 'totemism'; a *person*, Catherine Deneuve (or rather her image, what she signifies) is used as the binding symbol for a group of disparate things. She is the focus of their identity: so the difference between a perfume and a 'milk bath' is dissolved while a distinction between that perfume and another by the same manufacturer, is emphasised. This shows to some extent the arbitrariness of groups of identity in advertising. Things of different *kinds* are given the same meaning here, while similar things, perfumes, are given separate images.

It is the differences which are the connections; however, the ad system did not originally create these differences, but derived them from the structure of the referent system, by connecting the two.

A11

(*b*) *The Finished Connection: An 'Objective Correlative'*

The result of connecting two systems in the way shown above is that the links originally made, or rather whose logical basis exists, in terms of relationships, very soon take on an 'objective' or independent status and exist not as parts within a system but on their own:

$$\begin{array}{ccc} \text{C.D.} & (\neq) & \text{M.H.} \\ \| & & \| \\ \text{No. 5} & (\neq) & \text{Babe} \end{array}$$

Obviously, this 'result' does not take place temporally *after* the first connection as I have implied: I am simply trying to undo the logic of the advertisement's meaning process. And while the *logic* of the system, from which it derives its meaning, lies in the differences only (nobody would bother to find and push an 'image' for a product that was the only one of its kind on the market), the *appearance* of the system is one of 'logical' connections and similarities. After a while, we just start to connect Catherine Deneuve with Chanel and this takes on a sort of inevitability that seems to give the link status in some 'real' or 'natural' order. This is true of all ads but especially in those which claim to be either natural or scientific (in either case = objective), since both 'Nature' and 'Science' have in our society, or rather in its ideology, an objective status. ('Nature' and 'Science' will be discussed under 'Referent Systems' in Part II.) Thus once again we see that the *form* of advertisements is a part of ideology, and involves a false assumption which is the root of all ideology, namely that because things are as they are (in this case, because certain things are *shown* as connected in ads, placed together etc.), this state of affairs is somehow natural, and must 'make sense' simply because it exists. So when advertisements put two things side by side so that they co-exist, we do not question the sense of it. The form of advertisements, and their process of meaning through our acceptance of implications in that form, constitute an important part of ideology. Non-senses (the illogical juxtaposition of, say, a face and a bottle) become invisible—which is why it is important to state what may seem very basic, and once seen, very obvious, in this field; and sense is assumed simply on the basis of *facts*, that magical word whose original meaning is merely 'things already done'. It is certainly a fact that Catherine Deneuve's face *has been connected* with a bottle of scent, but that does not mean that it *is* (logically) connected with it. But the ideology embedded in *form* is the hardest of all to see. This is why it is important to emphasise *process*, as it undoes the *fait accompli*.

Images, ideas or feelings, then, become attached to certain products, by being transferred from signs out of other systems (things or people with 'images') *to* the products, rather than originating in them. This intermediary object or person is bypassed in our perception; although it is what gives the product its meaning, we are supposed to see that meaning as already there, and we rarely notice that the correlating object and the product have no inherent similarity, but are only placed together (hence the significance of form). So a product and an image/emotion become linked in our minds, while the process of this linking is unconscious.

However, a linking of the internal, thoughts and feelings, with something external and 'objective' is a crucial feature in any creation of meaning (a myth) and the need for some such connection is a basic one. It has been the function of art to make this sort of connection, and to bridge the Romantic abyss between subjective and objective, personal and universal: 'art' seems to elevate feelings or ideas that we may have experienced personally, to a plane where they appear to lose their personal quality and take on an 'objective' meaning, independent of any subject. T. S. Eliot describes this 'linking' or correlating aspect of art, as an 'objective correlative': 'The only way of expressing emotion in the form of art is by finding an "objective correlative": in other words, *a set of objects*, a situation, a chain of events, which shall be the formula of that particular emotion; such that when the external facts, which must terminate in sensory experience, are given, the emotion is immediately evoked.'[1]

It is now the function of the media to provide us with apparently 'objective' correlatives and 'meanings' (since art has become increasingly preoccupied with its inability to mean): and provide them it does. The formulaic reaction implied in Eliot's lines is shown in countless television rituals; one might think a Crackerjack pencil was the objective correlative for pleasure, by the obligatory shrieks and cheers of delight raised by the audience at each mention of the word 'Crackerjack'. And the moments on 'The Generation Game' when Bruce Forsyth holds his laugh like a 'still' are timeless tributes to an inexplicable 'joy'. Advertising too is based on evoking emotion, but not directly, only through a *promise* of evoking pleasure. In fact the emotional response is worked into the form, since it starts off as a signifier, giving meaning *to* the product, not as a signified.

Advertisements provide 'formulae' for emotions in so far as

[1]T. S. Eliot, 'Hamlet' in *Selected Essays*, Faber and Faber, 1932, p. 145.

the connections between feelings and things, which are actually only based on *differentiations*, come to be taken individually. Isolated from the systems from their place in which they derive their value, these connections gain status as facts, 'natural' or 'objective' correlatives. The technique of advertising is to correlate feelings, moods or attributes to tangible objects, linking possible *un*attainable things with those that *are* attainable, and thus reassuring us that the former are within reach. The myth that happiness or other states of mind may be directly conjured up by certain objects is not at all a new one (cf. Chapter 6, Magic): Eliot sees it as the crux of *all* poetic method, where the correlatives are *sufficient*: what *is* new is that the central rite in this creation of emotions is that of purchase and possession, and is thus displaced from the advertisement, functioning as its referent. It is not the ad that evokes feeling, it simply invokes the *idea* of a feeling; it uses feeling as a sign which points to the product. But then emotion is also promised when you *buy* the product. So the feeling and the product become interchangeable as signifier/signified: but, as with the process of 'differentiations' turning into 'correlatives', this is not a drawn-out process but a two-way process where all the meanings are involved simultaneously. However, just as it was necessary to imply that connections resulting from differentiations *came* (temporally) to be isolated from the differentiating systems, in order to explain the logic of the process, so in the last four sections of this chapter I will make the relationship between the product and the feeling/thing/person attached to it take on a linear form, for the sake of clarity.

(*c*) *Product as Signified*

The product, which initially has no 'meaning', must be given value by a person or object which already has a value to us, i.e., already means. Therefore at this stage something about the product is being signified and the correlating thing or person is the signifier. The following ads are all examples of products being *given* meaning; in A12 and A13 the correlative is simply an object; A14 shows a person as correlative, as with Catherine Deneuve in A8; A15 uses a correlative which becomes significant in its potential absence; A16 shows an example where I think the correlating process has defeated itself, by over-emphasising the product, at the expense of grasping the 'image' of the correlative. But all these ads use the same method of linking two objects (even if one of them is a person): the 'correlative' one acting as an intermediary both for the abstract quality, and for the product (which is the second object and a correlative of the abstract at one remove).

Cigarettes provide a good example of inherently 'meaningless' products:

A12

A12: The John Player ad uses the expensive car as a correlative for luxury and then correlates this to the cigarettes. The matching colours perform most of the connecting function: the beige and black of the cigarette packet are exactly the colours of the car. It is obvious that cigarettes cannot really 'be' or 'mean' luxury on their own. The car is such a classic symbol of luxury that its meaning is unquestioned, and this *signifies* the cigarettes as being luxurious, the car's value carries over on to them.

Notice the lay-out of this ad. It is completely mathematically logical in terms of the process I have just described and illustrates diagrammatically the way meaning is transferred in all ads. The title refers to two different kinds of luxury: those which are easy to enjoy, and those which are harder. It establishes the fact that everything we are to see in the ad is a luxury. This title is outside the two 'frames' of the ad: it refers to them both, links them, establishes their relationship. Therefore it is logical for it not to be within either of them.

Now observe that each of these two identical 'frames' or sections of the ad corresponds to one of the 'luxuries'. The luxury car, the signifying object, is in *apposition* to the Players cigarettes. They are equal and coexistent, given the same spatial weight and placed side by side in the ad.

But the car is leaning out of *its* rectangular frame, *into* the cigarettes' section; the curve of the running board sweeps down and round towards the cigarettes, where this curved movement is continued by the beige curves on the cigarette packet. So the car is also what *connects* the two, it has to push into the space of the cigarettes, just as its meaning is also pushed onto them: the luxury car is carried over both literally and in its value. So the implication is: 'Here's one luxury and here's another, but in case you're not convinced, see how this *known* luxury reaches out to the unknown one.'

Finally, the conclusion, 'John Player Kings—a taste of luxury at 35p' is located *in* the cigarette section, the lower frame, where the movement of the ad has been directed. This also makes sense, as only the general statement was outside both frames; the writing referring to each object separately is located within the appropriate frame.

So we see all of this ad's signifying process embodied in the form, the arrangement of signifiers: why should there be the two frames, and the car spilling from one to the other, if not to transfer its meaning, and why should the colours be the same? The answer does not concern 'aesthetics' or 'lay-out' in themselves, but the interchange of values and significance.

A13

A13: In the Belair ad we are shown foods which we *know* are fresh-tasting, and invited to ride on the accuracy of this information to the assumption that the other oral pleasure invoked, smoking Belair, is also fresh-tasting. How can a *cigarette* really be 'fresh'? Yet it seems to be, because of the dewy drops on the cucumber.

This cigarette ad and A12 and also A4 (where the quality is mildness) use a known correlative—a car for luxury, cucumbers for coolness—to sell us an unknown and unproved correlative. We have to make a leap of credibility and the known-correlative object is our stepping stone. The words in the Belair ad here make no claims: they are positioned close to two things and since we know their relevance to one, why not to the other?

The Sanderson advertisement A14 implies that the product has a meaning which fortunately corresponds to somebody's life-style, but that meaning is only created in the ad:

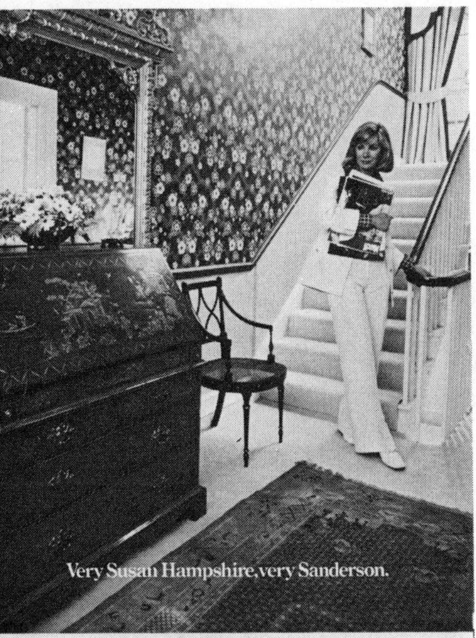

A14

A14: The Sanderson series of adverts—'Very (name of celebrity), very Sanderson' shows the Romantic tendency to latch personality to something/someone outside the self: ('Nelly, I am Heathcliff!'[1])—an emotional correlative. In the advertisement, Susan Hampshire *is* Sanderson, and Sanderson *is* Susan Hampshire: they are grammatically equated by being placed in apposition. The idea that the product can *be* her, its identity merge with her own, illustrates just how far the 'objective correlative' can go: you see somebody in their wallpaper. But Susan Hampshire is *used as* a correlative to *give* the wallpaper meaning; she is classy, impressive, desirable, a correlative for these qualities: the wallpaper, by connection, is classy, impressive and desirable too. Her 'personality' is the signified; the wallpaper is signified as having 'personality' as well.

However, there is a further implication in the wording of the ad: the fact that it is an achievement for the paper to be both very Susan Hampshire *and* very Sanderson, implies that Sanderson does have an image, a quality of its own, and that by a wonderful compromise, this quality can also suit another image, an individual's personality. Yet it is from this that Sanderson derives its image in the first place. The wording sets up Susan Hampshire and Sanderson as *different*, but *united* in the wallpaper: but in fact they are the same, united by Susan Hampshire since her image is what creates Sanderson's. And this wonderful vehicle of Susan Hampshire's self-expression, is, paradoxically, available to us all for a certain price per yard.

[1] *Wuthering Heights* by Emily Brontë.

And two more complex attempts at transferring meaning:

A15: This ad makes use of *cliché* and its fallibility as a correlative. The ring and the bridal veil stand for marriage, and in each picture the strong male hand stands for 'Promise, Confidence, and Security'. The pictures are clichéd illustrations of these three words, and provide a correlative for the building society's promise of them. But the point of the ad is to undermine the 'Confidence and Security' offered by the man.... 'The future never quite takes care of itself.... Now and then it needs a little help.' The cliché of masculine security and promise is exposed, to show the need for Halifax. Yet simultaneously, the image of the ad, the hand and the ring etc., undermined in its literal sense of marriage-as-security, is used in all its clichédness to represent the promise, confidence and security offered in reparation by Halifax. Despite breaking through the cliché of the signifier on one level, at another the ad uses it fully.

In other words, Security, *signified* by the hand, becomes a *signifier*, in its possible *absence*, of the need for Halifax: it is then returned to its original status of signified through the conduit of the product.

A15a

A16: The last example of this type shows an attempt at correlation which actually clashes with our perceptions. Portobello Road market is a Trendy Scene, and these people (shopping at the expensive end of it) clearly have a Bohemian but luxurious life-style. Because we like the antique market, or rather, see it as trendy and expensive, we are supposed to like the car, for which it is the correlative: the car is young, bold, elegant, but not too sedate (we assume). But actually the car looks out of place, it clashes with the environment, and is obviously parked in a most inconvenient place and is in everybody's way. (Perhaps this is also indicative of the owner's life-style.) Two very different things are connected, in my view unsuccessfully. The slogan is the connection, as in the Belair ad A13, since it refers to antique spotting on the overt level, though obviously intended to refer to the car. (This ability of language in ads to refer to two things at once is discussed in Chapter 3.)

Thus the signifier, the market, does not succeed in transferring its meaning to the car; the car is too blatant, it is a signifier in itself and does *not* signify quite the same as the market (which is crowded with pedestrians). In this case the only possible meaning the car can derive from the market is by an opposition: by signifying something different from it.

A15b

In A16 the product has begun to emerge from its modest place as signified; it is no longer purely the recipient of meaning.

A16

Style. It's hard to define, but easy to recognise.
The Marina Estate. One of 10 Marinas all offering a little more than you'll expect.
Morris Marina

(d) Product as Signifier

The next step, after a product has had meaning transferred to it from another object, is that the product itself comes to *mean*. It may start off as a reflection of something exterior, but will soon come to represent it.

A17 shows a product in the process of changing from a signified to a signifier:

A17: Here, the people are *literally* reflected in the product. It is a correlative for 'quality' (echoes of 'The Quality', i.e. upper class), for a rich way of life. There is however something of a crystal ball element in this reflection since most people will buy the cigarette not to reflect their life-style but to create it. The people could be us, if we had John Player Special to reflect in.

A product may be connected with a way of life through being an accessory to it, but come to signify it, as in the car ad which starts, 'Your way of life demands a lot of a car' and ends by making the car signify the life-style: 'Maxi: more a way of life'.

So the product and the 'real' or human world become linked in the ad, apparently naturally, and the product may and does 'take over' the reality on which it was, at first, dependent for its meaning. As product merges with the sign, its 'correlative' originally used to translate it to us, one absorbs the other and the product becomes the sign itself.

For example, 'Beanz meanz Heinz': the product has taken over a monopoly on the empirical reality of beans, originally used to *explain* the product, 'Heinz': i.e. the Beanz meanz Heinz slogan is a reversal of the first step in the link, which is that Heinz means beans. Once Heinz, the brand name, was *signified* as being beans—'Heinz means beans' places beans as the anterior reality; but now beans, all beans, are completely enclosed by the *signifier*, Heinz. It is the old difference between 'dogs are animals' and 'animals are dogs'. To say that 'beans means Heinz' is the equivalent of the latter; Heinz has appropriated all the meaning that was initially transferred *to* it from the exterior reality of beans as signifiers: but the product ends up as the signifier of reality.

Or there are the Guinness ads: 'As long as a country road', where the signpost reads 'Guinness $\frac{3}{4}$ mile' in one direction, and 'Guinness $5\frac{1}{2}$ miles' in the other. The reality *is* Guinness: what was used or would have been used (it is implied) to provide a meaning in reality for the product, has now been taken over by, and signified by, the product itself. It is Guinness that *means:* it is the sign on the signpost, a signifier of distance. Once, the signpost would have had to signify 'real' distance, to *mean* that Guinness was a long drink: Guinness would be signified. But now it is itself the signifier of length.

(*e*) *Product as Generator*

A product may go from representing an abstract quality or feeling, to generating or *being* that feeling; it may become not only 'sign' but the actual *referent* of that sign. It is one thing for a product to *mean* happiness, it is another for it to *be*, or create happiness. The product is always a sign within the ad: as long as you are not in possession of it or consuming it, it remains a sign and a *potential* referent; but the act of buying/consuming is what releases the referent emotion itself. A bath oil may represent excitement; this is all it *can* do in the advertisement, where it is inevitably a sign, because the referent is the real thing. Yet the ad shows us the product as generator in terms of its internal narrative, and we are promised that the product can *create* the feeling it *represents*; 'Things happen after a Badedas bath'. (This statement has the quality of a truism—how could *nothing* happen after a Badedas bath?—a truism which is disguised by the narrative material of the advertisement.)

To put this more simply: a product may be connected with an emotional referent but in two very different ways: you can go out and buy a box of chocolates *because* you feel happy; or you can feel happy because you have bought a box of chocolates: and these are not the same thing. In the first case the chocolates do

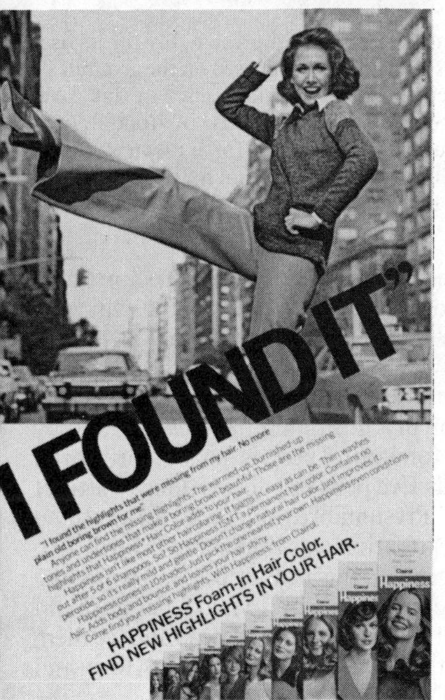

not pretend to be 'more' than a sign; they mean something, but in terms of a feeling which you had anyway. They are a *sign* for a feeling, which is the *referent*. But if the product creates the feeling, it has become more than a sign: it enters the space of the referent, and becomes active in reality. A18 shows how products start giving our feelings a little help.

A18: Babycham sparkles, not just the way she *feels* (reflection) but the way she *wants* to feel. It symbolises the state she desires, and presumably, drinking it helps her to achieve that state. The product, the object, has now started to do more than simply reflect a feeling already there, it stands for a desired feeling and is seen as *totally* identified with it: '*Just* the way I want to feel.' This is a crucial difference because an object reflecting an abstract quality may fairly accurately reflect one facet of it while not attempting to reduce the whole quality or feeling to its own limitations.

Once the product precedes the feeling, as in A18, there is a danger that it will set the bounds for the feeling and the two will become identified as the same. The result is not only speaking, but feeling in clichés. Happiness is shampooed hair, joy is a drink of champagne. There is a sort of Pavlov dog syndrome at work whereby after seeing certain products linked to certain feelings for a long time, by association the products *alone* come to create, to 'be' the feeling. 'Objective correlatives' end up by *being*, through this distortion, the very indefinable qualities they were used to *invoke*: putting everything in material and limited terms. 'Happiness is a cigar called Hamlet'. The connection of a 'thing' and an abstraction can lead them to seem the same, in real life.

The next example, A19, shows both sides of the meaning/generating process together:

A19: This Clairol ad, which deserves very careful reading, functions by a complete reversal of the apparent meaning. 'I found it', she says: and the product is named 'Happiness'. The meaning that one instantly assumes, because of the words, and because of the woman's ecstatic attitude dancing in the street, is that she has found happiness, that the feeling is what 'I found it' refers to. But actually she continues to tell us what she did find, in small print: 'I found the highlights that were missing from my hair'. We are being told, on the grammatical level, that she has found a new hair colour through 'Happiness' (the product). Yet the real message is the reverse: she has found happiness (the feeling) *through* the new hair colour. The product itself, the hair colour, is the means of obtaining something else, and here the connection has been made rather easy for us, as you can find Happiness and happiness at the same time.

Thus the product not only represents an emotional experience, but *becomes* that experience and *produces* it: its roles as sign and referent are collapsed together.

(f) Product as Currency

A19 showed a product made interchangeable with a feeling. When two things are made interchangeable and hence equal in value, they may be used as currency for one another. Of course, Happiness and happiness are only *seen* as interchangeable. They provide a currency on the level of signs. Yet this exchange value, because it exists in terms of *signifying* (Clairol means happiness/happiness means Clairol) comes to have meaning in terms of real buying and selling. The Happiness hair colour represents *access* to happiness; it is therefore a sort of money that will buy happiness. It provides an intermediary currency between real money and an emotion, because it has a value in terms of both: one, as genuine monetary *price*, and the other, a value as a sign, representing or replacing the feeling of happiness or whatever.

Thus as well as an external object 'buying' status for a product in meaning terms, the product is able literally to buy status in the external world.

A20: The product, face cleanser, is being sold presumably for its use-value. However the cleanser is really being advertised on the grounds of its exchange-value, its capacity to buy something else: in this case, crudely, a boyfriend (or three boyfriends in the case of Anne French cleanser). The product is pushed on one level for its own sake, its usefulness, and simultaneously on another level, not for itself at all, but as a currency to buy things that are intangible or hard to get.

These kinds of ads generate a connection between a product and a second 'product', love, happiness etc. which it will buy. 'Money can't buy you love'—but cleansing milk can (and money can buy cleansing milk).

Products are thus set up as being able to buy things *you* cannot buy. This puts them in a position of *replacing* you; they do things you can't do, for you. There is an ad for frozen vegetables which says 'Birds Eye peas will do anything to attract your husband's attention.' Presumably, *you* would do anything to attract your husband's attention. A woman and a Birds Eye pea are made interchangeable; the peas represent what the woman can't do, they have the same aim: to make her husband notice something at dinner. She must buy the peas and let them buy love for her. They are thus exchangeable both with love, and with her: they mean, and they make her mean.

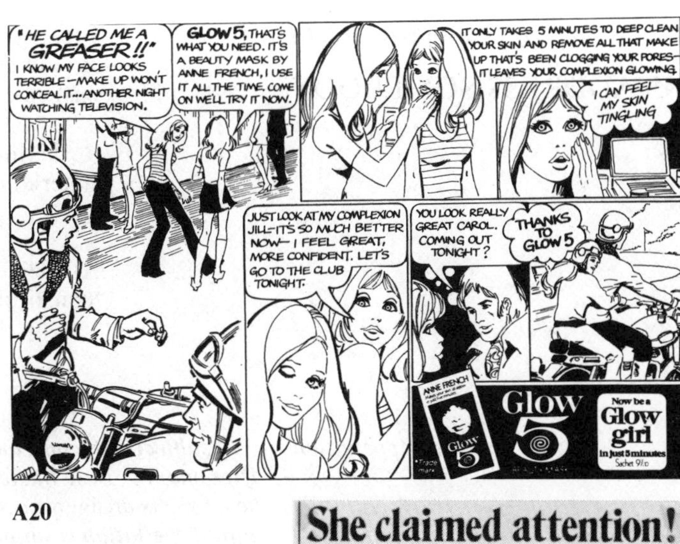

A20

She claimed attention!

with a clear skin

The appeal of a clear skin was a major step towards attracting the man in her world.

To make sure that your skin is clear and healthy you need to avoid the accumulation of natural oil and make-up as this is one cause of spots and blemishes. Use Lempak Cleansing Lotion to remove your make-up gently and to clear away excessive natural oil.

Lempak is no ordinary cleanser – it contains pure lemon juice which helps clear blemishes by correcting the conditions that cause them.

Used each night as a make-up remover or for a midday freshen-up, Lempak Cleansing Lotion will help you to a natural, clear skin to attract the attention of the man in your world.

LEM PAK CLEANSING LOTION

LEMPAK by Christy of England — Write for the free Beauty booklet: 'Keep your skin smooth, young and radiant…' Thos. Christy & Co. Ltd., North Lane, Aldershot, Hants

This chapter has examined signs as a currency in the way meanings are transferred; both through a transaction *within* the ad between an element of a Referent System and a product: and also in a transaction *outside* the ad, buying/consuming. However, since *this* transaction is usually also represented within the ad, it means that a series of transactions is carried on in its form: which takes on the status of a narrative when the transaction is represented in time: 'Things happen *after* a Badedas bath'; and the status of a given logic when the transaction is assumed by a juxtaposition of two objects simultaneously given the same value. In neither case, however, does the formal process take place within the closed world of the advertisement.

CHAPTER TWO
SIGNS ADDRESS SOMEBODY

'Ideology represents the imaginary relationship of individuals to their real conditions of existence....

... this imaginary relation is itself endowed with a material existence.'

'All ideology has the function (which defines it) of "constituting" concrete individuals as subjects.'

Louis Althusser[1]

Subject; Appellation

A subject is a 'conscious self', according to the concise Oxford Dictionary:[2] *I use the term to mean an individual who feels that he or she is an* agent, *acting out freely the dictates of a coherent ego. Appellation is simply the 'Hey, you!' process of ideological apparatuses* calling *individuals 'subjects'. (See below, Section c.)*

A sign replaces something for someone. It can only mean if it has someone to mean *to*. Therefore, all signs depend for their signifying process on the existence of specific, concrete receivers, people *for* whom and in whose systems of belief, they have a meaning. Moreover, signs are only signs in their actual *process* of replacing something; in other words, being exchanged with it *by* a particular person or people. It is in the dialectic between the 'for' and the 'by' that ideology maintains its momentum.

The exchanging of meanings in ads has already been described. An object 'replaces', 'stands for', an image or feeling; then the product 'replaces' the original object in this role, and appropriates the meaning of that image or feeling. However, this description makes it sound as though the product and object *themselves* perform the transaction. On the basis of the above definition that signs must mean something *to us*, it is clear that since the meaning depends on us, its transference must also depend on our co-operation. Thus, for the advertisement to succeed in turning products from signifieds into signifiers, the

[1]'Ideology and Ideological State Apparatuses' in *Lenin and Philosophy and Other Essays*, New Left Books, 1971.

Althusser's intervention within Marxist theory, formulating ideology as a material practice ('Ideological State Apparatuses'), has provided a crucial space for a sophisticated Marxist theory of signification and concrete representational structures.

[2]3rd Edition.

process shown in the previous chapter, it must enter the space of the receiver; it is he or she who completes the circuit through which, once started (and it has 'always-already' started, as Althusser says) a current of 'meaning' flows continuously and apparently autonomously.

Therefore, an examination of signs and sign-systems inevitably involves more than a structural analysis of those systems in themselves: such analyses are valuable as synchronic representations of signifying relationships, but to investigate the dynamics of these relationships we must enter the space between signifier and signified, between what means and what it means. This space is that of the individual as subject: he or she is not a simple receiver but a creator of meaning. But the receiver is only a creator of meaning because he/she *has been called upon to be so*. As an advertisement speaks to us, we simultaneously create that speech (it means *to us*), and are created by it *as its creators* (it assumes that it means to us). Thus we are constituted as 'active receivers' by the ad.

The 'vicious circle', in which we give meaning to ads, and they give meaning to us, will, as usual, have to be denied its simultaneity and dismantled into linear stages, for closer analysis and illustration. The next four sections describe, firstly, how we *create* the meaning of a product in an advertisement; secondly, how we take meaning from the product; thirdly, how we are created by the advertisement; and fourthly, how we create ourselves in the advertisement. The first two topics follow very closely from the conclusion of the last chapter; the second two take us further from the area of signs, towards the area of psychology; although semiology and psychology, as should be apparent by the end of this chapter, are inextricably connected.

And it is ideology which connects them, or rather, which provides the invisible cloak in which their intermeshing is rendered transparent: ideology is always precisely that of which we are not aware. It is only ideology in as far as we do not perceive it as such. And how does it become 'invisible', what keeps it hidden from us?—the fact that we are *active* in it, that we do not *receive* it from above: we constantly re-create it. It works *through* us, not at us. We are not deceived by someone else 'putting over' false ideas: ideology works far more subtly than that. It is based on false *assumptions*. This can be clarified as follows: there is a big difference between saying something is true (which admits the potential of the opposite), and saying that the truth of something *need not be questioned*—which admits nothing, and claims nothing either. In ideology, assumptions are made about us which we do not question, because we see them as 'already' true: time itself has been appropriated as a part of ideology in so far as it involves giving superior status, always, to anteriority. The 'already' is always stronger than the 'maybe'. (Time as an ideological referent system is discussed in Part II.) An assumption made about us inherently throws the substance of the assumption back in time, *further* back than the moment of the assumption itself. Ads create an 'alreadyness' of 'facts' about ourselves as individuals: that we are consumers, that we have certain values, that we will freely buy things, consume, on the basis of those values, and so on. We are trapped in the illusion of choice. 'Freedom' is in fact part of the most basic ideology, the very sub-structure of advertising. Outside the structure of advertisements themselves, it forms the fundamental argument always used to justify advertising: that it is part of the freedom of manufacturers to compete, and part of our freedom, to *choose* between the products of that competition. The idea of freedom is essential to the maintenance of ideology. I intend to show how, in fact, advertisements *work* by a process in which we are completely enmeshed, and how they invite us 'freely' to create ourselves in accordance with the way in which they have already created us.

(a) Currency Requires A Subject To Make An Exchange

Exchanges must be made, and currency used, *by* somebody; and that somebody is obviously the person for whom the currency has value 'in the first place'. Yet this value only exists in *terms* of an exchange; you only find how much money is worth when you make a transaction. In ordinary life we do not talk about the value of, say, food, but about the value of money. Money would seem to be what determines value—yet *its* value is determined by what may be exchanged with it. Its value goes down as *prices* go up.

This makes the important preliminary point that values are not fixed and inherent, but only exist *in* exchanges, or replacements. And since a sign involves a replacement it must not only represent but take over, perpetuate and *generate* the value of whatever it replaced. Thus, currency is a system of values emanating from exchange relations: 'objective correlatives' are, similarly, forms of assumed values which emerge in turning signifieds into signifiers, 'translating' a product in terms of an object whose value is only 'revealed' in, and in fact, derives from, its transference of meaning from one system to another.

So as money is given its value by how much food or clothes etc. it will buy, so signs are given their value as currency through use *by us* in our 'recognition' of what they stand for/(replace). In

A12, in transferring the significance of the car to the cigarettes, we are acknowledging that the car means something to us, luxury, and although we may not go around all the time thinking of such cars as luxurious, this value emerges in the fact that it can be used to transfer a *difference*—(A $\neq$ B, = a $\neq$ b).

Thus our first level of involvement in the ad's meaning is in our 'recognition' of certain signifiers from referent 'myth' systems. We *give* Catherine Deneuve's face its meaning, for use in the ad, in that it 'already' means something to us in terms outside the ad. The advertisement cannot claim to have created that meaning, for do we not 'know' it already? However, we do not know that we know it *until* it is used in the ad—ideas are maintained not in the vacuum of the abstract but through their active use: values exist not *in* things but in their transference.

Therefore, since any system of values constitutes *an ideology*, it is clear that an ideology can only exist in that its component values are constantly being regenerated by their transference; and the transference of values (perpetuated in monetary terms by buying and selling) means the same as replacement of meanings. In other words, where the values are *ideas*, they are perpetuated by our constant 'deciphering' or 'decoding' of signs.

The advertisement provides a supreme arena for this: a 'meta-structure' where meaning is not just 'decoded' within one structure, but *transferred* to create another. Two systems of meaning are always involved: the 'referent system' and the product's system; e.g. in A8, the world of glamour, and the world of perfumes. It has already been pointed out that the meta-system, the actual point of transference, is itself devoid of 'content'; a *relationship* (one of difference and contrast) is translated, but not an inherent 'quality'. So our cognition (in relation to a particular myth system) is appropriated to lock ourselves within a process, a 'form of knowledge' which is emptied of content (cf. the Saussure passage quoted in Chapter 1) and devoid of meaning, except in so far as meaning is constantly *assumed* through the form of its perpetual translation.

Thus the ideology of the 'Referent system' is always being regenerated in our relationship to the advertisement. Things 'mean' to us, and we give this meaning to the product, on the basis of an irrational mental leap invited by the form of the advertisement. In A12 the car has meaning; by a formal relationship that has already been discussed (see A12 analysis) the cigarettes come to have meaning. We are making an exchange between signifiers; the value that emerges is that of the common signified. Yet the very *fact* that we make the exchange, that we take part in the process, is itself constitutive of ideology.

I have shown how 'ideas', values, meaning, exist in *practice*, the process of making the ad mean, i.e. making the required leap from the referent object to the product: it is not only *meaning* that emerges in the space covered by this leap—but also, *ourselves*. We are not participants in an ideology until we are active within its very creation; paradoxically, ideology *means* that we are participants, *subjects*, i.e. 'initiators of action' in accordance with 'freely held ideas'. But just as these values which we hold only emerge in their being assumed as already existing, so similarly we only function as subjects in being addressed by the ad as *already* subjects: 'appellated'. By the time the ad has said, 'Hey, you—you know what Catherine Deneuve/a Rolls Royce/Susan Hampshire means, don't you? Well, this product means the same'—it has addressed you as somebody with a freely held body of knowledge (= first aspect of ideology) and as somebody able to think and act, able to perform an active part in creating something (in this case a meaning for the scent/car/wallpaper) on the basis of this freely held knowledge (= second aspect of ideology). In the process of the ad's 'saying' this and your 'understanding' it, the 'knowledge' referred to as anterior has been created by reference; and the active subject has been created by assumption. (The point about the 'hey, you' that Althusser describes as the essence of appellation, is that whatever you are *called*, you must *already be*.)

The relationship between 'ideology' and 'subject' is one of simultaneous interdependence. Thus when I refer to ideology, this also means the creation of a subject; and when I speak of the subject, this naturally involves his 'having' an ideology, as well as being created by it. The emergence of ideological values in the transaction of significance in an ad necessarily implies the existence of a subject. However, I shall make an artificial distinction and reiterate in terms of the *subject* rather than *ideology*, the way in which both are assumed in the formal working of the ad.

Let us go right back to A8. Nothing here even 'says' that Catherine Deneuve is 'like' Chanel No. 5, or that they have a similar aura. We are given two signifiers, and required to make a 'signified' by exchanging them. The fact that we have to *make* this exchange, to do the linking work which is not *done* in the ad, but which is only made possible by its form, draws us into the transformational space between the units of the ad. Its meaning only exists in this space: the field of transaction; and it is here that we operate—*we are this space*.

Now, if the meaning of the ad exists in the transformation of meanings between signs, and if this transformation takes place in us—(i.e. the signified exists in the transformational space and we, as subjects, are constituted in it too)—this is placing *us* in the space of the signified: which leads to an examination of *ourselves as signified* through transactions.

(*b*) '*Totemism*': *Subject As Signified*

If the connection between the product and the 'objective correlative' person or thing is made by us and in us, it is also made *with* us, in that we become one of the things exchanged (given the status of an object). Two transactions were summarised at the end of the first chapter. The double exchange-role played by the product can be seen in the Birds Eye peas ad described there. The peas are a stand-in for attractiveness, love; they are also a stand-in for *you*. Similarly Clairol (A19) means, and creates happiness: in its ability to buy that feeling, it replaces you, it does the buying for you at one remove. Thus there are two axes along which the product '*means*': there is the process of its gaining meaning, in a transaction we make between signifiers (Catherine Deneuve and scent bottle, car and cigarettes); and now it appears to have a second replacement value: it replaces, hence signifies, *us*. Having initially derived its meaning from correlation with things or people—and it is very frequently people—which have a place in external systems or groups, a product is then made to *give* meaning back to us, and create a new system of groups. Products whose only meaning derives from a re-hash of mythological elements already present in society, develop such an aura of significance that they tell something about their buyers and actually become adjectival in relation to them. There are the 'Pepsi People', the 'Sunsilk girls', and so on. The combination of the adjective's significance as *quality* and as *person* is shown perfectly in 'Is your Mum a Superfine Mum?' (Kraft Superfine Margarine). With a small 's' this endows the mum with the quality of superfine-ness. But with the large 'S' it identifies her as part of the Superfine group, a clan of Kraft Margarine users. Of course the synonymity of the two spellings indicates that the quality of superfine-ness is strictly limited to Superfine Mums. The product translates between the quality and the person; or rather, intervenes. You can only have the quality or meaning within its parameters. We are thus created not only as subjects, but as particular kinds of subjects, by products in advertisements.

A8 and A9 showed people used to differentiate products. But having been *signified* as different, the products then become *signifiers* of difference. If you use Chanel No. 5, you are signified as a different kind of person from someone who uses Babe.

Pepsi drinkers are not Coke drinkers. Superfine mums are not Blueband mums. Chapter One examined the transference of differences from one system to another, creating *product* differences: and we saw that relationships originally based on formal difference (Catherine Deneuve $\neq$ Margaux Hemingway, No. 5 $\neq$ Babe), come to be seen as 'inherent' relationships based on content (Catherine Deneuve = No. 5, Margaux Hemingway = Babe). Chanel No. 5 and Catherine Deneuve 'seem' to have the same quality, though they are only connected by a distinguishing function. The same slipping from differentiating signifiers, to similar signifieds (in other words, from contrasts generated between similar structures, to similarities made between *different* 'things') can be seen in the reverse process of products giving back significance to people. We differentiate ourselves from other people by what we buy. (The extreme form of this is individualism, see section c.) In this process we become *identified* with the product that differentiates us; and this is a kind of totemism. See, for example, the world/sect represented/created by Lambert and Butler: the people are even dressed like the product (A5). Lévi-Strauss describes totemism—the use of differences between natural objects to differentiate between human groups: '. . . on the one hand there are animals which differ from each other . . . and on the other there are men . . . who also differ from each other (in that they are distributed among different segments of the society, each occupying a particular position in the social structure). The resemblance presupposed by so-called totemic representations is *between these two systems of differences*.' He describes how there is a passage 'from a point of view centred on *subjective utility* to one of *objective analogy*' and 'from *external analogy* to *internal homology*.'[1]

However, there is a great difference between the totemism he is describing and the phenomenon I have described as analogous to totemism. As Lévi-Strauss says, 'The term totemism covers relations. posed ideologically, between two series, one natural, the other cultural.'[2] But the objects used to differentiate between us—No. 6 smokers, or Gauloise smokers, Mini drivers or Rolls Royce drivers—the objects that create these 'totemic' groups are *not* natural, and not naturally different, although their differences are given a 'natural' status. (See below, Chapter 5.) They are, as I have shown, given their

[1]Claude Lévi-Strauss, *Totemism*, Penguin University Books, 1973, pp. 149–50.

[2]ibid., p. 84.

meaning by the kind of people who supposedly smoke them, i.e. the kind of people, or accessories connected with them, shown in the ad. So what is involved are two sets of *false* differences: between products, and between people, each perpetually redefining the other, through an exchange of meaning in the ad, and an exchange of money in the shop.

We, as people, have thus been made to create the differences between products which then differentiate us; but it is also people who have actually *made* the products. One reason for my use of the word 'totemism' is that it describes a particular formation of groups which cannot be mistaken for the groups of class difference. Advertisements obscure and avoid the real issues of society, those relating to work: to jobs and wages and who works for whom. They create systems of social differentiation which are a veneer on the basic class structure of our society. Advertising refers only to consumption, to a sort of perennial leisure time which few people actually have. It emphasises what you *buy*, which in fact means you have to work *harder* to earn the money to buy. The basic issues in the present state of society, which *do* concern money and how it is earned, are sublimated into 'meanings', 'images', 'lifestyles', to be bought with *products*, not with money. The societal 'id', its deepest forces, are pushed under the surface completely. Things, products, can mean for us: so we are alienated from them, in that we forget their material process of creation in the workings of society, and we are also alienated from ourselves, since we have allowed objects to 'speak' for us and have become identified with them. As I have shown, signifieds are quickly transformed into signifiers: what reflects us will soon create us too, the symbols of our feelings will become the bounds of our feelings.[1] Real objects are lifted out of our physical reality and absorbed into a closed system of symbols, a substitute for reality and real emotions. Feelings become bound up with products, as with the happiness hair colour and superfine margarine.

This means, on one level, that the product 'produces' or buys the feeling. But the more subtle level on which the advertisement works is that of 'alreadyness', which is where 'totemism' becomes a part of ideology: you do not simply buy the product in order to *become* a part of the group it represents; you must feel that you already, naturally, belong to that group and *therefore* you will buy it. This is how advertisements maintain their hold on you in the gap between seeing them and buying

[1]cf. '*Totemism*', p. 141.

products. You should not be faced with a choice in the shop—the *sameness* of products was the starting point of this discussion in Chapter 1, and twenty brands of margarine all look and taste very similar. You do not choose in the shop, but in response to the advertisement, by 'recognising' yourself as the kind of person who *will* use a specific brand. You must have already chosen when you buy, otherwise the advertisement has failed in its purpose. This is why it is so crucial for the ad to enter you, and exist inside rather than outside your self-image: in fact, to create it.

Identification with a group involves the overcoming of several barriers—one of which is the inevitable *difference* between its individual members drawn together in relation to this one thing. The re-grouping of society in terms of consumerism must take place not only at the expense of recognising basic class groupings, but at the expense of individual differences—even those created by other products. Because of course, the 'totemic' groups existing around products must inevitably overlap, since we consume so many products; you cannot be a Gitanes man *and* a Benson and Hedges man, but you can be a Gitanes man and a Guinness man, and an Old Spice man, and so on. There are infinite permutations. The vast number of these groups and their overlap make them very different from those of tribal totemism; but there is still an analogy in that they involve the merging of some differences (those within the group) in order to create others (between groups). One group is differentiated from another only at the price of a sameness within them. We become the same, in each being made 'different' in the same way. However, the advertisement must remind you that you are special, and above all, must speak to you and through you as a uniquely individual subject. This appellation of the subject as unique is the topic of the next section. It is part of an inevitable contradiction: ads appeal simultaneously to us as different from other people, and as similar to them. They appeal to our specialness, yet submerge that in the totemic group of the product. A21 shows a typical way of coping with both these aspects of identity:

A21: This ad shows a subtle way around the group versus individual conflict. These people must be unique and have clearly defined personal tastes, since they disagree about liqueurs. Yet they (apparently unconsciously) appreciate the same kind of port, which functions as a highest common factor in their tastes. Beyond this point they are different: it is crucial that they be seen as *discriminating*: – yet at this stage they can still agree. The ad is really very clever since the fact that

Your friends probably disagree about liqueurs.
Let them discuss it over a bottle of port.

A21

the 'discussion' takes place over the bottle of port sets this product up as being connected with their *differences* (despite being their point of agreement): setting up an arena for, and participating in, a display of individuality. Thus it shows a group constituted around the 'totem' of Cockburn's port (as in the Lambert and Butler group of A5), but it also draws on the idea of individualism. Moreover, it *speaks* to you as an individual; and it assumes that the people in the ad *are* 'your friends'. (It is also arranged so that you are placed at the head of the table; in looking at the ad you are inevitably drawn in, since the space from which you are looking is also the space constituted by the form and perspective of the picture as the place at the end of the table. It leads right out of the page to where you are: you are created in the *absence* in the form—cf. the next chapter.) So you are described, involved, created by the ad: it assumes that *you* have these discriminating friends, that you belong to the Cockburn's group. Note that the name of the product is not even mentioned: the 'bottle of port' is just *assumed* to be Cockburn's. You are spoken to not as a *potential* member of a group, but *as* a member of it. (As with the well-known magazine policy of always assuming that their readership is one degree higher up the social scale than it actually is. Flattery is a better stimulus than exhortation.)

Thus, even discriminating people (or rather, not *even*—they *must* be discriminating to appreciate it) can be united by a product like Cockburn's port. In A21 the *totemic image* is itself discrimination. The people are united by their unique tastes and sensibilities—so that the individualism principle has actually become the symbolised quality of the product.

The fact that A21 shows people who are supposedly 'your friends' draws attention to the way ads address us as individuals, even while drawing us into a particular group. The same exchange—between the person referred to by the ad, the person whose friends these are—and *you* as you read the ad—is shown in A22 as well: an ad which provides an example of 'totemism'—the group of people who smoke No. 6, who are identified with it—but also leads on to a discussion of 'appellation', creating us as individual subjects. And the interchangeability of ourselves and the people in the ad leads to the idea of the 'mirror phase', described in the fifth part of this chapter.

A22

A22: This advertisement incorporates two processes: one is the correlation between the people shown and the product: they are No. 6 smokers, and endow it with its 'ordinary' image. But you are 'appellated' in relation to this correlation, because it involves the assumption that you are like the people in the picture: 'people like *you* are changing to No. 6', and *they* are actually the people who have changed to No. 6. Therefore, we become identified with them along the axis of the product; and the people shown here are carefully selected to look 'normal' or 'average'. The caption actually speaks to 'you', so that you cannot help becoming a part of its message. In the very form of address, you are trapped by its assumption that *you are* the person addressed.

(c) *Appellation and Individualism: Individuals Constituted As Subjects*

'All ideology hails or interpellates concrete individuals as concrete subjects, by the functioning of the category of the subject . . . ideology "acts" or "functions" in such a way that it "recruits" subjects among the individuals (it recruits them all) or "transforms" the individuals into subjects (it transforms them all) by that very precise operation which I have called interpellation or hailing, and which can be imagined along the lines of the most commonplace everyday police (or other) hailing: "Hey, you there!" . . . Assuming that the theoretical scene I have imagined takes place in the street, the hailed individual will turn round. By this mere one-hundred-and-eighty degree physical conversion, he becomes a *subject*. Why? Because he had recognised that the hail was "really" addressed to him, and that "it was *really him* who was hailed" (and not someome else).' (Louis Althusser[1])

'. . . it seems not untrue to say that some modes of classing, arbitrarily isolated under the title of totemism, are universally employed: among ourselves this "totemism" has merely been humanised. Everything takes place as if in our civilisation every individual's own personality were his totem: it is the signifier of his signified being.' (Claude Lévi-Strauss[2])

In constituting you as part of a group, advertisements must nevertheless address you as an individual. 'People like *you* are changing to No. 6'. I have examined our place in the transference of meanings in ads, a transaction between the people in it and the product; but since we ourselves are a part of this meaning, we can only make the exchange at the price of being 'appellated'. This appellation itself involves an exchange: between you as an individual, and the imaginary subject addressed by the ad. For this is not 'you', inherently; there is no logical reason to suppose that the advertisement had 'you' in mind all along. You have to exchange yourself with the person 'spoken to', the spectator the ad creates for itself. Every ad necessarily assumes a particular spectator: it projects into the space out in front of it an imaginary person composed in terms of the relationship between the elements within the ad. You move into this space as you look at the ad, and in doing so

[1] 'Ideology and Ideological State Apparatuses' in *Lenin and Philosophy and Other Essays*, New Left Books, 1971.
[2] *The Savage Mind*, Weidenfeld and Nicholson, 1966.

'become' the spectator, you feel that the 'hey you' '*really did*' apply to you in particular. The 'you' in ads is always transmitted plural, but we receive it as singular. Although the aim is to connect a mass of people with a product, to identify them with it as a group, this can only be achieved by connecting them with the product as individuals, one by one. Thus we are addressed as a certain kind of person who is *already* connected with a product: there is only one receiver of the ad, the subject 'you', already there in the very address. However, this address applies to all of us, and none of us: as an individual this imaginary subject does not exist, but in that we each 'become' him or her, he/she exists as a set, a group—the totemic group centred on the product. And as we each of us step into this totemic space, we *become* the person at the head of the table whose friends drink Cockburn's port, the person who is like the No. 6 smokers in the picture. We constitute a totemic set of one, we find our identity as part of a group the rest of which does not exist. We are appellated as already in a group of one.

Being connected with the product as an individual can in fact come to mean that we, singly, become the 'totemic identity' which the product must be endowed with *in order to* 'mean':—we give it its meaning by our own individuality. We saw a version of this in A21 where the product was given meaning by the variety of discriminating people who consumed the port. But of course, the ad creates these people. A6 shows how a person may be created to complement a product, and then treated as though they were actually the occasion for the product. Thus advertisements create their own consumers, they tell *you* what you are like: like Bruce Forsyth at the beginning of 'The Generation Game': 'You are a 34-year-old housewife from Wigan' etc. (It is interesting that this appellation, where 'Brucie' reads *back* to the contestants the information about themselves that *they* have previously supplied, is, though supposedly only the introduction to the programme, its dominant section.) Look at A9: Babe is 'a fragrance so fresh, so natural, *Fabergé named it just for you*'. *Naming*, use of a proper name, is where classification ends; it is the ultimate signifier of difference, of uniqueness. But 'Babe', the proper name of the perfume, is vague enough to appellate *all* women. We are appellated 'en masse', but *as* subjects; *subjects*, because we are spoken to as already-there-as-subjects—Babe is named *for* us, i.e. *after* us: we are not named *by it*. We are already 'so fresh, so natural'; we are always the anterior reality which the ad drags about after it, catching us in the trap of alreadyness. What is our present experience, in seeing an ad (being spoken to by it *as* somebody 'so fresh, so natural' etc.)—is displaced into the past: we already were fresh and natural, we were already 'Babe' because the perfume is named *for* us.

Sometimes the process of the product's taking on our qualities is, more realistically, placed *forward* in time; see A23 (1) and (2).

A23(1)

A23: Some advertisements recognise the problem of selling a unique person a piece of mass-produced machinery, and rather than implicitly denying the problem, try to find ways round it. The Pentax series—where celebrities' Pentaxes are shown—settles for the idea that the product *becomes* a part of you. This is more realistic and more sophisticated than ads where the product is seen as already connected with you; but it implies that you *have* a unique personality, extending to eccentricity, for the Pentax to become a part of it all. So the product *comes* to reflect and symbolise your uniqueness, instead of that uniqueness being generated by the camera. It is seen as already there; you have this individuality which will eventually show itself in your worn camera. But still the 'you' is very ambiguous. The cameras shown are not yours, but David Hockney's and Ken Russell's; Hockney's bit of uniqueness is the string, Russell's, the absence of string and the battered-ness. People are still totally identified with objects in these ads; they simply show a sort of mini-totemism, not a whole group.

That we are addressed as already having certain qualities is shown by:

MONTE CARLO 1975.
When a car makes you feel good about its looks, that's styling.
When a car makes you feel good about yourself, that's character.
CHEVROLET
MAKES SENS
FOR AMERIC

A24

A24: This example shows just how far the emphasis on the consumer can go. The car is supposed to be an influence on how you feel about *yourself*: it compliments your own taste, your own judgement—which presupposes that you *have* this taste and this judgement. The qualities overtly refer not to the car, but to the buyer; the heavy printed words are 'Feel good about your taste . . . ah! but what of your judgement?' By this emphasis on the buyer, on you, the advertisement is able to turn into individuality an otherwise stereotyped mass-produced product. The appeal to what is special about *you* and to undefined qualities that you have (whose details *you* can supply), is very clever since it is in fact a mass appeal, yet each individual reads it in relation to himself and therefore sees the *car* as a special product. Your own impeccable taste and judgement rub off on the product: it comes to represent taste and judgement, and therefore, since *your* taste and judgement are so perfect, you must buy it. The spectator/buyer has become the correlative from which the product derives its meaning: in him the roles of 'objective correlative'-person and appellated-subject are elided.

In A23 and A24 the advertisements invited us to read our individual qualities into the product, flattering us that we had them in the first place. So advertisements appellate us as unique;

ASAHI
PENTAX
Ken Russell's Pentax.
Your Pentax becomes a part of you.
ASAHI PENTAX

A23(2)

although this uniqueness is a universal one, since the ad speaks to an *imaginary* individual which then *becomes* us. By buying a Pepsi you take place in an exchange, not only of money but of yourself for a Pepsi Person. You have become special, yet one of a clan; however, you do not meet these others, except *in* the advertisement. This is a very important point, because the emphasis on individualism in ads reflects the social need for us to be kept separate: the economic and political world as it exists at present depends for its survival upon keeping its participants fragmented. This is the function of ideology: it gives us the assurance that we *are* ourselves, separate individuals, and that we *choose* to do what we do. It is crucial to maintain the myth that this choice is an individual one, that we act in accordance with our 'beliefs'—and of course, although these beliefs *are* ideological, and hence shared, we feel they are ours in particular.

In an advertisement, we are told that we *do* choose, we *are* free individuals, we have taste, style, uniqueness, and we *will act accordingly*. In other words, having been attributed with the qualities connected with a product, we are projected as buyers of it, precisely because 'given' that we 'have' the beliefs implied in the ad, we will act in accordance with them and buy the product that embodies those beliefs. It is a sort of 'double-bind'.

A25 shows just this kind of 'appellation': it tells us we are unusual and special—and so we must act accordingly and buy this unusual and special car.

A25

A25: 'It's the difference that makes all the difference': this ad is paradoxically telling a *mass* of people that they are going to be very unusual and buy a Fiat. The aim is to make you stand out, and not follow the flock of 'sheep' on the roads. Yet if all the readers of this ad *did* buy the Fiat, they would obviously not be all that unique.

This ad makes blatant all the contradictions involved in the advertisement's appellation of its subject as unique. It must create you as different; but it performs this *identical* function for everyone who comes within its reach. We are all the same, in being made different, but are each locked into the limits of the receiving-space created by the ad, an invisible one-man audience-place in front of it. When it says 'Hey, you' (to use Althusser's phrase)—we cannot but hear that singly. We become individual, yet not united.

It is the product that both appellates us and separates us, for it is the pivot around which the meanings of the ad, and our identity, are exchanged. In A21, for example, the product, the port, was like a central mirror; transforming heterogeneous people into homogeneous consumers. This is exactly what all ads do, because of their unique and imaginary receivers: they address different people as one (imaginary) unified subject. We can never be in the receiving subject-space at the same time as someone else; so the only people we can identify with are those *inside* the ad. In A9, where we are appellated as 'Babe', we cannot identify with other *spectators* of the ad, whose experience is the same as ours, because the pre-condition of *being* appellated as Babe is that you are the only Babe: it was named '*just* for you'. But yet, Margaux Hemingway is in the picture, obviously representing a 'Babe'. So our relationship to *her* replaces our relationship with other people; and she is also inevitably made a part of us, a sort of 'alter-ego', since there is *only one* Babe, and both she and us seem to be it. (See section e, 'The Mirror Phase'.)

Appellation, then, gives us imaginary blinkers in preventing us from looking sideways and recognising other people, contiguous to us; it only allows us to see forwards, into the ad. (As with the perspective in the 'Pearl and Dean' cinema ads, where we are sucked into the centre of the screen.) Our uniqueness as the ad's subject allows us to be nothing *but* that subject; and it must unite every aspect of us. Part of the myth of individualism is the idea of a consistent identity: you must *have* a coherent personality for it to be reflected in the product. A26 is interesting in its insistence on appropriating *all* your possible choices.

A 26

A26: This ad sets up a new dimension to the concept of individuality. The product is shown to suit, not different people, but the same person—you—on different occasions. The use of the same product in differing circumstances gives a feeling of identity, it flatters the image of a consistent self, thus embodying the individualist principle while giving it a new flexibility. The keynote of this ad is that of choice, of the flexibility of the *product*: the illusion of choice is given by the three different Carltons; but the actual aim is, of course, a *narrowing*, a limiting of 'your choice for every occasion' down to one object, this product. Each 'choice' is the same: Carlton. This shows one of the fundamental features of all advertising: a product is set up as reflecting your feelings, while thereby actually setting the bounds to what you feel you can 'choose'. You can choose, but only between given alternatives. You cannot choose not to buy.

So by 'appellation' we are trapped in the very illusion of choice; in the illusion of an identity choosing its action in accordance with its inherent characteristics. But this individualism is a forced one: you are not free *not* to individualise your Pentax, or *not* to 'feel good about your taste and judgement'. 'You' are created by the advertisement and *become* its currency, in the process of using it: you are signified by the very fact that you give it significance, in the process of giving it significance. Our creation of meaning in the ad, as active-receivers, and its appellation of us, as subjects, are synonymous and simultaneous. In reading the ad—'People like you . . .'—we *give* it significance: it cannot have significance until we appear in front of it. And in our reading it, it signifies us—makes us into its 'you'

A26 showed how an advertisement can cope with the idea of 'you' on different occasions, absorbing differences into a sameness; the way in which ads cope with the problem of different 'yous' *within* you, is the next refinement of the appellation process.

"Farouche"
The perfume created by NINA RICCI, Paris
for all the women you are.

(d) Divisions

From 'your choice for every occasion' we move to ads like the one for 'Farouche': 'The perfume created by Nina Ricci, Paris, *for all the women you are*.' Having constituted subjects in terms of a group, and then as individuals, the advertisement can then break down this individual into a fragmented ego to be reunited by the product. The subject is deconstructed, only to be rebuilt in a unity within the ad, and with the presupposition of a basic unity within himself, i.e. that 'all the yous' really are *all you*. The illusion of multiple identity *is* only an illusion: 'all the women you are' could be spoken to the general public—'all you women out there'—but again, the 'you' strikes us separately, and we take it to mean 'us' specifically; so that the multiplicity implied is still centred on you, and by the product. So, just as the totemic group can always ultimately be represented by you alone, so these fragmented aspects of personality are still summarised in 'you'. Whether 'you' join the 'Pepsi People', or whether several different 'people' are joined in you, the basic fact of individual appellation is the same.

However, this incorporation of divisions in the ego is really very clever since it short-circuits any potential breakdown in the 'individualism' ethos, caused by people's sense that they are probably *not* integrated subjects. This is one example of ads' ability to cope with and absorb *back into themselves* potential criticisms of their ideology. It is now very widely felt that people are not one particular 'character': developments in psychology—*The Divided Self*[1] etc.—though not accessible to everyone, do affect the general public in a watered-down way. It becomes harder and harder for the ad to say definitively, 'you are like this'. So instead, it says, 'you have so many sides to your personality'—but still claims to represent them all: a more extraordinary feat, one might think, than representing only *one* quality.

The multiple choice idea—with A26, Carlton, a choice of products (all the same one), with the following ads, a choice of selves (still the same one)—is closely connected with a whole type of lay-out, a 'gestalt' which, alongside the split-screen technique in cinema, has become increasingly common in visual advertising. In this type of ad it is the totality, the whole page which is more than a simple sum of its parts, that has meaning; the separate elements, not singly or one by one, but in their totality, create you. The point about the multiple lay-out page is that while it does represent different things, different aspects of you, it represents them all together, simultaneously, so that the separateness only has significance *within* the whole; which is the primary, enclosing entity. We cannot take the parts singly, because *visually* they are all seen together. This tension between the separated elements of a divided picture (which seem to emphasise divisions) and the actual wholeness of it (the fact that the divisions are superseded by their very coexistence) is a perfect way of conveying a similar tension in the 'self' created by the ad. Different aspects of 'you' are shown; but even in the process of being shown simultaneously, in the form of the ad, they are shown to be united.

A27: Here, many facets of the same person are shown: glamorous, sporting, careerist, outdoors, romantic; each picture has an obvious title, activities are simplified and labelled to fit certain functions of a

[1]R. D. Laing, 1960.

A27

A28

hair set. This splitting of personality (the career girl, the romantic date, the healthy sportswoman) suggests complexity while in fact simplifying and limiting. These divisions are united by the product; and by you. The words are 'When *you* set your hair at home . . .'—so you provide the totality, the pivot around which these different facets of personality come to *mean*. The totality of the page is only seen by you: you unite the different frames visually, in looking at the ad; although they are supposed to suggest a *narrative*—(your hair style lasts on Monday, Tuesday, Wednesday, etc.)—throughout a week—they are presented simultaneously and their overt narrative is subordinate to the implied whole. Note that no one image of the girl meets your eye: because no *one* of them is 'you'. You combine them.

So A27 is another example where in *receiving* the advertisement, in creating its meaning, we become its meaning. Only we can create the 'whole' woman, because of our simultaneous access to all the parts; we create the whole, the only place where that unity lives is inside us.

The multiple-identity type of ad is particularly relevant in relation to women. I have already suggested that it provides a way for ads to incorporate potential criticisms, and flaws in their own system of meaning. This applies especially to their attitude to women, who have for so long been seen as one 'feminine' entity by advertisements. The idea of 'Women's lib' has filtered into ads in that they are determined to show that their product suits not only all kinds of women, but all the kinds of women within you.

A28: In this 'Cachet' advertisement the lay-out itself has been altered from the equal-sized panels of the other split-up, divided page ad, thus indicating individuality more convincingly. There are just the same separated and labelled compartments for the woman's life (her appearance, her hobby, her job) but the variation in the shape and size of the panels in illustrating these generates the illusion of less rigidity.

Again, we create ourselves from the multiplicity of the ad: our individuality is implied in the presentation of these *different* kinds of individuality. The writing says, 'We know you don't want to look like the next girl', and then shows you girls who are all doing something 'different'—yet the sum of these differences is a sameness.

It is not really surprising that this creation of differences should be connected particularly with sexual roles (see section e on Lacan); and although with the two preceding ads showing *women*, they *seemed* liberated (i.e. you can be a career girl as well as a night-time beauty etc.) the limitations and implications of these roles show up more clearly in ads where the principle is applied to men. There is an ad for the Maxi car, with the caption, 'Both the car *you* want . . . and the car you both need'; where the first phrase goes with a picture of the man, alone, stepping into his car and impressing the boss; the second picture shows him and his wife filling the car with shopping. That 'the car *you* want' should be miraculously combined with 'the car you *both* need' shows as assumption that the car you want——*he* wants, to impress his boss, to bolster his ego, to improve his business relationships—is naturally going to be in opposition to the car for activities involving *her:* domestic chores, duties to be fulfilled, etc. The first 'you' is singular, addressed to the man: the second 'you' in the situation of obligation, duty, *needing* rather than *wanting*—encompasses the woman, and is plural. She is not connected with the desire, the glamour, the man's true 'wants': she represents the nagging, necessity side of life.

A29 shows another divided personality, united again by a car—

A30

As a bio-chemist I recommend Skin Dynamics.

A29: This example goes a step further than the 'Maxi' ad: there are now *three* cars in one. The 'gutsy', 'youthful', exciting car, for romance—the symbol of his virility; the sensible, practical, family car for 'the kids and the dog'; and finally, the stylish, spacious car for impressing 'the boys' and carrying the fishing tackle. The point of these different situations is not simply that each demands a different kind of car; the ridiculous thing is, they obviously *don't*, since the point of the ad is that one car will do for all three. Again, the separation and crude labelling of different aspects of life takes place only in order to bring out the product and prove that actually it can unite these aspects.

Who says you can't afford a sporty coupé, a family saloon and a handy estate?

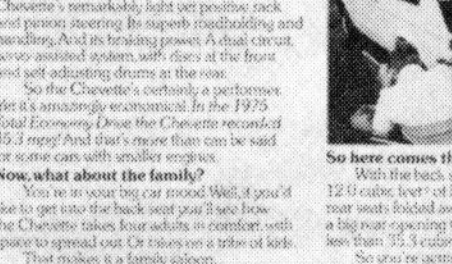

CHEVETTE
It's whatever you want it to be.

A29

These car ads, together with the 'all the women you are' ads, show us a very strange kind of relationship between men and women: men who separate their family from the truly 'masculine' aspects of their life; women who have to metamorphose from the practical office girl to a beauty queen (with hair still set!) for a date with HIM; and he, no doubt, in his 'racy, aerodynamic youthful mood' shutting out all thoughts of the kids and the dog, and maybe the wife.

The final example in this section, A30, shows a type of 'split-personality' advertisement which leads to the topic of the next section. It shows a divided woman, yet, in that one half represents the *advertisement*, and one half, the *consumer*, it also represents very precisely the 'mirror' relationship of same-but-differentness, an identity split around the product, into which our desire for a *unified* self is projected.

A30

As a woman,
I love
Skin Dynamics.
Skin Dynamics
From the laboratories
of Elizabeth Arden.

A30: The implications of this typically 'schizophrenic' advertisement are not at first apparent. (For extreme 'schizophrenia', see the American TV commercial where the same woman seen on a split screen in her kitchen and her living room simultaneously, holds a conversation with herself on the merits of a certain cleaning product, and recommends it to herself.) The crucial fact is that the model is seen 'as a woman' in *contrast* to her job-role 'as a bio-chemist'. A bio-chemist, goes the message, is not a woman. The model is only a woman when she relinquishes all signs of her career, her position in a man's world. Note that as a biochemist, her hair is neat, she wears a masculine-style shirt and jacket (not a dress) and most important of all, her mouth is closed. In the 'as a woman' picture the same woman has styled hair, and an obviously 'feminine' blouse or dress made out of something slinky, and her lips are parted invitingly. Her whole facial expression is now geared to an observing man.

This split-up woman also typifies the split between seller and consumer: on one side she 'recommends' Skin Dynamics; on the other, she says with a slight note of surprise, 'the great thing about Skin Dynamics is that it works'! As though the promises made on behalf of the product by the advertiser, and its results as experienced by the consumer, were inherently separated. As of course they are; but this bridging of the two with the one biochemist/woman model (what is she during the working day, androgenous?) is an interesting use of the 'split personality' genre in advertising.

It is the split itself that makes these meanings (described above) possible; each half of her is a symbol in relation to the other half. Different images of a single woman are here made to perform the same function as the opposition between Catherine Deneuve and Margaux Hemingway, in the two ads A8 and A9. They had a significance in relation to each other; and in order for this one woman to have significance, she must be divided, so that she can signify a biochemist (as opposed to a woman) and a woman (as opposed to a biochemist). This is a very clear demonstration that differences are essential to signification. One thing cannot mean in itself: it has to be in relation to others, and a completely unified entity cannot mean in relation to itself. The importance of systems of difference *between* people and things has been the starting point of this whole discussion (cf. Chapter 1); such differences can generate a meaning to a third party, ourselves. But since differentiation is necessary for *any* signification, it is obvious that for one thing or person to have significance to itself, it must be divided. Thus with this woman, each half depends for its meaning on what the other is not. Being a woman means non-biochemistness, and vice versa.

However, despite this division, and the fact that we actually see two 'different' women on the page, we identify them as one; we know that they are both 'her', a single person. Now, we do not *see* her as unified, spatially: we see her as divided; therefore our perception that she is indeed 'the same' is one that exists on the level of imagination. Her unity is not a visual, but an *imaginary* fact. That a spatial separation should be mentally grasped as an 'actual' unity despite the mutually signifying status of its two sides, is a paradox that will be explored more fully in the next section.

(e) Advertising And The 'Mirror-Phase'

I have shown how the work of advertising consists in an exchange of signs—a 'currency' which itself produces social relations and is founded in real monetary relations. The differentiation of products, through their exchange with images of value represented simultaneously in the ad, allows the differentiation and appellation of concrete individuals as subjects: a process located among the 'Ideological State Apparatuses' (see p. 40). What this section attempts to clarify is how and in what form there *is* a subject to be appellated, differentiated, addressed. A unified subject is the premise of communication. 'People like you . . .' assumes both a coherent ego, one that is in a position to compare itself to other egos, and an implicit 'non-youness'—a system of differences. It has already been pointed out that difference is crucial to signification: a sign is defined by what it is not. In order to be a sign at all, it must also point to an Other, the referent which it *is not*, but which it *means*. The subject may indeed be given a 'gestalt' of different subjective possibilities to be united in the product, as in the previous section: but it was shown there that this still presupposes a coherent self, a subject—or at least, it presupposes the *desire* for such a self.

What the advertisement clearly does is thus to signify, to represent to us, the *object* of desire. Since that object *is the self*, this means that, while ensnaring/creating the subject through his or her exchange of signs, the advertisement is actually feeding off that subject's own desire for coherence and meaning in him or her self. This is as it were the supply of power that drives the whole ad motor, and must be recognised as such.

Yet unless we are to suppose that everyone, everywhere, is born with this same desire for both coherence and individuality (and the importance attached to these things varies in different societies so they cannot be taken as timeless and universal) we have to turn around and look back into society and its signification for the conditions producing such an emphasis on the Self. I am not denying its real existence: but it is important to examine the way it is produced because this must be inextricably connected with the way it is *re*-produced in advertising.

The above definition of signification—a system of differences, in which each sign also points to an Other, its Referent, is clearly analogous to the system of Differences which is society, in which we are each a sign of ourselves: as Lévi-Strauss says, we have each become our own 'totem'. Thus the signifying practices of society are inextricably bound up with what we are—who we are. I am setting out this context for the discussion to follow in order to emphasise its extreme relevance to advertising. I am going to use certain 'tools' from Jacques Lacan, because I believe they are valuable in understanding the process of ideology as it reproduces itself in advertisements.

Lacan's psychoanalytic theory is important because it sees consciousness as *created* and not inherent: the subject is formed, not born. The idea of a creation of 'consciousness' is obviously related to ideological processes. See the Oxford Dictionary definition of the *subject* as a '*conscious self*': with Althusser's definition of ideology as constitutive of and constituted by, the category of Subject, this makes 'consciousness' itself necessarily ideological. This is not pejorative: ideology may be 'good' or 'bad'. But we must undo its transparency before we can even begin to decide what we think of it; then it may show its colours like a 'magic painting book'. Althusser says that our *reading* of Freud as revolutionised by Lacan, allows us to see that 'the "*meaning*" of speaking and listening reveals beneath the innocence of speech and hearing the culpable depth of a second, *quite different* discourse, the discourse of the unconscious.'[1] As the analysis of the tyre ad A1 makes clear, this is similar to the strategy of this book: a dismantling of the ad to reveal how it speaks in the apparently 'neutral' realm of the signifier. I do not intend to get entangled in a discussion of the 'unconscious' since it can only be known through its symbolic manifestations, and anyway, once known, it is no longer unconscious. That is why some of Lacan's terms are more helpful than the traditional ones of 'conscious' and 'unconscious'. He uses the terms *Imaginary* and *Symbolic* to describe realms of sameness (a kind of total internality) and difference (= signification).

The axis of the *Imaginary* and the *Symbolic* is the 'mirror-phase'. The theory of the mirror-phase was developed from observations of children in front of mirrors. At first the child is simply an unformed 'hommelette' (as Lacan calls it): flowing in all directions, as it were, he is neither physically co-ordinated nor able to perceive himself; at this stage there is no clear boundary between the child's self and the surrounding world. This primary realm of sameness, before the 'disengagement of the ego from the general mass of sensations'[2] is that of the *Imaginary*.

When the child is confronted by his image in a mirror, there is a process in which he *recognises* himself—it 'really is' him. The 'really is'—the perception that the image *is* himself—means that this process of self-appellation is not like appellation in the sense previously used, since the child still feels *at one* with what is

[1]Louis Althusser, *Reading Capital*, New Left Books, 1970, p. 16.
[2]Freud, *Civilisation and Its Discontents*, Hogarth Press, 1975, p. 4.

external. But the status of the image as a unity, a 'gestalt' in contrast to the child's as yet undifferentiated self, means that it is also perceived as *another*. The child is aware of his own lack of co-ordination and his inability to see himself all at once, and so although he realises that the person in the mirror is him, it is also *different* from himself since it has a unity he lacks. So, faced with an image of his corporeal unity, the child is required to place his identity in separation. Lacan calls this a 'prototype' for the world of objects, since the place of the *imaged-I* (the mirror reflection) is that of an object. That the image of his totality has this status, provides the subject with the permanent capacity to place himself in a similar relation to *an object*; this capacity is exploited by the forms of ideology.

In the Imaginary the child is still bound up with an image of himself in a unified position; the child and his image, 'subject' and 'object', are not differentiated. This fictional totality which Lacan calls the *Ideal-Ego* is formed by the imaginary capture of the ego by its reflection. Their 'unity' is a sort of leap of desire. Since the imaged-I is separate spatially from the child, the link must inevitably be an imaginary one: to consider the Other as the Same must by definition be imaginary. But in the mirror-phase, there is also an 'apprenticeship to language' in that the separation of the self creates the potential for signification of the self. An important point to emphasise here is the 'otherness' that is necessary for the construction of the subject in language. The *Symbolic* is a construct of differences in that the sign is no longer collapsed with its referent; the child is split from his image.

To summarise: the child's relation to his mirror-image involves two contradictory perceptions. One is that he and the image are the same; on the level of the Imaginary the barrier of the mirror is broken and there is a flow of identity between the child's self, and its representation, the image of the self. This imaginary unity is the *Ideal-Ego*. But paradoxically, for the image to represent the 'unified' self, it must be split from the self; because a sign must *signify* something, and for the image to 'mean' him, it inevitably cannot *be* him. So two areas are constituted: that in which *sameness* exists, the Imaginary; and that in which *difference* exists, that of the Symbolic.

But the existence of an 'Imaged-I' simply creates the *potential* for the Symbolic: which is a very suggestive idea in relation to advertising. The mirror image could be seen as an empty signifier of the self; because of its distance yet similarity it offers the form of a sign, but a hollow sign with no content. It can represent the child, but until he himself is differentiated from others, it cannot represent him in terms of a social identity, a 'social-I'. He does not yet have one, to *be* represented. Thus the mirror image may create a potential signification of the child's identity, but at this stage his identity itself is not defined, the symbol can have no differential meaning. There is still the capacity for the Imaginary unity of image and child.

The access to the *Symbolic* is afforded by the recognition of sexual difference. It is this which creates the 'social-I' Once the 'social-I' is formed it is impossible to return to the old, unified 'Ideal-Ego', because the mirror image now reflects the Social-I and this is a symbolic representation. The image has solidified, taken shape, because the child it reflects has been, as it were, cut out from what he is not. The mirror image now has a particular meaning in relation to the child, and so he can never again merge with it completely. It means himself, to him. And *he* means himself, in relation to others.

Once the boundary between the Imaginary and the Symbolic has been crossed, it is impossible to return. But though the fictional totality of the Ideal-Ego is broken, the subject is haunted by its ghost. Lacan calls this the *Ego-Ideal*, which implies the restoration of a previous unity but with the paradoxical aim of keeping the new, social identity *and* that former unity. The desire to become reunited with his mirror image once the subject has entered the realm of language, the Symbolic, is a desire that can never be fulfilled since the image is now a symbolic representation and as such, irreconcilable with its referent. So the 'Ego-Ideal', the *idea* of the unified ego *after* socialisation, is a sign, an echo, of the actual Ideal-Ego which existed in the pre-linguistic Imaginary. The unity which we desire with a *symbolised* self, is by definition only possible in the world of the Imaginary, which cannot be restored precisely because the self *is* symbolised. Thus the desire for the Ego-Ideal can never be fulfilled and involves the vain invocation on the Imaginary state.

It is precisely here that ideology, as a system of representations which also invites *identification*, can and does intervene. It was an image—(according to Lacan, a mirror-image) that first made us aware of ourselves as separate from others. But in signifying us in this way, it also became split from us because of the inevitable sign/referent relationship between image/self. I do not believe that the *mirror* image is itself crucial: there are many ways of learning to see oneself besides through the looking glass. I prefer to use the idea of 'mirror phase' as a *metaphor*, a shorthand for all social and external reflection of the self.

For Lacan says that the ego is constituted, in its forms and energy, when the subject 'fastens himself to an image which alienates him from himself' so that the ego is 'forever irreducible to his lived identity'.[1] Clearly this is very similar to the process of advertising, which offers us an image of ourselves that we may aspire to but never achieve. The idea of a 'mirror' offering a spatial unity of the self, but at a spatial distance from the self, has already been introduced in the previous section. I have also examined in section c, the peculiarly isolated position of the 'receiver-space' laid out for the subject in front of the ad. According to Lacan '... the mirror phase is a drama ... which manufactures for the subject, *captive to the lure of spatial identification, the succession of phantasies from a fragmented body-image to a form of its totality*...': it leads 'to the assumption, finally, of the armour of an alienating identity'.[2]

Advertisements alienate our identity in constituting us as one of the objects in an exchange that we must ourselves make, thereby appropriating *from us*, an image which gives us back our own 'value'. In the No. 6 ad, A22, *you* give the product its image/value (because it is people like *you* who smoke it) and then in buying the product you receive this image back. So *this* alienation takes place via the product. However, the people in the No. 6 picture are *also* giving the product its value—creating its image, 'signifying' it, and also using it. Therefore we are in the same relation to the product as they are; it becomes the 'mirror' axis which unites them and us, although we are spatially separate. Similarly, we are a 'Babe', and so is Margaux Hemingway (A9). But since 'they', or she, are *in the ad*, this is an identification which takes place across spatial distance. In A8, Catherine Deneuve's eyeline is aligned with ours, and this is true of most ads, where a face stares back at us with a gaze that merges with our own. In the 'gestalt' ad A27, however, the eyelines are all haywire; the point being, that the total subject is off-stage, absent. Here, the spatial identification involves a gestalt process: the totalisation of a 'fragmented body-image'; while with the single figure, in ads, our position is analogous to looking in a mirror, and seeing one *already* unified being. In other words, in the 'Divisions' ads, *we* are as it were looking *out* of a mirror, in that we provide the absent unity for a disjointed person; we are the total image, or would like to be. But with Catherine Deneuve or Margaux Hemingway, we are given a single representation whose relation to ourselves can be clarified by the use of the 'mirror-phase' idea, with the categories necessarily incorporated in it, the irreconcilable 'Imaginary' and 'Symbolic'.

[1]'The Mirror Phase', *New Left Review* No. 51.
[2]ibid.

For advertising as an ideological apparatus, as a signifying system within the Symbolic, is able to *re*present to the subject his place in the Imaginary. Ads set up, in your active relationship towards them, the fictional creation of an impossibly unified self: an 'Ego-Ideal'. They show you a symbol of yourself aimed to attract your desire; they suggest that you can *become* the person in the picture before you. But this merging with an 'objectified' image of yourself is impossible: the desire for it is simply a channelling of the desire for the pre-Symbolic, Imaginary Ideal-Ego. It is important to remember that the subject *cannot* completely be returned to the mirror as it were, since to understand an advertisement is to comprehend a system of differences that is of the Symbolic order. What the ad can do is to *misrepresent* the position of the subject, and to misrepresent its relation to him. It disguises its symbolic nature in offering you a unity with the sign, a unity which can only be imaginary, and hence a denial of the Symbolic. Yet the collapsing into unity of sign and referent (the ideological function of this is discussed in Chapter 3)—and of subject and image, means nothing less than the absolute accession to the symbolic. So ads form a symbolic system which appropriates and apparently *represents*, the Imaginary; therefore embodying the inherent contradiction of the mirror-phase. An advertisement dangles before us an image of an Other; but invites us to become the Same: capitalising on our regressive tendency towards the Imaginary unity of the Ego-Ideal. In offering us *symbols* as the objects of unity they ensnare us in a quest for the impossible.

In previous chapters the conflation of sign and referent was revealed in ads where Happiness was a cigar called Hamlet. But where the sign and its referent are the 'mirror' image and its subject (the self) this means that the gulf between the person *looking* at the ad and the other *in* the ad is effaced. What lies at the root of this process of the Symbolic, that drives to efface itself, is *desire*. Desire is directed both at the symbol and at unity with the symbol: thus it does not recognise the boundary between Imaginary and Symbolic. It blindly strives after the unattainable, constantly replenished because never fulfilled.

Similarly, in the ad, the sign never *is* the referent, the picture is not what it represents—but this is not acknowledged by desire. The function of this in the ad is to make up a fundamental imbalance: between one sign and another; between the signified other and the self. It is precisely desire that traverses this space and makes up a lack. We want to merge with, to be a part of, something that signifies us only through its separation from us: if Catherine *was* Heathcliff (see Chapter 1) they wouldn't mean so much to each other. Desire must always make a leap, across that gap between self and other, in its attempt to unite them. Christian Metz puts this very clearly in *The Imaginary Signifier*: '. . . desire is very quickly reborn after the brief vertigo of its apparent extinction, it is largely sustained by itself as desire . . . the lack is what it wishes to fill, and at the same time is always careful to leave gaping, in order to survive as desire. . . . It pursues an imaginary object (a 'lost' object) which is its truest object, an object which has always been lost and is always desired as such.'[1]

A31

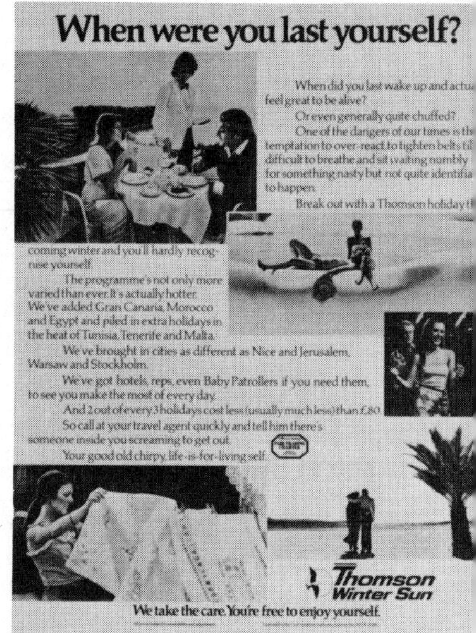

A31: This ad represents with peculiar explicitness a 'Lacanian' situation, especially in the fact that it is for travel, an idea wide open for appropriation in terms of traversing the distance between you and the 'real you'—actually going off, spatially, to find the 'lost' Self.

The first sentence is a question: 'When were you last yourself?' The ad being for *travel*, the terminus for this question is: 'We take the care. You're free to enjoy yourself'. The primary selling point is that with Thomson Holidays you can be free and happy, but the framework in which this is inserted is more central. Thomson Holidays don't just make you happy, they lead you to your 'good old chirpy, life-is-for-living self'. If you '*break out*' with a Thomson Holiday, you'll 'hardly *recognise yourself*'. Clearly, travel has departed from real holidays and has come to occupy the space between the Ego, 'tightening its belt and finding it difficult to breathe', and the 'Ego-Ideal', represented implicitly as what you really are. Travel here is the regression from the social-I to the Imaginary: notice that, e.g., 'baby patrollers' are available to remove what places you in a social relation. Travel decomposes the *difference* of Nice and Jerusalem; it forms them not as a chain in the Symbolic, which is what they are (in this context) but as *imaginary possibilities* for the ego, traversed by Thomson Holidays. Between the frightened self, waiting, apparently, 'for something nasty but not quite identifiable to happen', and the alienated-to-be-rediscovered self, 'something inside you screaming to get out', lies an exchange accomplished by a travel agent.

Every image that accompanies these words presents 'others' (collapsed into ourselves since the gap between the two is the travel that we may purchase), locked in a moment of stasis: eating, swimming, dancing, *looking*: the final image shows a woman observing something behind what looks like a sheet. She is probably about to purchase what is the object of her gaze. She has recognised something, just as we may recognise ourselves in travelling between our suffocating self and the 'real' self that awaits us in a Thomson Holiday. Behind the backs of the couple walking into the sun in the final image we may find our selves in an undifferentiated place where '*life is for living*'. This tautology reveals the spurious nature of the whole regressive journey, the 'finding' of the 'true' self.

[1]*Screen*, Summer 1975.

(f) The Created Self

The 'object which has always been lost' (see above) is, in this context, a perfect version of oneself. That the mirror offers this while simultaneously separating you from it, is shown clearly by the next ad:

2

When did your skin last smile back at you?
If you're not happy with your skin, get Glow 5. You'll soon brighten up. Because Glow 5 Beauty Mask works like a magnet on those impurities that dull your skin . . . draws out grime and old make-up. You can feel your skin starting to glow.
As Glow 5 cleans your pores, it makes them contract so they don't show. Your face ends up silky-smooth. Beautiful!
And that's something to smile about.
Glow* 5
BEAUTY MASK by ANNE FRENCH
*Trade mark

A32: This mirror image involves a separation—between you, 'not happy with your skin', and the version of you with perfect skin, shown actually *in* the mirror within the ad: a situation where your skin smiles back *at* you indicates a gulf between *you* and *your skin*. This illustrates the status of an object that the mirror image has. Your skin becomes a separate thing; though at the same time, the mirror image's status as *you* is emphasised by the non-youness of the people in the pictures in the corner of 'your' mirror—the man is the Other whom you wish to attract. In reality these pictures and the picture of 'your skin smiling back' are equally separate from you. But by representing the mirror within the picture, you are inevitably put in the position of the girl facing the mirror; your space in front of the ad is appropriated by its own structure. And in putting you in front of a mirror like this you are given the possibility of merging with the world of objects in the mirror, since despite the fact that she *is* Other, our spatial position means that we are supposedly able to be united with her.

While A32 showed your skin as an object, separated from you by the mirror, the next ad, A33, shows the logical conclusion of this separation; you and your skin may actually be set in conflict. Your body surface has been removed from 'you' and come to represent, in A32, a perfect, smiling you, but in A33, an enemy to you. Note that in both ads, the woman's eyeline is matched with yours—she stares straight back at you like your own reflection.

A33: Here, the idea that your skin can 'let you down' shows that it is seen as separate from 'you'. Again, there is a gulf between you and the woman pictured, since *you* are supposedly worried about your skin and whether it will let you down, while *she* has apparently flawless skin. Notice that she holds a mirror, but does not look at it. She looks directly out at the spectator: so it reminds us of the mirror-relationship, but since its back is to us, we substitute for it the invisible mirror between 'her' and 'us'.

It is not a coincidence that these two 'mirror' ads are directed at your face and skin. These are the parts of you that manufacturers literally do appropriate, in that their products may coat you with their thin masking layer of chemicals: the surface you see in the mirror may well be 'theirs', and not 'yours'. A32 was for 'Beauty *Mask*' by Anne French. In the mirror, your external appearance, your face, already has the status of an object; so it can easily become an object that is the property of the manufacturers—but one held up as purchasable. Thus our faces, having already been removed from us (you cannot *see* your own face) by the mirror, can be taken over completely, as the only time our face *ever* appears to us completely is at a distance, as an *image*; and in the following ads our face becomes, not part of us, the consumer, but the *product*:

Your age is no secret, if your skin lets you down.
These days it really doesn't matter how old a woman is. Both youth and maturity can be equally attractive. Advances in knowledge of health, exercise and diet have made it possible for the mature woman to go on looking lovely. As long as she cares for her skin.
Time passes and takes with it the youthful moisture that makes young skin young. Without this moisture the wrinkle dryness of age can start. Thanks to a remarkable substance called 'Oil of Ulay'* this is a process you can alleviate.
'Oil of Ulay' is a unique blend of tropical moist oils that almost exactly duplicates the skin's own natural lubrication. Apply it and it is quickly absorbed to enrich 'starved' skin cells. The skin regains the suppleness of youth, it feels soft and smooth. And all without a trace of grease.
Smooth a thin film of 'Oil of Ulay' beauty fluid on your face and neck night and morning. Its light, fresh texture penetrates easily into your thirsty skin to form the perfect base for a flawless matt make-up during the day. And a rich nourishment at night.
'Oil of Ulay' puts back the moisture that time takes away.

A3

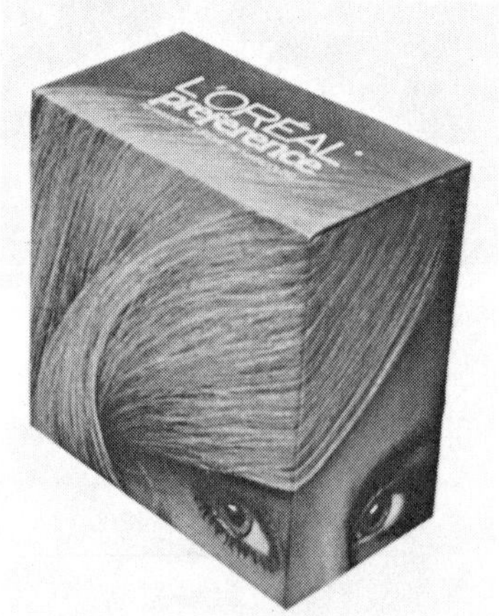
L'ORÉAL
préférence

A34

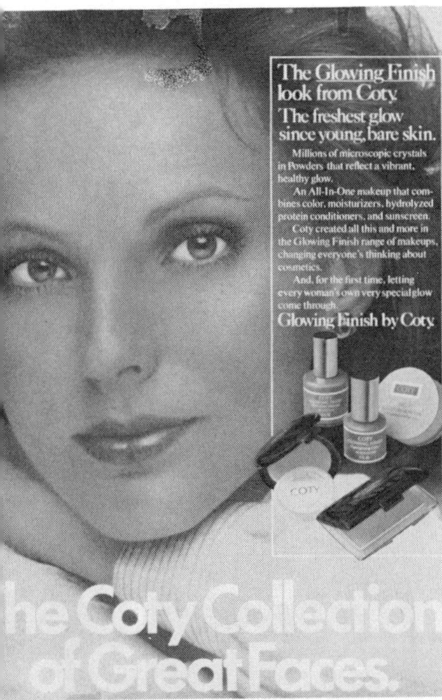

The Glowing Finish
look from Coty.
The freshest glow
since young, bare skin.
Millions of microscopic crystals in Powders that reflect a vibrant, healthy glow.
An All-In-One makeup that combines color, moisturizers, hydrolyzed protein conditioners, and sunscreen.
Coty created all this and more in the Glowing Finish range of makeups, changing everyone's thinking about cosmetics.
And, for the first time, letting every woman's own very special glow come through.
Glowing Finish by Coty.
he Coty Collection
of Great Faces.

and is sold back to us, to recreate ourselves. It is implied that we can recreate a unity with our appropriated image; our face is always Other in the mirror, yet is ours, so why should not these faces become 'ours'?

A34: The face as part of a collection: 'The Coty collection of great faces' shows that it is *owned* by someone else. It is given the status of a work of art: in other words an object. It becomes a thing, to be classed with others of its kind, not linked with a person or a body.

A35: As in A34, the face is seen here as an art object. The photograph is textured to resemble an oil painting. But here, the object-like nature of the whole face means that bits of it becomes objects, too: 'the hand-painted mouth'.

A36: Here, the eyes have become the particularly created part of the face. A crucial word here is 'creates': Revlon creates *your* face—which simply becomes 'the' face, any face. It is a product; Revlon actually creates only the make-up but make-up is equated with face. The eyes are the emphasised part; it is *the* face with *the* fabulous eyes. The '*the*' here particularly stresses the thingness of the face; the three small pictures show that the face is indeed mass-produced. In these little pictures the eyeshadow is shown in different colours but the face around it remains identical. This shows that it is merely a dummy, a *thing* for the eye colour to work on. Note also that the Fabulous Eyes here do *not* look into yours: they look just past you. Here, the Face and the Eyes are at their most detached, most object-like, not even linked to us by a meeting gaze.

A35

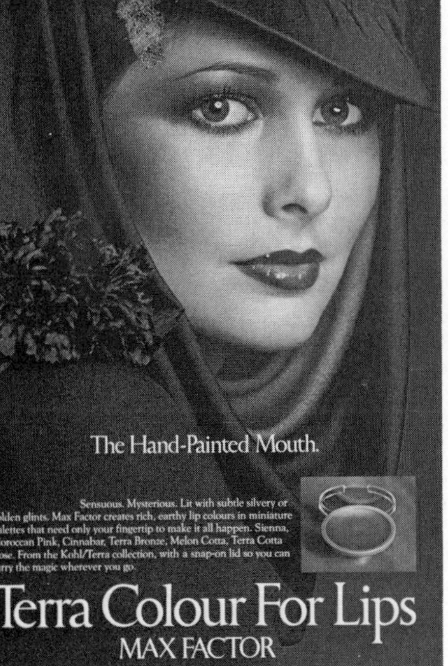

A36

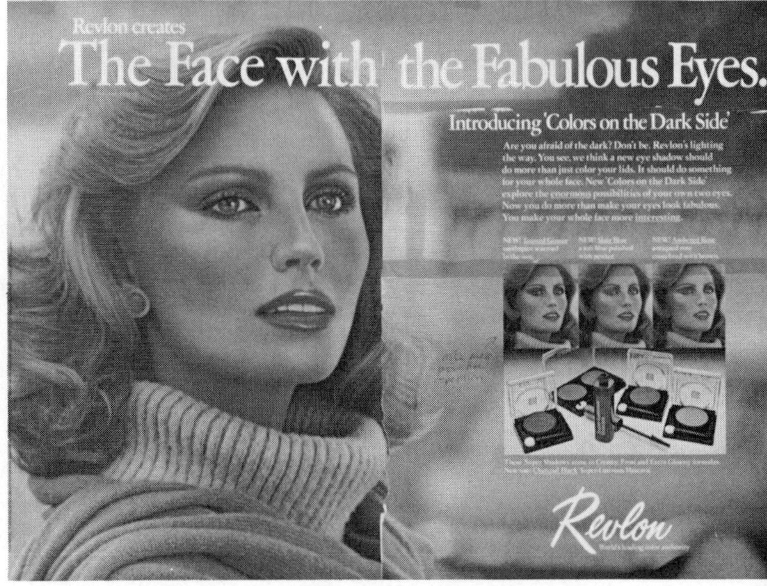

Since parts of you have been claimed as separate objects by advertisements, in order to get back these 'lost objects' you must buy them and recreate yourself out of your own 'spare parts'; a sort of 'Identikit'. There is an ad for men's clothing on underground escalators which shows a selection of clothes 'for all the lives you lead' and then a total outfit, described as a 'Lifestyle Kit'. This—a Lifestyle Kit—is precisely what ads offer us. In buying products with certain 'images' we create ourselves, our personality, our qualities, even our past and future. This is a very existentialist concept: existentialism is important in ideology because it endows the alienation of modern life with a philosophical inevitability. Sartre says of his early life, 'I never stopped creating myself: I was both giver and gift'.[1] What he describes here as a part of his growing up is one of the most alienating aspects of advertising and consumerism. We are both product and consumer; we consume, buy the product, yet we *are* the product. Thus our lives become our own creations, through *buying*; an identikit of different images of ourselves, created by different products. We *become* the artist who creates the face, the eyes, the life-style.

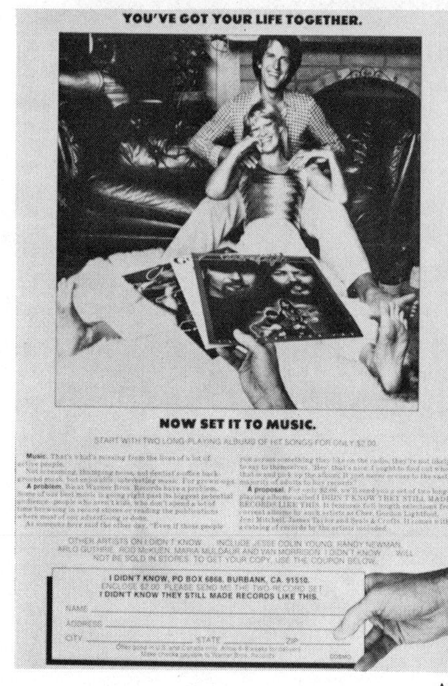

A.

A37: The kind of self-artistry implied by this ad is startling. 'Your life together' is a creation, a made thing; like an artistic creation of literature, it can be 'set to music'. This phrase is very revealing; it shows the people's *life* as a kind of movie always on display to which the records provide the soundtrack. There is also a terrible note of finality in these two sentences. 'You've got your life together'—that's finished, completed. It will not change. The next step, equally static and final, since it is only a parallel to the first, is to 'set it to music'.

Setting a ready-made life to music presents life itself as a purchasable artifact.

[1]Jean-Paul Sartre, *Words.*

CHAPTER THREE
SIGNS FOR DECIPHERING: HERMENEUTICS

'For while there is clearly a mask, there is nothing behind it; it is a surface which conceals nothing but itself, and yet in so far as it suggests there is something behind it, prevents us from considering it as a surface.'

J. L. Baudry[1]

Hermeneutics

By this I simply mean interpreting, but interpreting in the sense of deciphering a code, or translating from one language to another: it is an interpretation along given channels, which lead away from the interpreted object, to a 'meaning' behind or beyond it—or even 'inside' it. (In a way, Platonism and Empiricism are closely linked opposites: they find a 'truth' beyond and in *objects, respectively.)*

Advertisements enclose us more and more in a world that has to be interpreted: a world of significance. The very look of our urban surroundings takes on a symbolic form: objects supplanted from their usual places in our physical lives, from their material context, take on new symbolic meanings on the hoardings and posters where they are no longer *things* but signs. It is part of the 'Imaginary' function of ads to attempt to merge the two, so that these *signs* become things (cf. the Calligraphy section p. 91). In coding the material world around us in this way, ads produce a universe of puzzles—one that we cannot move in without 'deciphering', one that requires us to stop and work out a 'solution'; one where we must 'get' the latest Guinness joke or pun. As Lévi-Strauss describes, the natural world for the tribal mind is bristling with signs to be deciphered. This semantic universe provided by nature is now supplanted by a symbolic system: one that is invested with the *status* 'Natural'. I have already shown how ideology represents the subject (it forms and locates him) in a situation of freedom—one of the corner-stones of Liberal Democracy. It will become clear that in advertising the *exclusion* of products, people or language, as opposed to their customary plenitude, works to give the subject the impression that he is 'free' to produce a meaning for himself. The reasons why this '*production*' is actually *consumption*, have already been implicated—*freedom remains a position* given you by the advertisement.

[1]In *Afterimage* No. 5, Spring 1974, p. 27.

For, although *absence* in ads requires us to fill something in, and *jokes or puzzles* require us to 'decipher' and 'think', these hermeneutic processes are clearly *not* free but restricted to the carefully defined channels *provided* by the ad for its own decipherment. A puzzle has only one solution. A missing piece in a jig-saw has only one shape; defined by its contingent pieces. Since the introduction of certain advertising restrictions, Mackeson have been obliged to give up the claim that their beer 'does you good'. So now they show part of their old slogan: 'Looks good, tastes good, and by Golly. . . .' Now, we must fill in this space for ourselves. We are drawn in, openly, as participants in the meaning. But there is only one correct 'solution' to this: i.e. 'it does you good'. We are referred back to the ad itself (see Chapter 8), to its previous form, and it is *from this* that we derive our knowledge of what to put in the gap. This is simply an example to illustrate how the ad prepares us and guides us to participate 'freely' in its meaning, whether by filling absences, or by 'getting' jokes.

Absences and jokes are not fundamentally different features of advertising. Freud quotes Theodor Lipps on jokes: 'A joke says what it has to say, not always in few words, but in *too* few words—that is, in words that are insufficient by strict logic or by common modes of thought and speech. It may even actually say what it has to say by not saying it.'[1] Thus jokes involve an absence; what is absent is *meaning*. We must break through to it; a joke appears absurd until we have penetrated to its 'point', to what is behind its condensed and flawed surface. Indeed, condensation, one of the essential features of a joke, inevitably involves absence, that of the 'full' meaning, the things condensed. And an actual absence in an ad, as in a verbal puzzle (like crossword clues) always implies that something *should* be there, in other words that something is *meant*.

Therefore jokes and puzzles, humour and understatement in ads, are cases of advertising where certain gaps, and oblique references to what is missing, put us in a position of access to an absent meaning that may be reached through the ad. As I have said, all ads are signs; but this particular kind of ad gives us the impression that we can actually grasp the *referent* through the ad itself. By being such obvious signs, where we have to 'work out' the meaning (as in the Double Diamond series—see below), ads of this sort seem less like signs, in that they hold out their meaning as accessible, they are themselves a physical pathway to the referent—or seem to be—and this prevents us from

[1] *Jokes and Their Relation to the Unconscious*, Chapter one.

assessing the real relationship between sign and referent, finding out ads' real process of signification. The notion of the mask in the quotation above illustrates perfectly the overlooking of the materiality of the signifier in the hermeneutic pursuit of the signified, the apex 'behind' it. We have seen how many complex psychic processes are involved in the work of the ad, and the significance of absences and puzzles in ads is that they give us the opportunity for a 'conscious' activity that masks these unconscious processes. They present their 'manifest' meaning to us as latent, thereby concealing the real 'latent' meaning. In Chapters 1 and 2, I have concentrated on examining the ways in which advertising, as an ideological system, has appropriated systems of signification and psychic processes (which is why both semiology and psychology are valuable in the work of 'decoding' ads): these two areas merge where we ourselves become signs, part of an exchange system. But it is important that we appear, not part of a system, relegated to the status of things, but separate, 'free', and *in control* of such systems. In the process of *deciphering* signs, we are constituted as the discoverers of meaning, and are involved in a 'conscious' activity which keeps us looking through a certain opacity in the signifying process, to a message beyond; thus although involved in a hermeneutic and limited 'deciphering', we overlook the signifying process itself. Our 'active' involvement precludes an awareness of our more complex, unchosen involvement. I have been concerned with the way in which the formal structure of ads, their material surface, functions ideologically in 'signifying' the Subject. A crucial part of this is the ad's built-in *concealment* of it, by referring to a 'reality' or 'meaning' behind its surface: the mask 'conceals nothing but itself'.

In pointing to something concealed, or leaving absences in which this something may be revealed, ads of this sort, although sometimes appearing 'opaque' (needing to be deciphered) are aiming at total transparency: they are pretending to have a 1:1 relationship with their 'meaning', i.e. between signifier and signified. This denies all the complex workings of the signifier so far investigated: because if the signifier leads directly to the signified it becomes nothing but a window, a self-effacing route to the signified. The idea of 'meaning' as behind symbols and forms, directly represented by them, was rejected at the very beginning of Part One. But all the types of ad in this chapter re-introduce this idea. Although ads involving absence, puns, and calligraphy may seem very different, it is important to see the connection in their shared, underlying assumption that *the ad's sign system leads directly to a meaningful reality*. It simply represents what is 'already' there. This denies that the ad creates anything, or works on you, or diverts meanings—all of which we have already seen ads do. But the idea of signs as representational, of meanings as *pre*-existing and accessible to us, is essential to the ideology in which we seem to be free agents, able to understand a world which *has* order and meaning: which in turn obscures the fact that this 'order' and 'meaning' are, of course, determined by ideology, and are not 'actually' and 'already' in the world. But when a sign points beyond itself, it claims merely to reproduce a system of things as they are; it appears to have an external authority for its form. All the ads in this chapter lead us to feel we are interpreting *reality*, that the ad really does refer to *reality* in a direct and not a distorted relationship. The catch is that signs in ads do, of course, refer to a reality—real things are represented; lifted from the materiality of our lives. But these are set up as a symbolic system which does *not* represent the real *place* of these things in our lives: they are re-placed, given a new position ideologically, made to 'mean' something new. As I have said before, products are made, as well as consumed, but this is concealed. Ideology is the representation of *imaginary relationships* between *real things*: and in these 'hermeneutic' ads we discover meanings which, because they involve real things, seem to be real meanings. This is why ideology is so hard to pin down or unravel: because it constantly re-interprets while only claiming to re-present reality. And in the sign's setting itself up as a simple representation of 'reality', it contributes to ideology's claim to 'transparency' and 'obviousness'.

Since this chapter ends the first half of the book, I intend to reiterate some of the ways in which it follows on from the ideas of the previous chapters, and to show how these apply to the three sections of this one; absence, language, calligraphy. Chapters 1 and 2 give an indication of *what* is concealed in ads: this chapter is an examination of *how* it is concealed.

The use of absence and the idea of 'interpretation' in ads has been shown to have an ideological function, in that ideology consists of the creation of concrete 'subjects' acting 'freely'. In Chapter 2 we saw how our involvement in ads both constitutes us as subjects, and involves us, *as* 'free' subjects, in the perpetual reproduction of the ideology which 'appellated' us as subjects in the first place. Our brief exploration of the field of psychoanalysis showed how the process of becoming a subject coincides with the entry into the world of language, to the Symbolic: since becoming a subject entails a differentiation between the self and others, and this differentiation is also what makes signification possible (see Chapter 1). Language is always a system of differences. So is social identity. Lacan's work has shown how the subject is *formed* rather than pre-existent: he/she enters the social sphere and language at the same time, since both these are located in the differentiating area of the Symbolic. The subject is 'cut out' from the world in recognition of difference, of Otherness, of what he is not.

This description of how a subject is created is clearly very pertinent to the idea of filling an absence in ads since an absence is also defined by what it is not, by the contingency of objects *around* it (see A39 and also ads below such as A87). We are invited to insert ourselves into this 'cut-out' space; and thus re-enact our entry into the Symbolic. The things *in* the ad signify us, the absent; they refer to what is not there, the spectator. This is a *classical* form of representation: a sign is something *present* replacing what is *absent*. In ads the play of absence/presence produces a symbolic world where what is replaced by the spectator is formed in relation to what is present—his place is indicated by the *things* in the ad. Ideology is a concrete system of representations that *position* the subject: this *position* may be one of 'freedom'. And position always depends on contingency. We *mean* in terms of a set of relations, of differentiation: just as words mean in a sentence. We are positioned both *in* the ad, by filling an absence, and in *relation* to the ad, by deciphering it. The ideological illusion of freedom is seen in advertisements' holding out the possibility of being interpreted: we can 'consciously' work in 'producing' a meaning. But this is finally the same process as with Catherine Deneuve and Chanel: we make an *exchange* between what is present and what is absent, between signifier and signified. This 'interpretation' is *consumed* rather than *produced*—we do not produce a genuine 'meaning' but consume a predetermined 'solution'; since, as already shown, the process is bounded by the ad itself.

But the 'Symbolic', the difference that makes signification possible, is always disguised in ads by imaginary samenesses. In an exchange of present for absent, of sign for meaning, ads presuppose an *identity* of the two—that they are the same. In all the following ads, the relationship between what is absent and what is present is articulated in terms of symmetry: the signifier is a symmetrical reproduction of the signified. This symmetry can mean that the signifiers may totally 'stand for' the signified—which is absent but perfectly indicated by what is present: as with the ads in the first section below. This absence, which implies an insertion of the signified, is only an inverted form of the second kind of ad shown, where the *signifier* is so transparent as to be obliterated by the signified, which we get through to directly. In other words, where signifier and signified occupy a 1:1 relationship of replacement, either one may be absent, adequately represented by the other. These alternatives characterise sections one and two of this chapter. But the third aspect of this 1 : 1 relationship is that the signifier and signified may be merged in an attempt to collapse the sign with the referent itself: this is seen in calligraphy, making signs and things the same. It is only an extreme example, however, of the tendency in ads to make signs 'do for' the things they replace—investing their significance with a reality that supplants our own reality, from which these 'things' are stolen and made into alien symbols.

A38 is an excellent example of all that has been said in this introduction. By making ads as sign systems seem to refer to reality, they appear 'transparent' and 'natural' (see Chapters 4 and 5): we are *led through them* to the Real World:

A38: This ad invites our participation—we have to *do* something, to become involved; it is like a children's game or puzzle. The ad is relying on our *conscious* action in its meaning. Thus it illustrates the point that we are constituted as free and active: we do not *have* to cut out the screen; if we do participate, we *choose* to do so. Furthermore, we will then see *for ourselves* how the product works.

What we are invited to do, is to fill an *absence*: we are to provide a content 'behind' the empty screen. This content *is* the real world. It seems to have an existence of its own. Yet it is bounded by the frame of the TV: its significance is predetermined by the ad, it becomes limited to the ad's terms. So the world 'behind' the picture, with which we are invited to fill the screen, becomes in fact only a symbol, used to signify the *product*, to represent Sony's TV picture. Yet it also implies that the *ad* is representing a reality.

This ad makes 'filling an absence' into a game: it thus links the ideas of the first and second sections to follow. The absence seems to be filled at random, by our choice, yet is in fact limited by the *presence* of the TV around it; it is always the presence which provides the significance of the absence. This ad also illustrates the attempt to break through or bypass the signifier and see straight to the signified, behind it: or rather, it mistakes the signified for the referent, since what it *signifies* is a kind of TV picture, but the gap for the 'referent' of the picture, the reality represented on TV, diverts our attention from the signified to the referent and thus gives the ad a transparent status—it denies that it is a sign at all. This is relevant to the idea of calligraphy (where language becomes a sign) discussed in section three; since instead of describing a TV with an excellent picture, in *language*, the ad attempts to *show* it, to bring the referent onto the page, and thus collapse the whole signifying process to the level of an 'obviousness'.

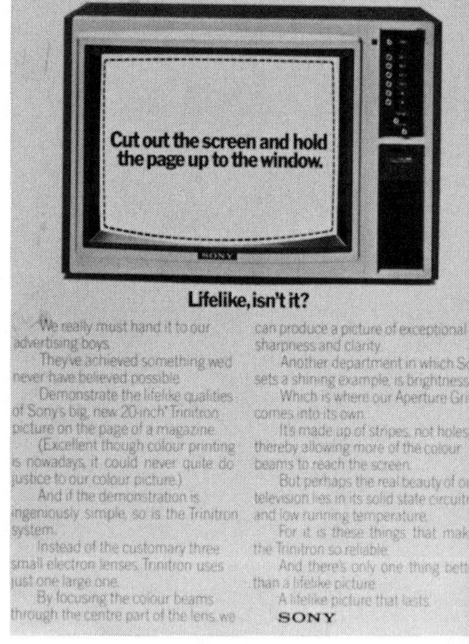

A3

(a) Absence The whole of the previous chapter was an examination of the way advertisements enter the space of the receiver: how their meaning process requires, and depends upon, their slipping into you. The work of the signifier, as endowed with 'latent' meaning, has been shown as very much bound up with the 'unconscious' areas of our understanding. But we usually focus on the 'message' conveyed by the ad—a message which we feel we receive over a distance—and are unaware of the process whereby the formal surface of the ad, the actual arrangement of *things* which carries the 'message', generates a meaning in a circuit through our own minds. The importance of this is that the ad actually *enters us to mean*, it appropriates the process of 'making sense' in us.

However, as has just been suggested above, advertisements conceal this aspect of themselves from us, by diverting our attention to the 'message'; and they are even more diverting if we have to hunt around for it. They function most effectively not by making their meaning immediately apparent, but by holding it up as the result, or prize, of a hermeneutic 'interpretation' of the ad. Having deciphered its surface, we then discard this surface as we 'break through' to the 'hidden' meaning. So this entails a reversal of the ad's slipping into you: you are invited to slip into it, to enter *its* space, drawn in to participate in a 'discovery' of meaning.

One of the most obvious ways in which you are invited to enter the ad is by filling an absence. Now, in a hermeneutic universe, meaning is always 'absent', in that it does not reside *in* things, but must be interpreted through their (limited) channels: it is found in the imaginary space 'behind' them. Therefore 'meaning' in the hermeneutic sense is always absent from the object to be deciphered: that is why decipherment is necessary. Of course, the catch is that this meaning, supposedly the ultimate 'reality', is in fact of totally imaginary nature; yet it is endowed with an ontological status superior to that of the concrete signifiers which are in fact our only clue to its existence.

So 'meaning' is always absent from a system that asks to be deciphered. Therefore absences in the signifying surface take on the nature of 'windows' to the meaning; (cf. A38); they must inevitably be the areas where the 'signified' reveals itself, though as suggested above, this is actually a *masking* of the signified by the *referent*. In the 'mirror-phase', for example, the 'imaged-I' in the mirror signifies the 'I', the person *looking* in the mirror; but yet he is always absent from the mirror, whose signification is a pointing outwards, away from itself, to the referent. I have shown ads where the imaged-person in the ad referred to you, the person absent from the ad. But as, by keeping us busy *deciphering*, ads defer us from *understanding*, so they also deflect the consciousness of this *fundamental* absence by *representing it* within the space of the advertisement itself. Ads produce internal absences: hollows that *anticipate* the receiving subject; gaps whose content has to be interpreted within the parameters set up. It is not as if we were free to *read* the material: by being given something specific to decipher, our comprehension is channelled in one direction only. Advertisements of the following kind reabsorb the 'self-creating' process described at the end of the last chapter—by creating a space for you to do it *in*. While on one level the advertisement surreptitiously, as it were, enters the subject, on another, the subject is given a space in the ad and thereby constituted as an active participant in deciphering it. It is the overt nature of this that is so deceptive; it conceals the meaning we create, by making us seem to 'discover' the meaning 'already' there.

The hermeneutic function of absences in advertisements can be demonstrated more clearly by the following examples:

(*a1*) *The Absent Person*

A39: In this ad there is no person, but we construct a self from the data given (the paper, the cards, the ticket, the hat, the location), the correlatives for a particular character; we 'read *in*' what kind of person has all these objects *around* him. These 'clues' signify a person—but he is absent; and so are we. In this shared absence we can easily merge: we can *become* the absent traveller. The perspective of the picture places us in a spatial relationship to it that suggests a *common* spatiality (as in all 'classical' art); everything is proportioned to the gaze of the observer—*us*, the absent person 'meant' by the picture. This 'deciphering' of the objects in the ad, and the potential coincidence of their 'absent signified' with us, the absent looker, draws us into the ad, which presupposes that we were at a distance from it in the first place. Yet, for their very ability to point to their 'owner', the objects depend upon us; *we* unconsciously assume their *primary* meaning, as signs: e.g. that the 'Times' is an upper-class newspaper, that Istanbul is an exotic place to be, that dark glasses are mysterious, and so on. It is these meanings which point, as *sign-posts* rather than *signs*, to the person who is conspicuously absent. Our knowledge of sign systems outside the ad is called upon; and we are called into it by them.

A similar phenomenon has already been observed in the A21 where the host of the dinner party was absent, at the point where the perspective of the picture opened into the space of the viewer. These ads are almost an invitation for us to *reverse* the mirror relationship: for us to *enter* the mirror and become the

A39

When travelling, a little gold can smooth the way.

A40

figure who, by his absence, is all the more like us. This removal of the imaged-I from the mirror-space of the ad makes obvious, and thus renders transparently innocuous, the invitation for us to enter them held out by *all* ads. Because the mirror space is empty here, no contradiction is implied in our entering and filling it; we can merge with the Other only because he or she is absent. This conceals the difference between ourselves and the Other; we are no longer enticed to an impossible dissolution into the 'Ego-Ideal' because it is absent, already dissolved into *us*. The imaginary unity remains so very imaginary that its imaginary nature is never noticed. It all becomes like a game—hide and seek the subject.

There are numerous examples of this kind of absence in ads—there is not room here to show a great many of them, almost all of which would precisely duplicate A39 in structure. More of them are, however, to be found in the chapter on Time, Chapter 7. Once you start noticing how frequently a subject is lacking in pictorial ads, the elision between you as absent looker and the absent subject becomes a very obvious and widely noticeable feature of advertising. Here is one other of this type, where the hollow for the missing person is a whole room: which is the product.

A40: Here, the angle of the photograph creates the illusion that you are actually in the room, standing just behind, and to the right of, the surface with the tomatoes. *You* are the missing person. Again there are clues about this excluded person forming an outline like a shadow: accessories which point to a life-style—the Scott Joplin music, the wine bottles, the old-fashioned syrup tin.

The wine and glasses and the four bowls also suggest a dinner party: there is a story involved here. The narrative proceeds across the perspective of the picture, from foreground to background (see Chapter 7): the tomatoes and onions lying right next to 'you', the spectator, will be cut up and cooked, then the wine in the background will be drunk, the record played, etc. There is a merging of spatial and temporal movement as the space of the kitchen is crossed by the suggested narrative in this way; yet there is still an asymmetrical relationship between the duration of looking time and the duration of the implied narrative. We are thus given a position in this empty kitchen, both spatially and temporally: constituted in an absence that defines us by crowds of surrounding signifiers. Here there is a kind of 'gestalt' where the sum of the ad's parts creates a totality—the absent subject.

One other point to be made about these 'absence' ads is that they involve a narrative. (Narrative is, of course, all contingency.) In A39, someone is in Istanbul—travelling, card-playing, possibly involved in diplomatic dealings, possibly in something shadier (like his dark glasses). In either case, the scene is set for a story. The same is true with the kitchen, A40. This temporal aspect will be examined in greater detail in Chapter 7. The point in this context is that the leading actor in this narrative is the absent you: you are invited to become locked into a place in a closed narrative which has been hermeneutically revealed, and thus appears open. But it is only open to swallow you up.

The Absent Man

Another type of absence is that of a spectator, and this is usually connected with sex. Here, it is important not to confuse the entry into the ad *as* spectator, with entry by identifying with the person shown, which was the mirror-relationship. In the following example it might seem that there is *not* an absence, since there is a person in the room; but someone *is* conspicuous by his absence, and this is The Man. The 'clues' in the room signify him; and the *woman is simply another one of these clues*. In this case, the hollow in the ad is a sexed one.

A41 The Invisible Man: This woman is looking at a man (who may coincide with the reader: he is drawn in): her words are in reply to his 'what will you drink?' Her dress is unbuttoned provocatively, indicating beyond doubt that the invisible character *is* male; the final factor is the chess set visible behind her, implying a second person, an intimacy, yet defining her intellectual quality in relation to the man, as does her decided preference for a certain drink. The message is that she is at home in a man's world, yet is sexy; and not in a passive way, as is shown by her unbuttoning of her dress. Women (in media) are 'entirely constituted by the gaze of man'. This woman *is* alone, *is* decisive and intellectual: 'Femininity is pure, free, powerful; but man is everywhere around, he presses on all sides, he makes everything exist; he is in all eternity the creative absence. . . .'[1] The man in this picture is nowhere and everywhere, a pervasive presence defining and determining everything, and in whose terms the woman must define herself. She is doomed to see herself through *his* eyes, describe herself in his language.

A4

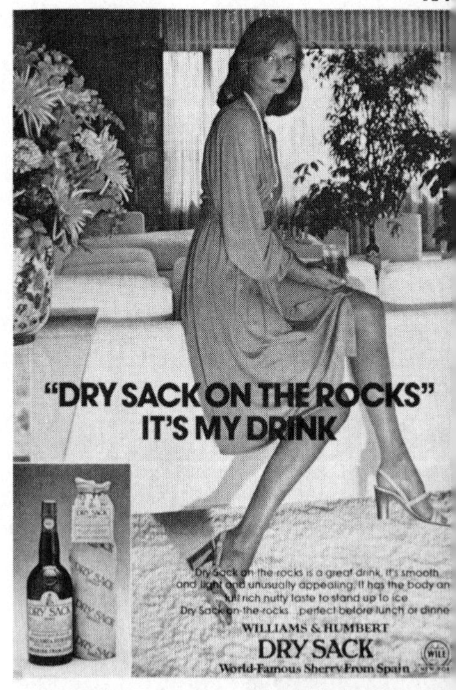

This happens literally in an American ad for a shampoo called 'Gee, your hair smells terrific'. The very product is named in a man's words. He creates the woman, even her shampoo is a means of seeing (or smelling) her via *his* perceptions. And in the ad for the shampoo the caption is 'Gee, you'd look terrific in Hollywood': the invisible man is heard, not seen.

Occasionally the situation is sexually reversed, but this is rare, and the tone is different.

[1]Roland Barthes, *Mythologies*, Paladin, 1973, p. 51.

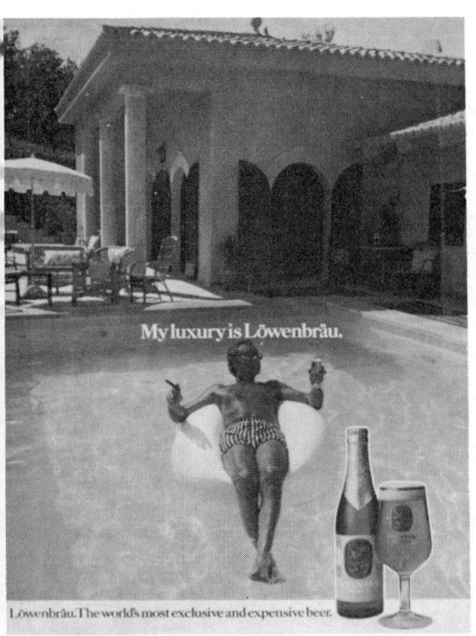

My luxury is Löwenbräu.
Löwenbräu. The world's most exclusive and expensive beer.

A42

A42: Here, a woman seems to be necessary to appreciate the man's luxury and *independence*. He has 'got away from it all' with a drink and a cigar; his isolation, his independence, his masculinity are bound up in this. He, unlike *all* woman models, does not look at an 'audience': he doesn't need to, the audience looks at him. He is not looking out of the ad. He does not have to seek out, to please; he will fasten his gaze on whatever interests him and at the moment it is his beer. We are sold the product by looking *with* him, not *at* him (as with women). The provocative positions of the women in the ads discussed are exaggerated to break through precisely this situation; to attract the free and choosy male.

Thus ads invite you to constitute yourself in coincidence with an absent person, and in relation to certain given objects—one of which may be a member of the opposite sex.

(*a2*) *The Absent Product*

We have so far discussed the 'absent person' in ads. But since this person is always signified by objects (and above all, the product) in the ad, interchangeable with them in that they represent his absence with their presence, it follows that the other side of the exchange, the *product*, may likewise be absent from the ad, and signified by the *people* in it. There is a series of lager ads on TV where the lager itself is never there. In one of these ads, two workers in a factory pick up two empty glasses from the conveyor belt and start 'drinking' lager from them. The foreman comes up behind them and tells them to 'drink up' because it's nearly 'closing time'. In another ad the two men come into a pub which turns out not to have this particular brand of lager when they order it. So they take two empty mugs and again 'drink' the invisible lager. Although the product is actually absent in these cases, it is sufficiently signified in the ad—by the two men—by their attitude towards it, by their taste, and so on. There is also a definite space for it to fill: the surrounding presence of the *mugs* makes the actual presence of the lager redundant. Thus with absence in an ad, the thing meant to fill the gap is always defined, not by a simple replacement but by what is *contingent:* it is what *surrounds* the gap that determines its shape. It is the contingency of the replacing object/person that makes these ads differ from others. As already suggested, *all* ads involve a replacement, they all exchange something present for something absent; what makes the ads in this section special is that they represent the absence *in* the picture—making it part of a chain of contingencies. It is *next to* what replaces it.

The idea of contingency necessarily leads to *narrative*. In ads where people were absent we saw a narrative structure: e.g. the 'story' of the traveller in Istanbul, the 'story' of the dinner party. Giving the product a place in a narrative always involves this sort of definition by contingency: when it is seen as *humorous* however, it is because the 'gap' in the narrative does not completely fit the product. In the Benson and Hedges cinema ads, for example (where Spike Milligan and others are doing a gold robbery and put a packet of Benson and Hedges cigarettes in the alarm bell to jam it, but then one of them cannot resist pulling it out so the alarm rings and they rush off only to sink in their boat because the gold is so heavy)—in these ads the product is made to fill a place in the story that it does *not* adequately fill in reality—it is defined as valuable *by* the story around it and the things (gold, money) shown as exchangeable with it in the story. The joke is the inadequacy of the given cause, in explaining the effect: a discrepancy between the product and its place in the narrative (who would 'really' risk being caught robbing a bank just for a few cigarettes?). We can return to Freud's discussion of jokes as based on '*insufficient*' words or logic. It is the fact that a Benson and Hedges packet of cigarettes is *not* adequate compensation for setting off a burglar alarm and getting caught thieving, which makes the ad funny (and indicates an exchangeability of Gold with Benson and Hedges, which is the main point—a sort of pun). And where 'treasure' is represented by packs of Benson and Hedges in a chest, the joke is again the fact that the cigarettes are *not* treasure. The joke involves an absence—the absence of *real* treasure—an absence that still exists precisely because Benson and Hedges does not adequately stand for treasure and fill that gap in the signification. There is a further dimension to the joke because it is based on the idea of Benson and Hedges being 'Gold': this is a joke on the level of the Symbolic, as the gold packet *stands for* gold; but the identity of packet and real gold is purely *imaginary*. Where the contradiction between the Imaginary and the Symbolic is made overt, there is always a release of humour, since it means that a sign is made to function on the level of the *impossible*. Further, there is an element of 'calligraphy' here in that the slogan 'Pure Gold' is not *written* on the cigarette pack but *shown*, by its *being* pure gold (the colour, not the substance).

These Benson and Hedges ads—which, because of their complexity and subtlety will crop up time and again in this book—unite many aspects of humour and hermeneutics in ads—but centred still on absences, gaps (including those formed by a *misfitting*). The following, A43, indicates a product by its

A44

A 43

absence: it is even Lacanian in that the TV has become the 'lost object'.

A43: Here, the product's contingency in the narrative is used to signify its quality: 'The first time. . . .' Although the TV is absent it is defined by the other objects in the room—the lush plants, the numerous small sockets (they must have lots of electrical appliances), the TV stand. Its absent place is also invested with a sort of *glow*, an aura that places the lost object in the realm of desire. If the 'I' of the slogan ('*I* lost a clear sharp picture . . .') regrets the loss of the TV ('pity'), we, at least, have found it—in the inset 'mini' ad or *alternative* ad, at the bottom of the page. (In as much as we identify with the 'I' in the ad, *we* can recapture what is gone, imaginarily). Thus we are given access to presence and absence simultaneously; the absent thing of the picture is defined by the narrative so clearly (and sharply?) that it virtually becomes present, and this is realised at the end of the 'story'. The only regret we are allowed to experience is that we do not *yet* possess this TV: so in a sense we are implicated in the narrative in that our future purchase becomes contingent to it, giving the story of absence a full and happy ending.

Since the absence of products and the absence of people are interchangeable with their presence, which we 'read in', ads can clearly double the process, in making the presence of one side of the equation contingent on the absence of the other, within the same advertisement.

A 44

This is what they don't watch it on.
do it Murphy style.
Murphy
RANK RADIO INTERNATIONAL

A44: In previous examples I showed how the ad produces an exchange between people and products. This example shows a much more sophisticated method of doing this—precisely by denying the connection in one way and yet relying on it in another. In A44 the absence of people and products is possible in the same picture: we have a choice of either 'removing' the TV and keeping the people, with the world they belong to and signify, or, 'removing' the people, keeping the TV and producing an 'outline', as it were, demarcated by smart people (who cannot be watching the TV and therefore are a potential absence) in which we may place ourselves. It is quite clear that something in the picture does not fit, it is illogical, and this provides a sort of negative potential where we may insert ourselves.

It is important that the couples watching the TV in the picture (or rather 'not watching' it) are somewhat removed from the other party-goers who are standing on a level above them. This is crucial because in 'removing' the couple, who by definition cannot be watching TV, we do not affect the place of another sign for wealth and chic, the 'smart people' generally. The relation between the two groups of people (one watching themselves, the other watching TV) is once again a narrative one—the couple got bored and have gone off to do something else. The function of this narrative separation is to allow us to place ourselves within the ad, without changing its social terrain. Our place is defined in the play between the absence and presence of the exchange formed by a contradiction achieved through language, between the representative couple and the TV. If they can be smart and still watch TV, so can we: if they are 'not watching it', neither are we. The importance of the two groups is that we see 'smart people' both watching and not watching. This is very much having your cake and eating it. The central point, however, is that it is enough for signs to be in relation, even negatively, for them to be meaningfully coexistent and exchange values (i.e. since they are *smart* people 'not watching' the TV, the unwatched TV is smart, too). It is this co-signification that is exploited here: a system of interchangeable *invisibility* is produced. Since smart people *don't* watch TV, either *they* cannot be there watching it, or *it* can't be there to be watched. But this exchange, even of *absence* for *absence* is still one of *value* for *value*. And this implied exclusion of either the people or the product, is produced by the negative relation of the *language* to the *picture*.

(*b*) *Language*

In A44 it was the language that gave opacity to the ad, as it did not make sense in connection with the picture: smart people who don't watch TV were shown watching it. Thus it was language that cracked open the absence in this case: it created a gap of *negativity* in the fact that what was described was pictured in reverse. It was only the language that made a difficulty, an absurdity that we had to interpret; the same phenomenon is seen in A45:

A45: The caption in this ad is 'She's miserable'. Here again, the words and picture catch our attention by their incongruity: we are drawn in, by attempting to understand the 'contradiction'. It is resolved through our 'deciphering': we learn how to assimilate the two elements by reading the small print, where the mystery (she looks happy/she is unhappy) is solved.

Thus language is the basic element in creating a 'hermeneutic' of the ad: the two preceding examples show how we need to 'interpret' its 'misrelation' to a picture—drawn in by an absence of *logic* between the two (which is the definition of a joke). Language is the primary *Referent System* (cf. Part Two) used in ads, in that we bring our understanding of it *to* the ad, it is a system of meaning whose frame the ad can use, but does not generate. Our knowledge of it can be manipulated—as in A44 and A45, where our very ability to understand the 'logic' of words created the tensions within the ads. So our ability to decipher one system—language—creates the difficulty and opacity which in turn lead us to feel we must decipher a second system, the advertisement. But once deciphered, the language, instead of being a system of signs, has become a sign complete in itself, which can then be exchanged with different forms of signs, i.e. pictorial ones: which is what happens in A44 and 45. We can see language used as a pivotal sign in A46:

A46

A46: Here, the slogan 'sex has never been a problem for us' can be read either up or down in the page. Because it is inside the pictorial part of the ad, it functions like a caption for the picture: here, it implies that the couple have no problem with their sex life. But these words, simply because they *are* words, are linked to the block of language beneath them; and read downwards, the phrase has a quite different meaning: that 'Minis' are made for both the sexes. This gives the picture and the block of words the status of signs, because they replace each other—they are exchangeable around the central axis of the slogan. Thus the verbal section of the ad is, *in itself*, a sign.

Having established that language can function as a sign, not only as a group of signs, it can be shown that ads may use language in exactly the same way as pictorial signs: it can be present, to be deciphered, or absent, to be filled in.

(*b1*) *Words: Deciphering Language, Puns and Puzzles*

Language can make very precise references, which we decipher as part of the 'real world', since it is the most accessible to us of all the forms used in ads, and we use it ourselves—it almost becomes *our* speech. Ads can use language closer to or further from our own, to produce different effects—we decipher a certain meaning from the *style* of the language used, the *way* in which it is written.

A47

A47: Here, very colloquial language is used, so the product is linked to everyday life, valued in a child's terms—'I'll swop my prize marble for a finger'. The writing itself joins in this significance, as it is a child's writing. There is also a sort of narrative implied: a playground 'deal' between two children. All this is signified purely by the language in itself (= connoted: see Part II).

A48: Here, on the other hand, we see an ad which uses the reverse technique: unfamiliar language intended to convey 'class', something special; we are told, through the language, that this is something just a little bit different.

But not *too* different. The ad has made use of a well known proverb, 'smile and the world smiles with you'. Using a colloquial phrase, as the *structure* of the ad, keeps the foreign word within a familiar framework, and this prevents it from alienating us. Using an English proverb and a French word conveys the precise meaning desired; that this rather groovy French product will be very much at home in the English context. The balance between novelty and familiarity which is an integral part of the message, is actually contained *in* the language used.

Fume
and the world
fumes with you
GAULOISES
DISQUE BLEU
GAULOISES
Fume a Gauloises: It's French. For to smoke.

Thus we see the use of language as a conveyor of decipherable meaning, not in its spoken 'message' but in the very style, even written (calligraphic) style (with the Kit-Kat ad)—in other words, it functions as a *sign* in itself, signifying childishness, or Frenchness, in the above two examples.

This ability of language to refer to particular worlds, to invoke certain areas of 'reality' *besides* carrying a direct message, clearly gives it the capacity for uniting several meanings in one. It is capable of 'double meanings' precisely because it does refer to and represent things, areas of life, social circles, at the same time as 'telling' something directly. The *way* you speak 'says' a great deal about you. Thus language is not 'transparent'. The Kit-Kat ad did not merely convey the desire to swop a marble for a finger of Kit-Kat: this 'signified' is also a 'signifier'. The language here described the kind of person speaking, the situation it was spoken in, a world to which it belonged. So like all signs, language refers back to the wider system in which it has meaning—not as a sign system *transmitting* meaning (i.e. sentences which make sense, etc.) but as an opaque *thing* which has a social setting and social meaning, like everything else. It is in this sense that the two preceding ads had to be deciphered: the language *as a sign-object* referred to two worlds. (That of the playground, and that of French chic.)

So the 'transparent' meaning, i.e. the meaning *carried* by the words, and the 'hermeneutic' meaning, the meaning implied by them, can be used to create an elision of two things *in* the words, which refer outwards to these two different meanings: one, the direct 'message', the other, the 'referent system' or referred-to world. Puns provide a short cut between a product and a referent system—we do not have to 'get through' the product to the reality it connotes, because the elision in *language* of the product and world brings them into a frame of reference

A49

Get into Bacardi shorts.
You start with Bacardi rum.
Take a measure to suit you.
Then splash it with lemonade.
And you're into Bacardi shorts.
Shorter drinks that are
longer on the unique, mellow
flavour of Bacardi rum.
Or try a different style—
neat or with a dash of tonic.

simultaneously. This is a further example of the assumption of a 1:1 relationship between signifieds and signifiers, product and words: puns actually condense two meanings to fit together perfectly, in the same space—so they *must* be symmetrical (it appears). The symmetry is rendered 'obvious': it is disguised by the condensation which creates an 'Imaginary' unity of two meanings into one symbol.

The fact that puns are an instant connection between product and world 'meant' by it (thus giving the product an inevitable 'meaning', produced automatically) is shown in A49.

A49: The caption refers on one level to the product—the drink. But in all this series, the people (usually decapitated) are shown wearing shorts; the words also refer to *these* shorts and the meaning on this level is not so much a direct 'message' as a *reference* to a whole world, where one wears shorts because it is so hot and luxurious. The people in these ads are always nearly naked and have sun-drenched bodies, usually dressed very provocatively. There is an aura of luxury and richness. All this is the world around the product, which the product is meant to signify: by referring to this style of life, as well as to the drink, the pun facilitates this meaning process (which is the basic process of all ads, cf Chapter 1), making it something to be deciphered, to be 'got' as one gets a joke.

The writing is, in fact, as a concrete *object*, 'getting into' her, very nearly into *her* shorts; since it intrudes across her body in precisely the place where her shirt is pushed up—the fullstop of the sentence coincides with her navel. So the writing, as a thing, has a definitely sexual connotation here—which backs up the whole idea of 'getting into shorts', and the 'image' of the drink.

Have you the cheek
to let him touch you?
Let him feel your skin.
Is it touchable?
Don't worry the answer could be simple ... Neutrogena.
Other soaps and cleansers leave a film on your skin—impurities which your make-up can "lock-in," causing untold trouble.
Not Neutrogena. Its rich soft lather first cleanses then rinses off without a trace, leaving your skin clean and fresh.
The perfect base for a perfect complexion.
Give your skin a chance—Give it Neutrogena.
Neutrogena

A50

Thus puns perform the correlating function seen in all ads, but in a way that begs to be deciphered. Condensation is the central feature in all the following examples; and condensation draws together both the denoted and connoted meanings of the ad, therefore making a deterministic connection between them, so that this deciphering involves, not finding a meaning, but finding the (hidden but inevitable) link between two meanings.

A50: This pun unites, verbally, both a physical and an emotional meaning. 'Do you dare let him touch you?', the meaning of the sentence taken colloquially, intensifies the physical point made by the other meaning, of whether your skin, your face, is good enough to let him touch it. The two meanings combine to create the idea that if your skin isn't all right, it would take a lot of nerve to let him touch it. This fear is condensed into a short question because of the pun, and the product becomes connected with the fear, brought in as a solution to it.

A51

A51: This pun relies on the difference between 'entertaining' as transitive and intransitive. Is *she* entertaining because of her sparkling character (which is suppressed when she has to get a meal without the Hostess trolley) or, is she entertaining *them*, her guests, by providing a meal (on the Hostess trolley)? The slight verbal twist here manages to emphasise, besides the practical side, the woman and her qualities, thus adding weight to the point that she should be able to participate in the dinner party talk rather than be stuck in the kitchen. The practical and the social argument for the trolley are united in the pun.

A52: The 'More' advertisement is a good example of using condensation to perform the basic advertising function of linking the product and a quality or idea. 'More' cigarette, the product, becomes synonymous with MORE the measure of quantity. On one level, that of our own language, it is obvious that 'If you aren't getting more you're getting less'. By the naming of the product this truism seems equally obvious as regards the More cigarette. *Of course* More is the opposite of less; and the ambiguity in the words does not allow you to separate the product from the 'fact'. 'More' is made into an absolute, despite its (linguistically) relative quality: you can only have More, or less; there cannot be *more* than More.

Condensation is a way of translating between absent meanings (the 'full' meanings) as I have said above. Thus all the preceding examples, varied though they were, still involved our finding a 'meaning', getting *through* the condensation to its signified ideas.

In the case of the 'Double Diamond' puzzle ads, the condensation is not merely that of ideas into words, but of words into letters, so that the deciphering process functions to reproduce the *words* absent from the ad.

YYUR
YYUB
ICUQ
4ADD

The letters are lifted from their *alphabetical* place, to the status of *words* in a sentence.

In some cases the pun can work to lift *words* from their contingency in a *sentence* and place them as *things* in reference to a picture. There is an advertisement for a man's suit with the caption 'Oriented to embrace both style and elegance', which shows an oriental-looking woman with her arms around a man. The caption is split, so that 'both style and elegance' is on a separate line. Now, the words 'Oriented' and 'embrace', although they have a perfectly logical function in the sentence about Dormeuil suits, also refer to the woman—they read,

A52

'embrace an Oriental', as a sort of caption. She is clearly Oriental and *is* embracing the man in the suit. Thus two 'key' words have resonance quite outside their place in the structure of the sentence. They have become signs on their own, as is shown by the fact that they may be exchanged with the picture. Thus it is ultimately the picture, the woman, that is referred to by the words, though obliquely: *it* provides the 'grammar' that is the structure for their underlying meaning.

Since we do have to 'get through' the condensed or dense language, to an 'idea' or to a picture, language might be seen as a barrier, an opaque obstacle brought in to exercise our hermeneutic skills; if we end up getting through to the picture it might seem simpler to have *only* the picture. We can see how the hermeneutic process of language is undone and finally discarded, in the next section; yet the ads in it still presuppose a direct link between the ad and its meaning. Thus the ads in this section have, in their *use* of language as dense, disguised the actual redundancy of language in their process (since as we have seen, an ad makes correlations anyway, through its visual structure). Hermeneutic interpretations may be made difficult or easy; but their fundamental nature is the same.

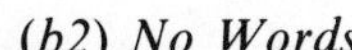

(*b2*) *No Words*

3

Since language is a sign, it may be replaced by signs. In many of the ads already shown, while the words do say *something*, they do not directly convey the meaning of the ad. The Benson and Hedges series provides many examples of ads where the significance is all in the picture:

A53: Here the important feature of the picture *is* the product: displayed almost without words. The joke in the only three words of the ad is related to the attempt to *produce* this picture of the product, the crucial image. Also a part of the joke is the attempt to get the words onto the packet—the name, 'Benson and Hedges'. In a way, this shows the need for some words in the ad; yet also part of the joke is that we *know*, before it appears (and would know even if it did not appear) the name of the product. Everyone knows it because of the *packet*, the visual symbol; it is actually the gold box that mutely provides the image of the ad, and the joke is its struggling to produce an unnecessary name for itself. The ad is about the creation of words and yet could not be so confident of its humour if it were not sure that these words are superfluous to the basic image.

In the effort to produce the third packet we are given the illusion of 'breaking through' to the *meaning*, getting to the point of the ad, but actually it was there all along: in the signifier, the goldness of the first box, not the words on the last. So we again see that it is the signifier that carries the meaning of the ad, and that our attention is diverted from this in an attempt to create a verbal signified, words carrying an abstract, ideal 'message'.

Thus the meaning is already *in* the ad—not absent from it in the realm of the ideal, to be deciphered and reached through words. This point is made conclusively by the following pair of ads:

A54 (1) and (2): These ads have different captions but the meaning, held in the picture rather than the words, is the same. Both pictures convey an image of confidence, authority, masculinity: the words are superfluous. It would be impossible to say that the ads have *different* meanings. So it seems that the ad generates the *illusion* of a hermeneutic meaning, while actually the meaning is 'right there' in the ad, not separable from it.

A55: The Chanel ad here realises this fact: it does not use other sign systems but the ad is *itself* a sign. There are no words at all, except the name on the bottle. This is pure advertisement: the very essence of all advertising. The ad just *shows* us the product visually, and does not need to tell us anything. (The Chanel ad already seen, of Catherine Deneuve for Chanel, is almost equally silent, deriving its success from the tacit assumption that words are unnecessary to sell *this* product.)

However, this example introduces a confusion that leads to the idea of 'calligraphy': it is a sign, but it is trying to present its *referent*, the Chanel bottle. Obviously the picture can never be more than a sign for what is real. But we have the impression here of 'breaking through' the ad, by-passing the more complex hermeneutic process of language, to a hermeneutic that simply involves the replacement of the present sign by the absent referent; so this 'transparent' ad is still very much in the hermeneutic genre.

A56: This ad actually makes a joke in drawing attention to the redundancy of words. It shows how all the language of the ad is merely a false screen set up precisely for us to *penetrate* to the 'meaning', the signified, which is, simply, the product—in this case, Jaffa. So, as in A55, we are *directly presented* with the meaning: 'Jaffa'. The idea of 'the Perfect One' reflects the Platonic nature of the hermeneutic meaning: the referent, grapefruit, is elevated to the level of the ideal—in the senses both of imaginariness and of perfection. This shows how the referent of the sign is made its 'meaning' (signified)—and is thus abstract and concrete at the same time, a 'real thing', grapefruit, yet an ultimate, perfect 'meaning', the apex of the *concept* grapefruit: in other words, it is a symbol. The *meaning* of the ad is grapefruit—and meaning is ideal: there is only one 'meaning'. But the *referent* of the ad is all (real) grapefruits everywhere: what we see in the shops. In eliding the two the ad makes *real* grapefruit a symbol, and simultaneously makes the idea of 'perfect' grapefruit seem *real*. This brings us back to the starting point of the whole chapter: the appropriation of reality by advertising, in creating symbols, transparent and opaque, all offering 'meaning' behind posters and pages and screens, rather than in material life.

A54(1)

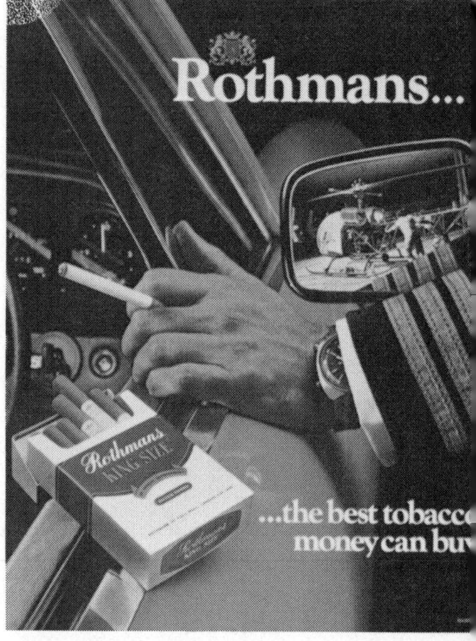

A55

A54(2)

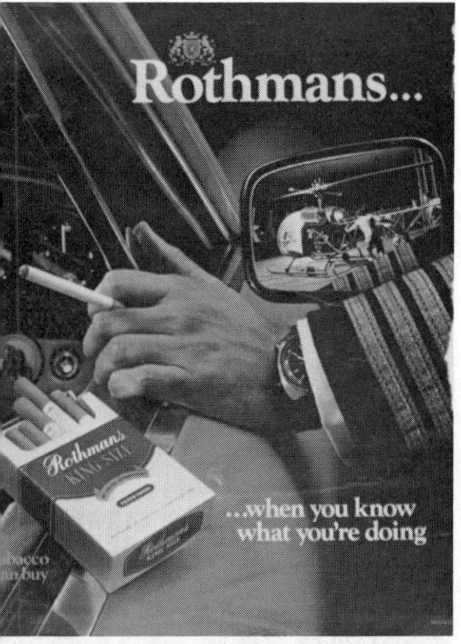

A56

We have seen that language is frequently superfluous in the hermeneutic of ads, since its referent is absent but can be 'shown' directly, without words. But a way round the problem of language and the absence of its meaning, is Calligraphy: the only way to make language signify the product directly is by uniting it with the product.

(*c*) *Calligraphy*

'The calligram makes use of this double property of letters to function as linear elements which can be arranged in space and as signs which must be read according to a single chain of phonic substance. As sign, the letter permits us to establish words; as line it permits us to establish letters. Hence the calligram playfully seeks to erase the oldest oppositions of our alphabetical civilisation: to show and to name; to figure and to speak; to reproduce and articulate; to look and to read. Pursuing twice over the thing of which it speaks, it sets an ideal trap: its double access guarantees a capture of which mere discourse or pure drawing is not capable. It undermines the invicible absence over which words never quite prevail by imposing on them . . . the visible form of their reference. . . . The signs summon from elsewhere the very thing of which they speak. . . . A double trap, an inevitable snare. . . .'[1]

Calligraphy ties up the two previous sections on absence and language because it is the way in which language deals with absence. In hermeneutic systems, referents are always absent, but the calligram tries to unite referent and sign, again giving the impression of producing 'transparent' meaning, as in A55 and 56. The *thing*, the product, signified by language in the ad, is made to *be* the language of the ad: in A55 the product spoke mutely, and in A56 it spoke only one word, its name; but the next examples show language as a *form* taken over and 'filled' by objects. The signified product is organised in space according to the shape of language. In examples in the 'language' section we saw the materiality of words enable them to function as signs: the child's writing in the Kit-Kat ad, or the physical shape of the caption in the 'Bacardi Shorts'. But here the words become not only signs but referents. In Calligraphy words cannot be merely signs, either in their signifying function or material appearance; they must appear to incorporate the referent itself. The masking of the absence of the referent in its represented presence is clearly the furthest you can go in a one-to-one relation of the signifier and signified, sign and referent: their conflation must

[1] Michel Foucault from 'Ceci n'est pas une pipe' in '*October*' Vol. I, p. 9–10.

be *imaginary* and thus a denial of their *symbolic* function. (See above, p. 62.) In calligraphy, the sign is apparently formed *of* the objects to which it can really only refer.

A57

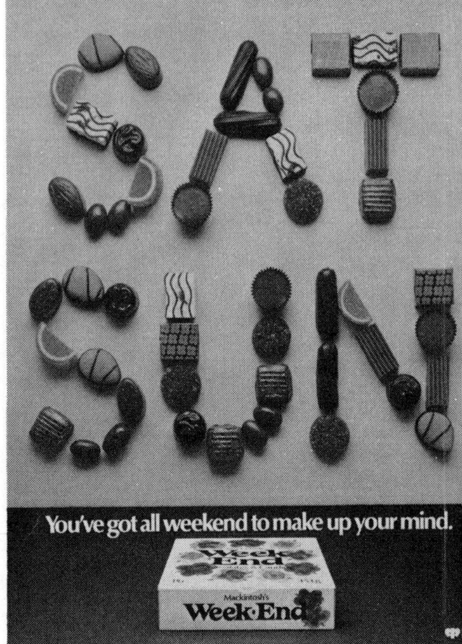

A57 and 58: These two ads have been placed together since they use different calligraphic methods based on the same pun: 'You've got all Weekend to make up your mind'. In the light of Chapter Two, the common phrase that is exploited in these ads can no longer retain its familiar innocence. To *make up* your mind is to be constituted as a subject: here it is possible in choosing between different chocolates.

In A57 the contents of the box, all 'Weekend', are arranged according to a form of language. This functions as a sort of demonstration of *why* you've got all weekend to make up your mind, since the chocolates are arranged in the space of the abbreviation SATSUN, which cryptically covers all of a weekend. The ad represents a perfect coincidence between the 'material' space of the product and the temporal space that the product is named after. A box of chocolates allows you to make up your mind in time. And it is the function of calligraphy here to make these co-exist.

The calligraphy in A58 is more radical since the chocolate is present while its name is not: the name of the chocolates in question will presumably be given to us when we buy a box of 'Weekend'. It is important to remember that chocolates contained in named boxes are themselves named: so that in buying one thing by saying 'Weekend, please' we are obtaining access to a kind of hidden language which we only discover at the moment of consuming them. The calligraphy in A58 rests on the desire to replace the objects with their names—which we will discover by deciding to eat them. Words, of course, come out while chocolates go in. Words are produced, chocolates consumed. So even on this small scale, consumption replaces production in emphasis. And actual objects are turned into words, appropriated by a language that claims to *be* 'reality' in being 'made' of objects.

Time in A58 is the time of speaking. The implication of a nearly infinite choice in a weekend/Weekend in that the sentence is never closed ('No, I'll . . .') further suggests that if we possess a box of these chocolates then our speech for SATSUN can be produced entirely from the names of these objects. An entire body of language is congealed into the brand names of 'Weekend'. We buy our language which gives us freedom to choose. 'Weekend' becomes a kind of *logos*: 'In the beginning was the word, and the word was Weekend. . . .' It provides access to all else. Ideologically this serves a double function: it suggests that language is in some sense absent, that objects can signify without being named (i.e. forms and structures are used, those *of* language, but we are denied knowledge of their content *in* language), a suggestion allowed calligraphically. At the same time it is indicated that a collection of names may be used as a corpus of language, a system of differences (the chocolates are different from each other as words are) within which we may choose. We can see why Foucault says that

A58

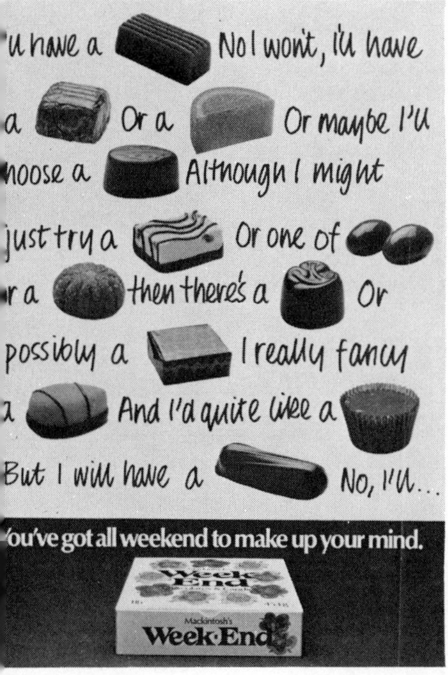

calligraphy is a 'double trap, an inevitable snare' since we are required to make a choice, that desirable process, between words and objects. Or rather in a false space occupying the no-man's-land between sign and referent, we are caught endlessly *making up our minds*.

The third Weekend ad makes the notion of choice completely explicit:

There is one group of examples that should be mentioned in this context: the Brook Street ads on the London underground. In these, either the hands or the feet of two people are shown, with a dialogue printed above, which we assume to be that of the partially seen speakers. These ads approach calligraphy in that the dialogue is printed in alternating colours which are the same colours as the objects that signify the speakers: blue shoes, blue words. Looking at the ad we assume that the person in blue shoes is the one who speaks with blue language. In one case the coloured speech is correlated with drinks held in the hands of the unseen speakers: a green drink and a pink one are held by absent people, whose speech is printed, respectively, in green and pink lettering. This is particularly striking because there is a further, unstated connection being made; the drinks are destined to *go in* where the language has *come out*. As suggested in the 'totemism' section and in relation to the three ads above, consumption is used again and again to conceal production, with language as much as with material goods. But here, language *is* a material thing too. In these ads linguistic signs are both given a materiality in their colour, and, following from that, a referent not signified in the words themselves. A coloured block of language refers to coloured objects which are not spoken of in the words of the dialogue. And the objects metonymically signify the *source* of the speech—it is connected with them, not with the people, thus the *objects* are seen as producing the speech. Unlike the above calligraphic ads, the referent is not incorporated in the signs; rather, the speaker and spoken are placed within the same material space which is one of colour. What is spoken of is the job that the bureau may obtain for one of the speakers. But labour is misrepresented in terms of consumption since the coloured objects that the coloured words refer to are already possessed. These contradictions indicate the ideological place of the Brook Street Bureau itself in that it sells labour that is then possessed like shoes or consumed like drinks.

A59: In the 'White Horse' ads, the sign and referent co-exist in the brand name. It is the language on the bottle, specifying the type of whisky, that becomes calligraphic, in this case outside the writing proper. The function of picturing the horse itself, in this example, is to make more 'real' the *natural* signification that the brand-name gives the whisky. But the *system* of the 'White Horse' ads as a group lies in the slogan: 'You can take a White Horse anywhere'. On one level, this whisky is universally consumed and is never out of place wherever you are. More importantly, the ads operate an *interchangeable incongruity*. In the example here the bottle is present in a quasi-realist fashion resting on a rock; but its excessively foregrounded position in fact both compensates for *and* makes clear the bottle's out-of-placeness in the Highlands. What allows it to be present is the object status achieved by its name. A white horse should not be out of place on a hillside. It is the whisky's name that places it here and makes it the receptacle for the significance of the landscape and its horse—that which is the shared property of the bottle and the landscape. Here, the calligraphy allows a separation between the whisky and the world so that we may exchange the two in a way prescribed by the White Horse/white horse equation. In other examples, in this series, the incongruity is reversed: it is not the bottle out of place in a landscape, but the White Horse (a horse) surrealistically present in a drawing-room. Now the whisky can retain the significance of the white horse as a natural object while through the strength of its own cultural status overcome the oddness of the horse in a drawing-room. What calligraphy makes possible in these ads, which function all together as a system, is a doubling of the significance of the

A

product: the bottle can be placed outside in nature, or the horse inside in culture. But 'Nature' itself is a sign and hence cultural, as will be seen in the next chapter.

With calligraphy, the advertisement reaches a final point in its imaginary joining of sign and referent. The analyses in this section attempt to show what ideological function this can serve. But there is a further point to be made. The organisation of the material in the ad, the chocolates in the 'Weekend' example A57, is according to what can be termed a 'Referent System' (to distinguish it from the referent of the sign). The arrangement SATSUN appeals to our pre-existent knowledge of the forms taken by language itself. SATSUN is a simple puzzle whose shape produces its solution: it means the weekend. Part Two looks at the way in which the subject's *knowledge* is appropriated by advertisements, in their appeal to major Referent Systems, like nature or time. These are systems of meaning that can be used, *referred to* by ads, just as language refers to objects which are what it 'means' or represents (—and these two *different* things are confused in ideology, which makes *reference* do for *meaning*). Language is the meta-referent system, a structure of denoting signifiers, while other referent systems are structures of *connoted* meanings. In calligraphy we have seen how language provides a *structure* for referent systems while these systems themselves provide structures of meaning that flow through the elements from them as structured by the ad. Advertisements structure *outside* elements, while in calligraphy, language structures elements within it, like sweets. This shows that the meaning is literally *in* the structure; language provides not a system of inherent meanings but a system of relations that can carry meaning (in the Weekend ads, this is the product). Similarly, advertisements use already existing structures of relations filled with a new meaning—the product. In Calligraphic ads the structure (language) is very clearly refilled by the *ad's* own meaning, which is the product, but this is simply an exceptionally clear case of what *all* ads do. They work an exchange between meaning and system using structures of relations hinted at by elements *from* them (e.g. Catherine Deneuve suggests the whole system of the world of *chic*) but once these structures have been evoked they are used purely *structurally* (to create differences)—and so there is a permanent robbery, of materiality from structures and of structures from their material. Symbolic structures come to replace and confuse our perception of the real structure of society.

PART II: 'IDEOLOGICAL CASTLES': REFERENT SYSTEMS

'Mythical thought builds structured sets by means of a structured set, namely, language. But it is not at the structural level that it makes use of it: it builds ideological castles out of the debris of what was once a social discourse.'

Lévi-Strauss[1]

'... the peculiarity of ideology is that it is endowed with a structure and a functioning such as to make it a non-historical reality, i.e. an omni-historical reality in the sense in which that structure and functioning are immutable, present in the same form throughout what we call history, in the sense in which the *Communist Manifesto* defines history as the history of class struggles, i.e. the history of class societies.'

Althusser, *Ideology and The State*[2]

[1] '*The Savage Mind*', Weidenfeld and Nicholson, 1966, p. 21.
[2] *Lenin and Philosophy and Other Essays*, New Left Books, 1971, pp. 151–2.

Denotation, Connotation

Denotation *is the work of signification performed 'within' a sign (q.v.) as it were: it is the process whereby a signifier 'means'*—denotes—*a specific signified (q.v.).*

When I discuss connotation *I am concerned with a similar process but one where the signifier is itself the* denoting sign: *the sign in its totality points to something else. That something else I term a Referent System. See the discussion of 'staggered systems' below.*

What has been said in the previous chapter indicates that the subject drawn into the work of advertising is *one who knows*. To fill in gaps we must know *what* to fill in, to decipher and solve problems we must know the rules of the game. Advertisements clearly produce knowledge—otherwise the Chanel bottle in A55 could not stand in such a blank space—but this knowledge is always produced from something already known, that acts as a guarantee, in its anteriority, for the '*truth*' in the ad itself. This has already been shown to be a central part of ideology: the constant *re*-production of ideas which are denied a historical beginning or end, which are used or referred to 'because' they 'already' exist in society, and continue to exist in society 'because' they are used and referred to; and which therefore take on the nature of a timeless, synchronic structure, 'out of' history', although this structure as a whole clearly does exist in history. It only seems 'timeless' from the inside: obviously, an ideology can never admit that it 'began' because this would be to remove its inevitability. Thus although systems of knowledge do have a beginning and ending and a place in historical developments, their internal workings must be purely structural, and self-perpetuating not from any movement *onwards*, but from a process of translation and retranslation between systems, vertical rather than horizontal momentum; so that as with a chemical 'dynamic equilibrium', the movement is internal and imperceptible and never constitutes a *disturbance*. I emphasise this at the outset because my concern in this half of the book is with precisely such systems, those referred to and drawn into the work of the ad, and although I will be looking at these systems *as* systems, rather than tracing their historical development, I want to make it quite clear that I am not denying this historical development, and investing them with the very 'inevitability' that I seek to expose. Synchronic structural analysis is very valuable in areas of ideology, precisely because these areas set themselves up, and function internally, *as* synchronic structures: but in examining them it is important not to forget that they *are* ideologies and this necessarily implicates the very tools that fit so well the job of describing and deconstructing them.

Thus when I speak of our 'anterior' knowledge that is brought to the advertisement, I have no intention of endowing this knowledge with a 'true' status. I am simply pointing out that *it* endows the *ad* with such a status. With 'objective correlatives' we saw how an object with a *known* quality was used as a way of transferring this quality. To make the exchange between Catherine Deneuve and Chanel in relation to one between Margaux Hemingway and Babe, requires us to be already in a position of knowing. There is a cognitive outline in which the product is inserted: *we exchange because we know*.

The assumption of pre-existing bodies of knowledge allows reference to take the place of description, connotation of denotation, in ads: this reference must inevitably take place on the formal level, by pointing at another *structure*, since the 'content' or substance of the reference is the product itself. So the 'referent system' is always a connotation because what is denoted is the product. However, there is a circular process involved because having introduced the referent system by means of connotation, it is then made to denote the product—'place' it in a system of meaning. This denotation is basically the process described in Chapter One. In this section, we are concerned with *connotation*. In his discussion of 'staggered systems' Barthes says that he is dealing with 'two systems of significations which are imbricated but are out of joint with each other'.[1] Catherine Deneuve is signified by a photograph, but 'she' in turn becomes a signifier: for wealthy—chic-Frenchness. The 'out-of-jointness' of these two systems is compensated by the spectator's knowledge, without which connotation is not possible.

A 'connoted system' is one 'whose plane of expression is itself constituted by a signifying system.'

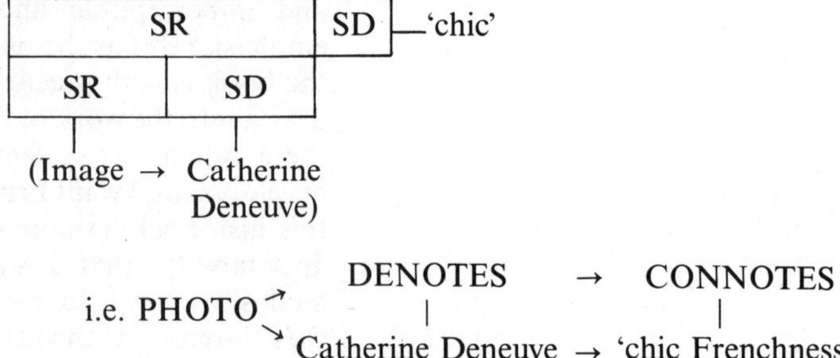

[1]*Elements of Semiology*, Jonathan Cape, 1967, p. 89.

'The signifiers of connotation . . . are made up of *signs* (signifiers and signifieds united) of the denoted system. . . . As for the signified of connotation, its character is at once global and diffuse; it is, if you like, a fragment of ideology. . . . These signifieds have a very close communication with culture, knowledge, history, and it is through them . . . that the environmental world invades the system.'[1]

It is important to recognise that in no sense are we leaving the 'realm' of the signifier: a realm I have already suggested is all-embracing (in the '*invisible*' perpetuation of ideology). In signification, signifieds are continually being formed as signifiers. The *signified* 'Margaux Hemingway' becomes a *signifier* for 'aggressive femininity' on the level of connotation, and so on. What the ad does is to provide a 'meta-structure' in which these transformations may take place. It draws together disparate objects which are initially *signified* by their place in a system of knowledge, but then made to signify, i.e. become signifiers, in terms of that place so that it is their *position*, rather than themselves as the 'content' of that position, that signifies. Indeed, since they have been taken *out* of their positions, these are necessarily empty, merely *forms* of knowledge. Referent systems must be referred to *as* systems, as whole areas for ideas and not single, specific 'ideas'.

The gathering of objects which are signifieds *in* ideological systems, making them signifiers *of* these systems (hence 'referent systems') by arranging them in terms of another structure (the ad), is described by Lévi-Strauss as a kind of 'bricolage'; a word which derives its meaning from the work of the 'bricoleur' who does odd jobs making and mending things, not with new materials, but with bits and pieces left over from previous jobs and constructions. This metaphor is clearly very apt for the process I have described as taking place in ads: they can only use odds and ends from ideological thought that already exists. In this sense ads are similar to the rites and myths which, Lévi-Strauss suggests, 'like "bricolage" . . . take to pieces and reconstruct sets of events (on a physical, socio-historical or technical plane) and use them as so many indestructible pieces for structural patterns in which they serve alternatively as ends or means.'[2] And a crucial feature of these odds and ends of thought used by ads is that they do not exist 'independently' but in *our* thought: it is *we*, as subjects, who are appealed to as the *providers* of these elements. Thus, where a purely structural

[1] ibid., pp. 90–92.

[2] *The Savage Mind*, Weidenfeld and Nicholson, 1966, p. 33.

analysis can become too abstract in areas like this, a sound understanding of the role of 'appellation' (see above) and the constitution of *the subject* in creating/perpetuating ideology can bridge the gulf between the 'system' of knowledge (which as a *system* becomes 'autonomous') and the actual, historical and social situation in which it functions. For it is individual people, real people, who are the connecting link here: they, we, clearly exist in time and space, in a changing world, but also provide the arena—unconscious—for the ideological structure of ideas. This only exists in so far as it exists inside our heads. It is therefore *through us* that mythical structures partake of historicity.

It is perhaps helpful in this context to distinguish between the '*knowledge*', which, as suggested above, we must have as a prerequisite of the ad's connotation process (a knowledge which must inevitably be specific and historical), and the system of signification *of* this knowledge, which as a system cannot have a specific 'existence' in one place and consists of a series of formal relations. At all levels, denotation *and* connotation, signification intersects with knowledge—which produces the movement between levels. But in dealing with *connotation*, as opposed to the *work* of denotation, we have to look at the 'forms' of knowledge that advertisements employ—that they turn into signifiers. If, for example, previous significations (e.g. Romanticism—which is situated historically) have produced the *signified* 'NATURE', this can be 'emptied' and used as a *signifier* in relation to a product. A product is placed within a hollowed-out knowledge, and draws its significance from that.

The chapters in this part of the book do not cover all the referent systems available to advertising. They do, however, seem very central to an examination of ideology since they all involve relations of transformation—we are placed in reconstructed and *false* relationships to *real* phenomena. We misrepresent our relation to nature, and we avoid our real situation in time. I have placed 'magic' as a topic between these two because in a way it combines the other two fallacies—transforming our *temporal* relationship with *nature*. Nature is our fundamental spatial environment, time (obviously enough) our temporal one. Ideology functions to misplace us in each: advertisements *refer* to this misplacement as to an inevitable and 'natural' fact.

CHAPTER FOUR
'COOKING' NATURE

Nature is the primary referent of a culture. It is the 'raw material' of our environment, both the root of all technological development and its opposition; that which technology strives both to improve and to overcome. If a culture is to refer to itself, therefore, it can only do so by the representation of its transformation of nature—it has meaning in terms of what it has *changed*. In the first part of this chapter I discuss some advertisements which refer to this change itself, its process, by giving 'natural' objects cultural forms. I shall then go on to examine images of 'science', including their place in human relations, at which point it will become clear that the scientific image feeds back into an image of nature itself: 'The Natural' (cf. Chapter 5).

(*a*) '*The Raw and the Cooked*': *Representations of Transformation*

Lévi-Strauss describes the cultural transformation of natural objects as a process of 'cooking': society requires food to be cooked and not raw for it to be acceptable. In cooking, nature, in the form of raw material (e.g. meat) enters a complex system whereby it is differentiated culturally (for example it may be roasted or grilled). In just the same way, images of nature are 'cooked' in culture so that they may be used as part of a symbolic system. In the ads that follow, both sides of the 'cooking' process are presented *simultaneously within the product*, so that it carries the *charge* of the transformation itself: natural, 'raw' things are shown in the terms of the product—like the orange that has been formed into the outline of a marmalade jar (*A60*).

0

CHIVERS
Olde English
THICK CUT
ORANGE MARMALADE
There's nothing quite like an Olde English breakfast.
CHIVERS

There is an advertisement poster for Heinz mushroom soup which shows a mushroom whose stalk is a tin of soup. Here, the cultural artifact, the *tin*, has appropriated the raw mushroom, and *stands for it* in that it represents the mushroom stalk—it has 'taken over' the natural object. Yet the cap of a real mushroom, pictured on top of the 'tin-stalk', ensures that we retain an image of *what has been transformed*, thus defining the extent of the process in indicating both its source and its result.

The image of manufacture is very apparent in all the examples to follow: lids, screw-tops and bottles are given to natural objects, demonstrating the value of 'cooking', improving nature, lending it their seal of approval only in this technologised form. In the next chapter, the reverse will be described. Once nature has been drawn into culture it is given a meaning: one that can be transferred to products. In this sense, nature has been transformed into 'the Natural'. It can become a symbol once it has been 'cooked': because 'science' introduces it into a system of differentiations, giving it an order and cultural place which enable it to 'mean'. However, here 'raw' nature *means* precisely because it is a symbol of what culture has transformed: the Sanatogen vitamin pill ad in this section, for example, (A64), shows how messy orange peel is compared with the clean bottle that contains 'cooked' vitamin C. Yet at the same time, even here we have a slight suggestion of 'the natural' in that the raw element, since it *has been* safely transformed, also has the function of giving the cultural product a 'natural' status, so that the supposed *quality* of the 'natural' is retained, but not its *form*. This is obviously a false distinction, yet it arises from the fact that the whole of society's relationship with 'nature' is very much one of having cake and eating it.

The two sides of this relationship, the systems of connotation described above, are perpetually slipping backwards and forwards into each other, but here we are primarily concerned with the referent system as the 'cooking' process, not as 'nature' itself. 'Nature' has simply become a referent of a 'cooking' society: it has meaning in terms of its relationship with what has transformed it, but is not valued in itself. Thus the 'raw', the natural object, becomes in this context a symbol, not of *nature*, but, ironically and in alienation from its original place, of the *culture* that has worked it over.

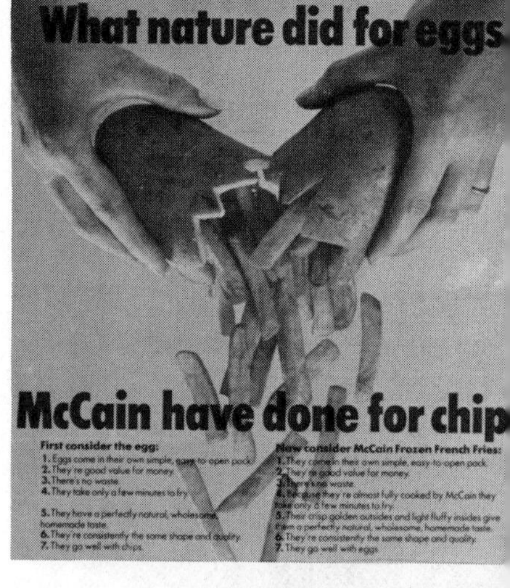

A61: 'What nature did for eggs, McCain have done for chips'. Raw nature, the potato, is 'cooked' by being transformed into frozen, ready-made french fries: in fact they have been so 'cooked' by the manufacturing process itself, that you hardly need to do it yourself: 'Because they're almost fully cooked by McCain they take only a few minutes to fry'. You are thus saved any direct contact with the raw object—that the cooking should be so thoroughly performed by the manufacturers provides a literal example of the idea that I have been using metaphorically to apply to all cultural transformation. However, this ad, besides being an ad *for* a cooked product, the chips, relies on the system of the cooking process for its referent; on several different levels, which feed into one another. The image of the chips coming out of the potato shell is a simultaneous representation of the 'raw' and the 'cooked', the two ends of the process. The potato reminds us how different potatoes and chips are, how annoying potatoes are to clean and peel; in seeing the difference between the two we become aware of all that must be done to turn one into the other—cutting up and frying. All this gives chips a superior status since they are the result of this process, they eliminate it for us. But the whole process is turned back to front temporally, while not detracting from this superior status of the chips: they are, in addition, given an *anterior* status, by coming out of the potato, they were there 'already' inside it. Potatoes are full of chips—this picture shows that potatoes are *made* of chips, not chips of potatoes. So the product gains status in two completely different ways, which are actually contradictory, or rather, work in opposite directions around the raw/cooked axis: chips are both connected with, and simultaneously distanced from, potatoes. The distance is filled by the cooking process (it is the referent of the potato/chip gap, as it were) and the contingency gives this process a 'guarantee' of 'natural' order.

This advertisement does not do all this 'unconsciously', however: it actually provides a parallel to its own image, in the image of the egg and egg shell. McCain is doing what nature has already done to eggs: so it is copying nature, but of course, copying it to *improve* on it. And the egg is described in manufacturing terms; *not* manufacturing, in natural-egg terms. 'Eggs come in their own simple, easy-to-open pack . . . they have a perfectly natural, wholesome, homemade taste.' So this ad still very much depends on the image of *cooking* as its referent, as a criterion for efficiency and desirability: to extol the virtues of the egg, we must say that it is easy-to-open and tastes 'homemade'—for these cultural terms are indications of goodness, value.

The advertisement rounds off by connecting the two 'cookings'—the actual 'cooking' of the raw potato into the chips, and of the raw idea of the egg into a cultural way of looking at it: by suggesting that you literally cook the two together and have egg and chips. This ties the McCain-cooked chips and the technically described 'cooked' egg in a way that allows them to exchange values, so that the naturalness of the egg (after all, *nature* 'packed' it) *and* its culturally defined convenience, attach to the chips, where a manufacturing-cooking has slipped in between the simultaneous qualities (rawness and convenience) of the egg, transforming the former into the latter. Finally, in that McCain foods are 'Europe's largest processor of frozen potato products', they are endowed with some of the omnipotence and ubiquity of 'nature': the '*size*' of the manufacturing company makes it technologically impressive and its work effortless, almost 'natural'.

A62

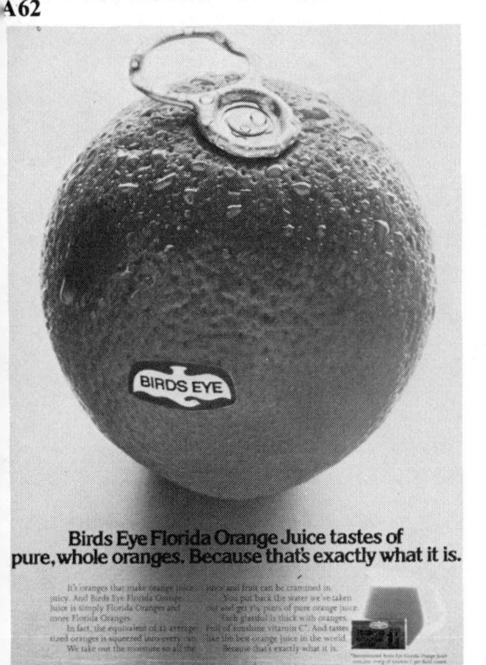

BIRDS EYE
Birds Eye Florida Orange Juice tastes of pure, whole oranges. Because that's exactly what it is.

A62: Here again, the *image* of nature is actually 'cooked'—the orange may be showing that Florida Orange juice is made from oranges, but it does not do this by presenting a 'raw' orange. In giving the orange the features of the product (can top, label) it emphasises the 'cooking' that has transformed the orange into the can of juice. When the small print says that 'each glassful is thick with oranges' it is obviously referring to oranges as a 'cooked' term, in their transformed and symbolic form—because a glass could hardly be thick with real, untouched oranges. It is thick with Florida-ised oranges, in other words, canned juice. The label on the orange in the picture shows that the manufacturers have appropriated the reality of the 'natural' orange, even though it is allowed to retain its shape (not like the Chivers ad A60): the orange is only allowed to signify as a Birds Eye can, it can only mean *as cooked*, and what it *means* is that it has been cooked. It shows us what Birds Eye can *do* with oranges, not what oranges are like in themselves. The orange is made to signify the product literally, in the picture, rather than the product signifying the orange. This illustrates how the signified orange becomes a signifier in its 'cookedness': thus 'cooking' is the *system* referred to, and the orange hollows out an empty place in it, in which the product may be inserted.

A63

A63: This shows the 'cooking' of the sun. 'Sunshimmer' imitates the sun, in that it tans you, but it compensates for all the sun's inadequacies: it tans you evenly, unlike the sun, moisturises your skin, unlike the sun, and above all, is *available*, unlike the sun: 'Some days the sun doesn't even come out. But Sunshimmer comes out anytime you squeeze the neat, little tube.'

As in the previous examples, we thus see that the natural thing, the sun, is used as a referent for what Coty has *improved*: it is the *difference* between Sunshimmer and the sun, that is the chief selling point of the ad. In a 'neat, little tube' you can buy 'cooked' sunshine; the whole advertisement is an exposition of the *gulf* between the 'real thing' and Coty's product. Yet Coty is presented as the real thing: with a little help from Coty, the sun '*really*' shines. The advert has taken the reality of nature, scooped out its actual content (i.e. the real sun) and placed the product there, so that it *means* in terms of a certain system, it appropriates the *place* of the sun, while filling this place with a transformed content, a tube of fake tan. The advertisement draws attention to the difference between the two actual objects, the sun and the tanning gel—showing (as with the chip ad) how much more convenient the gel is—but an exchange is made whereby the transformed object, the product, which is the 'cooked' version of the sun, is given significance in *terms* of the sun; in a 'referent system' that endows the sun, and hence the product, with the connoted meanings of 'naturalness', 'health', 'beauty', 'perfection' and so on.

Thus a system of meanings, a referent system, is used in its entirety to give significance to the product. And since the product cannot have a place in a pre-existing system, its link with the referent system is provided by an intermediary object, that both belongs within the system, and is also tied to the product. This was the thesis set out in Chapter 1, and I have demonstrated how the link between the product and correlating object can be made by colour, by formal arrangement, by a linguistic connection like a pun, by replacing one for the other in a narrative, and so on. Here (A63), the basic process of exchange remains the same, but the product and the object are linked by the fact that the product is actually a *version* of the object: it is the technologically 'cooked' model of a natural phenomenon. Catherine Deneuve was linked to the Chanel bottle by a simple juxtaposition: the bottle then took Catherine Deneuve's place in a differentiating system, a system of meanings. It is in this sense that I refer to the place in the referent system as a 'hollow', since it is referred to by the presence of one of its elements, simultaneously with the exchange between that element and the product, so that the product ends up filling that place—a *position*, merely. With Coty and the sun, the transference is blurred because not only does Coty replace the sun 'semiologically', that is, in the sense I have just described of exchange along the axis of a *form* of knowledge—it replaces it literally, in terms of *content*. It even retains the original in its name—'Sunshimmer'. There are thus two links between the element from the referent system, and the product: one, is that the product is equated with the sun, the element of the system, by being put in exactly its place as regards connotation; the other link is the opposite since the product gains meaning by being different from the sun, *not* being it, by-passing its inadequacies. Nature thus participates in both a symbolic and an imaginary system—given meaning by being drawn in to a system of differentiation created by culture, being significant by its very opposition with culture, but in being given a symbolic status by this, it merges on an imaginary level with that '*other*' that was used to give it symbolic status. The ideology of culture appropriates all the network of images and connotations, the structure of significance, of nature; but devoid of its real content.

All the advertisements in this section show this very clearly. The product (the equivalent of the Chanel bottle, to keep referring back to my 'paradigm' example of A8) and the correlative object from the referent system, are merged, present simultaneously in one image: the orange *and* the Florida can of juice, the orange *and* the Chivers marmalade jar, the chips *and* the potato—these are elided, because the 'cooking' process performs the function illustrated in other ways under the heading of 'objective correlatives'. The product takes on simultaneously the properties of *orangeness* and *non-orangeness* (A62), sun-ness and non-sun-ness (A63). It is essential to recognise the contradiction here: not for the sake of making a semiological point alone, but because this contradiction embedded in the sign itself, inherent *in* the signifying process, is the contradiction in the very relationship between nature and culture, as seen (ideology) and represented (sign systems) by our society.

The categories of imaginary and symbolic have a precise value here as areas both of which are fundamental to human 'consciousness', yet irreconcilable: constantly attempting to merge and yet in their inability completely to do so, providing a perpetual momentum in the form of desire, along which the subject is carried to regions purporting to fulfil such desire. These categories need not remain entirely the property of psychoanalysis, and their ideological meaning and function must be very clearly defined. The so-called 'unconscious' denies many of the contradictions in ideology, since the Symbolic, the creation of meaning, depends on an A/not A dichotomy, while Freud said that the imagination does not know the word 'no'.

If we apply this to 'nature' and 'cooked nature', in the light of the examples above, A60 to A63, it becomes clear that the 'cooking' process is one of differentiation, of entry into the symbolic, but in these ads is simultaneously placed in such a way as to suggest an imaginary *unity* of the two 'ends' of the process, the 'raw' and the 'cooked'. McCain's chips are an immense improvement on ordinary potatoes, but they *are* potatoes, and moreover, this improvement has simply been carried out in imitation of Mother Nature's own idea, as manifested in the egg and eggshell. Technology is always using nature's '*ideas*' (this can be seen also in the eyeshadow ad A78, in Chapter 5 below). Everything done by society is always already there: it is ratified by Nature (the primary system of Order—although of course, it is invested with this Order by science, a cultural practice)—this is how *ideology* conceals the transformations of which it also boasts, but deprives of origins—of a place in a historical process.

So, 'cooking' is the way in which we transform nature, but the products of the transformation are reinserted in the place of their object. This second part of the circular process will be examined in more detail in Chapter 5. However, the first part, the 'cooking', as represented in the ads in this section, functions as a sign, in the way described above: by referring to the 'natural' system, while also defining itself *against* it, differentiating the product from the natural object. This differentiation and the fact that the replacement or exchange which is always the essential generator of meaning in an ad, must be made *between these differentiated things*, whose material content if *different*, means that it is only a *form* of knowledge, emptied of content, that is ultimately referred to by the ad. Coty fake tan is *not* the sun. But the ad generates *connotative* meaning for the product in terms of a system of knowledge *about* the sun, its qualities, its 'place' in 'nature' etc.; and in filling this place yet denying its original content, it is clear that only a hollow structure, an ideal or imaginary *system*, is used. Our knowledge is denied all material content because on the level of *denotation* Coty is not *like* the sun, but *unlike* the sun. We do not make an exchange which involves a real concrete element of our knowledge and experience; only the *form* of this knowledge is appropriated—so real things and our knowledge of them, are constantly being both assumed and denied. We feel as if we know, because we certainly know the things about the sun that the Coty ad refers to and uses as a framework for its product: yet *what* we know is actually negated by the replacement of Coty for the sun. In other words the connotation and denotation work in opposition: Coty is denoted as *not* sun but connoted as *like* sun. The sun, or an orange, or a potato, are as it were *shells* of signs: there is nothing *in* them (except tans, juice, and chips—literally, in A61) since they are hollowed out and the product inserted as the '*reality*' that fills their inherent vacancy as symbols.

This is all part of the argument of the last chapter, where I suggested that in ads real things are constituted as symbols, forming a system of 'pure' meaning that can never be brought down to the ground and connected to the materiality of life, precisely because the symbols are stolen from that materiality, and also refer to it—they are its *meaning*: this amounts to a tautology of 'it is what it means, and it means what it is', but one which takes place through circuits of signifying systems (of which advertisements are only one example) whose materiality (hence the importance of the signifier, the *material* carrier of meaning) guarantees this tautology a solidity, an inevitable 'realness' since it is a 'meaning' found through 'real' things. (Cf. Chapter 3: the hermeneutic discovery of meaning 'behind' reality.)

Nature is absolutely fundamental to all this because it is *the* hunting ground for symbols, the raw material of which they are all made. But as nature is ransacked for symbols, it is, of course, transformed. I have stressed the fact that in the ads of this chapter the *images* are 'cooked', the *referent itself* is 'cooking' nature. We are never shown a 'raw', whole and untouched natural object: even the potato which appears in A61 has fancy-cut jagged edges and is unnaturally hollowed out, filled with chips: a perfect illustration of the metaphor I have used for this signifying process, where the natural thing signifies only as an empty form, to be filled by the product. The orange becomes a symbol only with a label and can top on it: or with a label and the shape of a jar. This shows precisely that symbols involve differentiation, *are* a differentiation; since the orange, the potato do not mean anything by themselves, they only mean when brought into a contrast: here between nature and culture; *both of which* are represented in the image of the product itself.

A64: This Vitamin C ad plays strongly on the 'raw and cooked' idea; the 'cooked' form of Vitamin C needs no peeling, like the 'raw' orange skin shown. The vitamin is, paradoxically, more available—'you don't have to peel it, wash it, or cook it . . . it's never out of season or expensive or difficult to get'; one obtains it 'as easily as opening a bottle'; while it is, at the same time, more remote, removed from us physically, inside the glass of the bottle and the screw-top lid and the cardboard packaging. You cannot hold or *touch* these pills, as you would an orange. The only feature of our relationship to the natural object retained is that of consumption, the only function of a product. There is no other point of contact with the manufactured vitamin: you touch the bottle, the box. Mechanisation and packaging *enclose* nature, attempt to bring it under control, and at the same time remove it from us completely while seeming to bring it closer, 'more available'. We are denied actual contact with natural objects: again, the *shell*, the *orange peel* is the sign: an empty signification to be filled by Sanatogen, which is *exchanged with the substance of the orange*.

The process of reaching the 'Natural' goodness, through the product, *instantly* ('as easily as opening a bottle of Sanatogen') and the *microcosmic* nature of the pill, the streamlined version of nature, a force encapsulated only to be re-released, lead to the idea of *magic*, in Chapter 6. Magic is the process of *undoing* the 'cooking' and condensing of nature shown in this chapter (cf. such products as 'WonderMash' where the magic and *wonder* are in the *release*, the retransformation of potato powder into potatoes—*instantly*).

Introducing
Sanatogen Vitamin C,
you don't have to peel it.

It has all the Vitamin C goodness of a whole orange in one good-tasting chewable little tablet. It has as much Vitamin C as a normal portion of cabbage or cauliflower. But you don't have to peel it, wash it, or cook it. And it's never out of season or expensive or difficult to get. Sanatogen Vitamin C tablets are the easy way of making absolutely sure that your family is getting the right amount of Vitamin C—especially in the winter.

There's not much you can do about flu bugs or cold weather. But you can be sure that you and yours are getting their Vitamin C every day as easily as opening a bottle of Sanatogen Vitamin C tablets.

Sanatogen Vitamin C. For all the family.
Nothing could be easier.

The 'cooking' process in representation, then, is one of appropriating form without content; of manufacturing symbols and products simultaneously out of the raw, meaningless and undifferentiated mass which is nature, and then substituting these symbols and these products *for* nature. The products symbolise both nature and anti-nature, embodying the inherent tension of a society which both ravages the natural world and violates natural human needs, yet seeks to represent its workings *as* natural, hence inviolable.

(*b*) *Science*

'... the scientist never carries on a dialogue with nature pure and simple but rather with a particular relationship between nature and culture definable in terms of his particular period and civilisation and the material means at his disposal.'[1]

'The raw and the cooked' showed how society's conception of its relationship with nature produces certain images of transformation in which the tensions of this relationship are held in a perpetual dialectic. 'Science', at once the most prestigious and, as we shall see, the most transparent of society's 'cooking' processes, produces and justifies these images, and is also conditioned by them, as the image of 'science' first defines, and then supersedes, the image of 'nature'. 'Science' can really only be defined in relation to nature: which is its object; yet as

[1]Lévi-Strauss, *The Savage Mind*, p. 19.

the second section on 'science' will show, science can take on the nature of a referent system in itself—endowed with a mysticism which equals that of the 'Romantic' vision of 'Nature', and an authority which partakes of the inevitability of Nature. As with the chips and the potato, or the fake tan and the sun, it acquires some of the connotative qualities of what it replaces, while seeking to define by contrast precisely that which it replaces: 'The Natural'.

As Science investigates the world, it defines (thus differentiates) 'The Natural' constantly and necessarily, since 'The Natural' is the object for science's subject, for the 'knowing entity' which science appears to be. A science, it has been suggested,[1] should be 'subjectless', yet in our society Science is one big subject, a sort of 'meta-subject' whose knowledge is somehow far greater than that of all the particular people in whose heads this knowledge exists, put together: it is a kind of giant brain which *already knows*, into which actual 'scientists' can only feed in hope of a glimpse of this wonderful bulk of metaphysical knowledge. Clearly I would not wish to deny the possibility of a science in any field nor to underestimate the value of real scientific research; but I am here talking about the *image* of science, its ideology—which means the distorted representation of our relationship with something that may very well be real and valid, only we are misplaced in relation to it, with science one might say displaced, completely. For 'Science' is never *our* knowledge, indeed, is never anyone's knowledge: yet it is not truly subjectless because instead of being simply *a science*, it is Science—it has a proper name, almost a character. It is spoken about as having achieved things and discovered things, as owning knowledge which, as I have said, no actual person is credited with knowing; it becomes a unified *entity*, rather than a practice.

I have emphasised the existence of 'Science' as an independent area because it will be shown as a referent system in my second section here, and as such its disembodied quality, an ethereal system of True Meaning, reintroduces the idea of hermeneutics, already shown to be a central part of ideology. But Science can never maintain for long this detachment which is, as it were, the turning point or apex of an elliptical curve around which it feeds into, and out of, nature and the natural, forever turning towards it and away from it, reworking nature *into* 'the natural'. Science comes at a central point in this inevitably rather blurred

[1]Althusser, *Ideology and Ideological State Apparatuses.*

discussion of 'cooking' nature and returning to nature, because it is a product of culture that studies what is natural: it appropriates nature for culture by placing it within an order of things.

A65

Your car breaks down here, you're dead.

(b1) Ordering Nature

Just as in the last section, manufactured *forms* imposed an order on the *image* of nature (and this section was put first deliberately because, as Lévi-Strauss suggests above, the relationship expressed in these images is what *conditions* the 'content' of scientific research, rather than the other way round)—for example, the form of the marmalade jar on the slices of raw orange—just as this ordering of nature in images provides a way of formally controlling it, so the actual achievement, the 'content' of science, is seen as literally to control it, to capture, review, and reinterpret it. Of course, the physical ordering of nature and the production of images of order go hand in hand: to know is to classify, to classify to order, to order to overcome. The following three ads differ fundamentally, however, from those previously shown, since it is not so much the image in the ad giving meaning to the product, that involves controlling and improving nature: it is the product itself that provides an image by the fact that it actually does this in real life, is a scientific instrument that can defy nature, or at least claims to.

A65 (a) The Battle With Nature: Here the product of technology, the car, is shown as still *in* nature, engaged in combat with it. The machine can withstand and fend off the dangers of an extremely 'natural' environment, that is, one far removed from culture—in this case, the location is the North Pole. Nature appears as a referent connoting danger, isolation, destruction: the car provides safety, enclosure, and above all, a means of getting *out* of nature, away from it literally. 'Your car breaks down here, you're dead': in other words, you must be able to get away and drive back to 'civilisation', and the car provides a literal escape route from nature to culture, the technological means of getting from one to the other.

The verbal side of the ad emphasises the precision and durability of the product—words like 'stress bearing component' help, conveying rather a tone and general idea (i.e. connoting) than a precise message. ('He knows every stress bearing component and every casting is crack-tested and scrutinised.') There has to be (as in the next example too) the convincing detail of a *minor* fault ('the only problem he's had is a little trouble with the rear door lock'): this is the ultimate guarantee for the truth of the whole ad; clearly it conceals nothing. And that something

A66

can go wrong (though not with the stress bearing components, of course) serves to give us a surreptitious reminder that this *is* a dangerous situation, serious business: this is For Real. The terse caption, with its grammatical insufficiency (lacking the 'if') adds to the sense that this is all very *basic*, nitty-gritty: down to the bare bones of nature *and* of sentence structure, as it were.

So technology overcomes the raw and provides safe transport from its uncooked dangers; although here we see the product *before* it has escaped from nature, placed within the referent system from which, by opposition, it derives its image of safety and control. (For a further analysis of this placement in nature, see A65 (b), page 130.)

From an example where the product is situated in nature, we move to one where nature becomes located in the product.

A66 (*a*) *Capturing Nature:* While in A65 the car was still there in the landscape, here the landscape is captured in the camera—which has provided the picture photo for the ad. This photo represents the experience of the struggle with nature, but also draws attention to the fact that the photographer has come back, and is no longer engaged in that struggle, but is able to represent it in its absence. Chris Bonington has to bring back 'faultless transparencies'—technological transparencies through which we can perceive nature—but at a safe distance.

That the photograph in the ad *is* the one produced by the camera is shown conclusively by the fact that the camera and Chris Bonington are not in the picture, but the camera is pictured separately, in the area of the words—the conveyors of truth, camera and language, share the right hand half of the double page lay-out: the camera coming first, since it is what has told us—pictorially—about the mountain, and then the words, which tell us in turn about the camera. The coupon at the end of the ad, in the bottom right hand corner, is a sign of available information, of our further access to truth and scientific knowledge. There are thus three grids through which the perception of nature must pass, a triply removed lens: the camera, which describes the mountain, the words which describe the camera, and the space for us to enter the whole process for ourselves, via the canonical persona of 'David Williams'. Nature is captured and interpreted by *subjects*: Chris and David, these two friendly people who offer us a frame in which *we* may insert nature, too.

Apart from the crucial development of having captured nature and returned home with it, rather than being pictured as still within it, this ad works in a similar way to the Peugeot one. There is a whole genre of camera, wristwatch, and suchlike, adverts that has developed: the 'I took it to the North Pole/up a mountain/fifty degrees below zero/smashed it on a rock/dropped it in the sea' kind of story. The emphasis is always on the instrument's precision in *measuring* (light meters, watches, thermometers etc.) or otherwise ordering nature (the photograph imposes the order of a frame), and on its endurance in

It stood up very reasonably to absolutely appalling conditions. One or two faults did develop – for example, a bit of grit got into the works – but you'd get this with any camera. At the end of the trip, all the equipment was still working.

I took seven lenses, all of which gave excellent results. In particular I thought the standard and zoom lenses were first class.

Probably the most impressive thing was the meter, which went on working far below the minimum temperatures claimed by the manufacturer. In normal conditions it was remarkably consistent, although as with all but a very few meters, you had to use a bit of judgment above the snowline. In fact, I've never had such a consistently exposed set of transparencies.

It's a very nice, neat camera.

I like it. I'm going to take it on my next expedition."

If you'd like to find out more about it, send the coupon to David Williams.

To: David Williams, 5-9 Glasshouse Yard, London EC1A 4JF. Telephone: 01-253 2772.
Please send me more information about the Olympus OM1 and OM system.

Name

Address

Olympus OM1
from David Williams

withstanding nature, overcoming the most extreme natural conditions. (Of course, these conditions never affect 99 per cent of us. Hence the unreality of this 'For Real' ness: cf Chapter 5, A65 (b), and A66 (b).) The camera in this ad is shown to be impervious to nature—it gets 'knocked against rocks' and, we are told, 'mountains are not good places for cameras'. But transparencies are good places for mountains. The camera can reproduce nature, on a page instead of in the freezing cold outside. However, as has been shown in previous examples, a bit of the mountain does rub off onto the camera—literally: 'one or two faults did develop (the validating detail)—for example, *a bit of grit got into the works....*' Of course it did: and highly necessary too, because the working of the camera must have the image of being nitty-gritty, it needs a piece of real grit to ensure the rock-like, basic, hard and compact quality that the camera must have, in order to oppose exactly those features of the natural landscape. As in 'the raw and the cooked', some of the mountain's image thus attaches itself to the cultural, 'scientific' artifact, as a fragment of the mountain lodges in the mechanism itself.

A67 Re-organising Nature: We now have the landscape actually brought into the scientific enclosure of the greenhouse: to be observed, not only *through* Science, as in the last ad, but *by* Science; and of course this is very different from A66 in that nature is brought back within the confines of culture not on film but in its physicality. These are real plants taken over by science—which controls more than their image; it controls their growth, their very existence: the plants are as streamlined here as products in a factory. On the other hand, the light bulbs grow down from the roof of the greenhouse, from a network of pipes and wires: an inverted image of the root and the plant. In this hot-house nature and technology interact—as natural minerals are made into 'chemicals', and chemicals applied to natural plants, which in turn produce minerals, and so on. Science here is intervening in the natural cycle: killing bugs....'We try to control them...' and weeds, but protecting crops. So science tries to reorganise nature according to the needs of society: this is its final goal and of course it can be very beneficial, but this is not the issue. In ordering nature like this, 'Science' steps between us and it, between 'civilisation' and wild 'nature', only preserving 'The Natural' for our organised enjoyment. The natural environment that is left for us is described in totally 'cooked', cultural terms: an 'attractive landscape' populated with 'interesting wildlife'. These double words like landscape (= land) and wildlife (= animals) and the adjectives 'attractive' and 'interesting', which inherently imply a subject (someone to whom these things *are* attractive and interesting), show the way that cultural terminology distances the real phenomena by translating them through concepts. 'Landscape' and 'wildlife' are abstract terms, ideas: they are connotative, they do not denote an actual field or a specific animal. That we have turned land into landscape, seeing the former always through the conceptual glass of the latter, shows how it is the imagery and language *of culture* that actually

A67

determine *what* we see as nature—because how we see it is inseparable from what it 'actually is', to us. 'Wildlife' is, similarly, a concept that can never apply to any specific creature, and thus is always an image or translation of nature; it denotes what is 'Natural', but not nature. The notion that nature must be attractive and interesting further shows that it is seen through the eyes of culture: a value judgement is attached to it.

It is interesting that this very 'cleaned up' and Romanticised (cf. Chapter 5) view of nature as attractive landscape populated with interesting wildlife, should be part and parcel of the view that seems so different, of scientific contact with nature, tackling the raw. Yet of course, they go together. They also go with making a profit: as the ad itself says, 'There's a connection'. But the sceptic who voices and thus anticipates our fears and criticisms of ICI and chemical research, precludes any further criticism: the very form of the ad, a transcript of an interview, has the aura of *research* (research into research—creating an ideology of ideology) and of scientific 'truth': it is less an interview than an experiment, a challenge put to ICI and scientifically rebuffed. Thus the form of the ad signifies a certain faith in science, as well as testing that science and hence allowing it to justify itself. There is a current idea (particularly prevalent on TV discussions on Ireland, Africa, and on advertising itself) that if two opposing views are juxtaposed the result is total objectivity. This is clearly nonsense: but it provides the basic structure of the verbal part of this ad, the internalised opposition somehow making it more genuine (as with the admission of faults in the last two ads), = objective = scientific.

A67

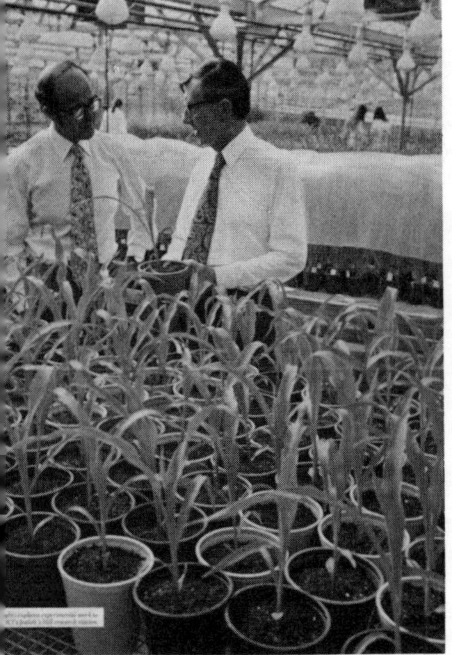

Finally I repeat, this does not pretend to be an analysis of science, but of the presentation of science through the ideological form of advertising.

(*b2*) *The Natural Order*

Once nature has been brought into the enclosure of the greenhouse, under the eye of science, it is no longer necessary to go outside to investigate it, out to the 'raw' undifferentiated natural world: nature can be investigated, as A67 showed, within the parameters of science, *through* science. However, once science has interpreted nature we are invited to interpret science, instead of nature: what was once the 'transparency' that brought us nature, the grid of differentiations through which it was revealed, has now become a transparency which reveals nothing but itself. This has partly been shown in the linguistic self-enclosure by which culture defines what it sees, and sees what it defines, a point which arose in the analysis of A67. Inevitably, as science orders and classifies nature, it sees nature in terms of those classifications, and so on: this is simply a basic feature of all language. But it is one thing to represent reality, another to replace it. In Chapter 3 I have discussed at length the creation of a world of symbols, the interpretation of which ultimately replaced the interpretation of the world that *they* claimed to interpret. A certain opacity in the signifying system is enough to deflect our attention from what it deciphers, to deciphering *it*. Thus the means of knowing becomes all that need be known: this is the same as my argument in 'the raw and the cooked', that only *forms* of knowledge are appropriated by advertising, so we always use the grid by which knowledge is culturally ordered, but never actually find *what* is known. The obvious ideological function of this is to make the subject feel *knowing* but deprive him of *knowledge*. (Hence the trap of a structural analysis without a context: it slips *around* a historical reality, merely.) Similarly, in culture things may be *natural* (how many products use this word) but they are never *nature*.

The ideology of science tends very much towards the kind of closed, symbolic system described in Chapter 3. In that science creates or formulates a system of nature, complete with laws, hierarchies, internal relations—in short, law and order—it then works on this system, so that in a sense it is working on itself, as I have already said: but the significance of this system for the *ideology* of science, is that its complexity renders it mystically incomprehensive to nearly everyone and so instead of helping us to understand *nature* we are confronted with our difficulty in understanding *it*, with its strange words, cryptic diagrams, and magical, mathematical symbols.

This density which we must decipher to find 'science', let alone 'nature', can exist, paradoxically, alongside the other image of science, that of clarity and perfection. The necessity of penetrating to the complexity of science is illustrated in a whole genre of ads for scientific equipment etc.:

A68 A Hermeneutic of Hi-fis: The clean surface of science masks a complexity which is just hinted at: 'It looks even better on the inside'. We now 'read through' science to science itself; it becomes its own referent, indeed, comes to reveal its own 'raw and cooked' system:

A69: Here, the 'cooked' surface is partially removed to reveal the 'raw' workings of the washing machine. The numbers attached to different parts of the picture, the various internal components of the machine, are used in the text, in the description of the machine: we are thus offered a 'key', invited to participate in interpreting the workings of the washing machine. Its secrets are 'revealed' in image by the removal of the machine's outside, so that we break through the surface of science to get drawn into its internal system. But this system is not immediately comprehensible to us and the verbal part of the ad provides the other part of the hermeneutic revelation, a sort of 'interpretation by

A68

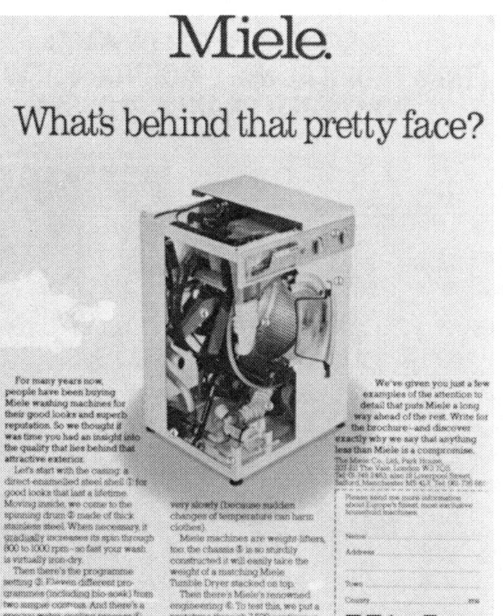

A69

numbers'. Of course, numbers have a particular 'scientific' significance of their own: they are signifiers far more than signifieds, for who understands what the expressed claim of '800–1000 rpm' really means in terms of drying washing? The point is that the numbers signify scientific *fact*, and 'objectivity'.

The exposure of inner workings achieved in A69 by the removal of the outside of the machine, is a permanent feature of much electrical equipment nowadays—for example, the stereos with transparent covers that show all the works—a sort of ideological metaphor. It is this self-revealing, innocent transparency which gives science the status of a 'natural' because 'obvious' order. Thus science, by offering itself to us as something to be seen and understood, rather than the means by which we see and understand, is always something already there, like nature, something full of 'facts', like nature, something Natural—replacing nature.

There is a whole nexus of connotation around this idea of the obvious, the natural: what is *revealed* is always assumed to be more basic than what concealed it, transparency always gives the illusion of getting right there to the bare bones of something; it also implies *proof* simply by *showing*: 'there it is, it must be so'. Everything is revealed, and nothing explained.

The transparency that replaces the decorative with the *visibly* functional has a great deal of the puritanical in it: especially in the sense of an anti-aesthetic tone. 'Beauty is more than skin deep': and 'you might not believe it to look at the CS705D cassette deck (A68), but Akai think that what's inside is more beautiful than the casing.' In A69 Miele showed us what was 'behind that pretty face', using the same idea. The connection between science and puritanism is an obvious one: both have a clean, clinical image, and both claim to ignore appearance, superfluity and irrelevancy and to get 'down to the basics'—the basics always being *natural*. But the irony of puritanism is that it also believes in covering up: it is rather like getting made-up to achieve the 'natural' look, as is seen in many cosmetic ads. This parallels the way that science in exposing its own incomprehensible intricacies, achieves the look of the 'natural'.

The anti-aesthetic image, always so closely associated with 'truth', comes to be applied in advertising to advertising itself:

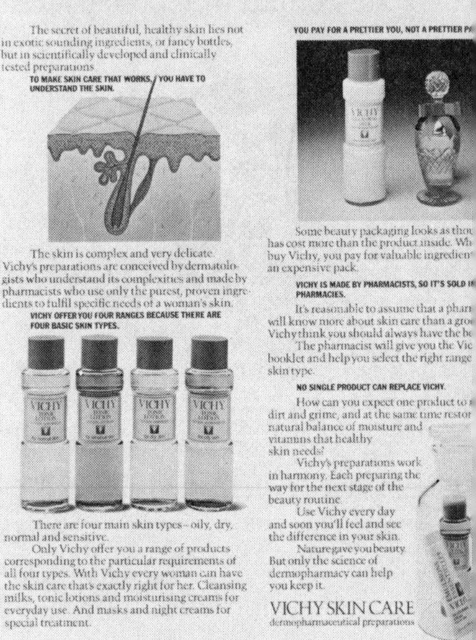

A

A70: This ad shows a conscious rejection of the 'romantic', 'pretty' ad and packaging, of flowery language like 'powdered orange blossom' and so on, claiming to be 'serious' and 'scientific'. 'The secret of beautiful, healthy skin lies not in exotic sounding ingredients, or fancy bottles but in scientifically developed and clinically tested preparations.' Thus we are at the outset offered 'science', knowledge, rather than exotic *words*. The caption for the diagram, a 'scientific' diagram showing a cross section of the skin magnified, is 'to make skin care that works, you have to understand the skin'. Then underneath the diagram, 'The skin is complex and very delicate. Vichy's preparations are conceived by dermatologists who understand its complexities and made by pharmacists who use only the purest, proven ingredients. . . .' We are told that the makers of Vichy understand the skin, but *we* do not understand it: the diagram tells us *nothing*. It is just a picture of the skin: it represents, but does not explain. So again we see how representation is a closed circle: the diagram *shows* us, it conceals nothing, it *is* the skin, enlarged to make it even clearer; but it does not help us to know anything. While seeming to be an explanation, it is really a *symbol*: it denotes the skin, but connotes *science*, *facts*, *seriousness*; it represents the whole miraculous system of science but is empty of meaning in itself. This shows that science, supposedly a system full of knowledge, is for ads (and ideology) a referent system like any other, and our knowledge *of* it is exploited (Vichy takes from this diagram all the connotations of purity, certainty etc. of science) while our knowledge *in* it is denied. (We never find out how Vichy works or how the skin works.) If you use Vichy every day 'soon you'll feel and see the difference in your skin': feeling and seeing are supposed to be the ultimate test, but they still do not *explain*. Obviousness, transparency, 'The Natural' (it's only natural etc.) become attached to Science as a referent system, but defy the possibility of *a* science.

The preceding ad showed the prevalent idea that knowledge of things resides *in* them, to be revealed by looking closely, by feeling or touching, rather than in systems of relations between things. The entire hermeneutic idea is based on everything revealing its own meaning, that to know something is simply to know it, rather than to know *about* it. To know something directly involves purely a relationship between you and the thing, between subject and object: while to know the relation between two things involves a relation between two objects, and though the subjective position can never, of course, be removed completely, its central and privileged role in the process of knowledge is superseded. In any case, a *subject's* relationship with an *object* places the whole process in an arbitrary position, like trying to find your bearing by only one landmark: while in looking at two or more things, at relations *between* objects, the observer's position is much more clearly defined.

It is therefore clear that knowledge of relations can be far more valuable than knowledge of 'things'. It is an opportune moment to comment yet again on the benefits and dangers of 'structural analysis', an area which I think has not been considered carefully enough by either Marxists or 'structuralists'—who seem to have been placed in an opposition based on historicity versus 'structure'. Because of the way ideology is structured, in fact the way society is structured, a stress on structural relationships is invaluable; it removes the myth that anything can be known in isolation, and removes the emphasis on the subject. But as I started by saying that knowledge of particular things is found not in them but in their relations, it is crucial not to forget that it is, ultimately, particular things and social phenomena that we wish to know and understand. The knowledge of systems is important because they are not, in reality, empty structures but systems of things and people, and systems of signifying the relationship between the two—which is the concern here.

Having argued for a kind of knowledge that *can* have substance, I have not, I hope, gouged all meaning out of the word 'science' and made it as hollow as it becomes when merely a referent of advertisements. The diagram in A70 merely 'referred' to 'science' in this way: what should be *signified* by the diagram, the workings of the skin, is replaced by the diagram's function as a *signifier* of a vague, connoted *image* of scientific knowledge. This same replacement, an exchange of connotation for denotation, of reference for explanation—an exchange disguised by the fact that the referent *seems* to be there in the sign (cf. Chapter 3)—can be seen in A71, where the whole advertisement functions similarly to the Vichy diagram.

A71

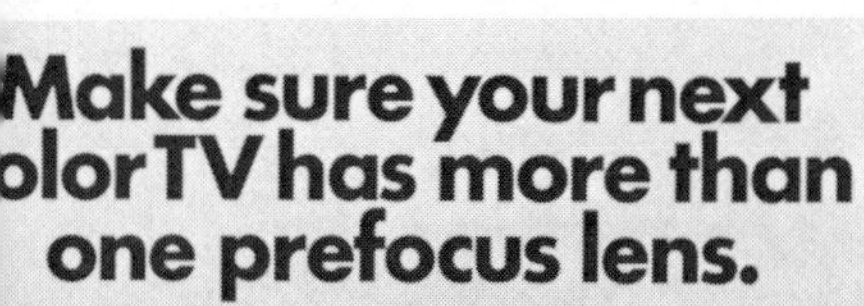

A71: Nobody reading this advertisement can have any idea what a 'prefocus lens' is: here again, the diagrams conceal nothing but themselves, the language seems explanatory but like the picture, only refers to scientific knowledge and does not actually offer it. The entire advertisement is a sign pointing to Science, but empty of science.

Science has thus become constituted as a referent system in itself, completely separate from nature, against which it was originally defined. It protects us from nature, but this protection becomes so complete that science itself seems to be the basic order of things, full of symbols for our society, just as nature provides a universe of symbols for tribal society. But science has never finished with nature. The relationship between the two is one of dialectic: science both conceals and reveals, it protects us from nature and then presents us with 'the natural': in its own 'natural' laws, but also with the 'attractive landscape and interesting wildlife' that ICI promised us in A67. This *re*-presentation is the subject of Chapter 5, where the circuit of imagery is completed by the location of culture *in* nature.

(*c*) *'Cooked' Sex: 'Civilisation and Its Discontents'*

Lévi-Strauss' dichotomy of the raw and the cooked applies not only to natural objects but to sex. In this area we can see all the tensions, the 'cooking' process yet the appeal to 'the natural', that have been discussed so far in this chapter. Here, however, the 'cooking' does not simply involve 'nature' or our view of 'nature', it involves ourselves; our bodies and our passions and our images of them. Sex becomes a referent system, always hinted at, referred to, in innuendo, double entendre, or symbolism: but never 'raw'. Thus again the illusion is that sex is being revealed, while in fact it is concealed behind its own references.

A

A72: Here the referent is wildness: 'for those of you who've been civilised long enough' implies both discontent with civilisation and simultaneously, culture as an élite group—it is for those of you who are at the apex of civilisation. Coty claim to be '*unleashing*' this 'most sensual, frankly arousing fragrance', throwing off the control of civilisation: yet, 'Now Coty's *coaxed* the dangerous Wild Musk (like an animal) into its *own* creme fragrance compact'. That the compact should be *its own* implies that it 'naturally' belongs there. As with the Florida orange ad, A62, and the others in that section, the opposition between nature and culture is represented in a way that overcomes it—so that we may have both civilisation *and* its discontents. We can be made to feel both 'tamed' and 'unleashed'.

The product, having 'cooked' nature, can then offer a safe passage 'back' to it. It can re-present nature to us in a form where it may be consumed.

A 73

lines; steady road-holding;
speed of 107.6 mph; 0–60
seconds* and the sort of
space you need when
just want to get up and
that's the MGB GT. A worthy
companion to cars like the Midget,
MGB and MGB GT V8.
Look out, too, for the 'limited edition' of 750 specially equipped MGB GTs, built to commemorate MG's fiftieth year.
When you're behind the wheel of an MG, you're driving a true thoroughbred.
MG
BON 18IN
You can do it in an MG.

A73: This example is similar to A46 in that the caption may be read in terms of the car's acceleration rate, described in the verbal part of the ad, above the picture, but 'IT' also has the connoted meaning of sex. We all 'know' what 'it' means—another hollow referent.

The product involves a double cooking in that it offers a cultural version of riding a horse—'when you're behind the wheel of an MG you're driving a true thoroughbred'—which is in itself a metaphor for sex. And its implicit offer is that you can have sex in an MG. Not only is the product, the car, a 'cooked' version of a horse and a vehicle for enclosed sex, it is also itself located inside a strong cultural referent—it is parked in the courtyard of a Tudor house. However, the couple who have previously occupied the car, and presumably 'done it', are walking outwards into the garden. Having 'cooked' their sex in the car, they may be 'unleashed' into the garden, a controlled natural environment.

The couple's entry into the garden obviously connotes a sort of return to Eden—this is denoted literally in the following ad.

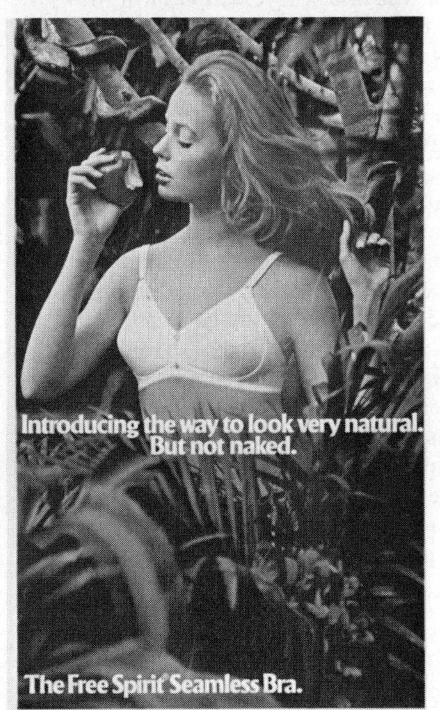

Introducing the way to look very natural.
But not naked.
The Free Spirit Seamless Bra.
If you don't want to go around looking naked to the world, and you don't want to look phony, either—here's what you do want. The Free Spirit Seamless Bra.
With body-soft cups that shape like a bosom, not like a bra. Cups without a single seam. And comfort? Eve herself never had it so good.
Free Spirit Seamless soft cup bra . . . also available in fiberfill or fully padded styles with cups in a new polyester tricot that won't stretch out. Only from Playtex.*

A74: Here, the snake and the apple literally refer to the garden of Eden—which itself connotes both innocence and wickedness combined and thus is a suitable image to represent what is both desirable and undesirable about 'raw' sexuality. The element of naughtiness suggested here will be seen again in images of nature—cf A81 below. Yet the only way the idea of temptation really fits into the ad is in that *we* are being tempted to go out and buy the bra. In doing this we are improving on our natural state: 'Eve herself never had it so good.' But in this improvement we are also returning to perfect freedom: although the bra encloses and confines the body it is also the release, apparently, of a sort of Hegelian Free Spirit: it is, after all, the Free Spirit Seamless Bra. It has a natural form—'body-soft cups that shape like a bosom, not like a bra' (although it comes in 'fiberfill or fully padded styles') but an unnatural function.

However, it *claims* to be '*introducing* the way to look very natural': the product actually creates, introduces 'the natural' (thus showing that 'the natural' is a cultural concept, since it is introduced by an artifact) while also preventing nakedness.

Setting up naturalness and nakedness in opposition is using the 'raw' to give status to the 'cooked', and indicates that culture, having once given nature a significance, may then safely lead us back to it.

CHAPTER FIVE
BACK TO NATURE

'La Nature est un temple où de vivants piliers
Laissent parfois sortir de confuses paroles;
L'homme y passe à travers des forêts de symboles
Qui l'observent avec des regards familiers.'[1]

Baudelaire
Correspondances

Nature, having been 'cooked', is then returned to 'the natural' world to inherit its place in a system the components of which have all been similarly 'cooked': a network of romantic symbols. When you have cooked your food, you arrange it in a nest of fresh watercress, or sprinkle parsley on top of it: it is relocated as 'the natural' which inevitably becomes symbolic, since the water cress is there to signify something about what is cooked. Nature is on one level channelled through technological processes, the result of which is The Product—whether food or machinery or sex. But when this product is replaced in nature (quite literally in a field or among flowers, as the following examples will show) it can never be nature undifferentiated and raw, because a transaction of meaning is required, and 'nature' is supposed to invest the product, which was torn from it in the first place, with the status of 'the natural'. In other words, 'nature' as a referent, is hardly closer to raw nature than the manufactured product which it signifies as 'natural'. For example: there is an advertisement for instant coffee which shows in a series of pictures the process of transforming the coffee beans into a jar of granules. The final picture shows the jar and a cup of instant coffee: the raw beans have been cooked to make the product. However, the 'cooked' picture retains an image of nature, in a bowl of flowers which has suddenly appeared next to the coffee cup. A *romantic* symbol of nature now replaces the actual natural form of the product. The whole idea of 'nature' and its connotations has been channelled into the flowers, just as the beans have been processed into the granules. Therefore, the product can never quite get back to *nature*, because it can never be signified *as* nature, only as natural: 'the natural' is the meaning extracted from nature, and there is an invisible but

[1]'Nature's a temple where the pilasters
Speak sometimes in their mystic languages;
Man reaches it though symbols dense as trees
They watch him with a gaze familiar.'

Joanna Richardson tr., *Penguin* 1975.

impenetrable barrier between the two. 'The Natural' is the meaning given by culture to nature; that it is socially determined and not a fixed quality is shown by the change in what constitutes the 'natural' from age to age, throughout history. It becomes the justification for whatever society approves and desires. But precisely because of this reference to Nature as the determinant of what is good, as though it were an independent arbiter, 'the natural' becomes the meaning given *to* culture, *by* nature—although it is culture that determines 'the natural' anyway.

Thus society works on nature in two ways: with technology, to create manufactured goods, and with ideology, to create symbols of 'the natural' which are then juxtaposed with the manufactured goods so that meaning may be exchanged between the two. In the previous chapter we have seen how our culture 'cooks' nature to produce not only these manufactured products, but *images* of manufacture, of the 'cooking' process, of 'science': images, that is, of itself, as defined against nature which is wild and raw and dangerous. But to admit this process of self-definition would be for culture to undermine that definition, its self-image of superiority and efficiency, 'civilisation'. Thus it must ultimately turn back to the natural world it has overcome, replace itself in the context it has defined as 'natural'. This chapter sets out to examine that context, images of 'the natural' as opposed to the images of science and manufacture shown in Chapter 4. Besides images of the 'natural', which are shown in the first section below, we can also see in 'Surrealism' images of *the replacement in 'the natural'*—a parallel to the 'raw and cooked' section in that the process itself, though here of reinsertion in nature rather than removal from nature, is presented. Then in the last section I shall discuss the significance of the relocation of cultural objects and indeed culture itself, within 'the natural' order.

(*a*) *'The Natural'*

'The natural' is, I have suggested, a symbol in culture: *what* it signifies varies greatly as will be seen in the variety of examples below, where it is used to connote such different qualities as 'perfectibility', 'danger', 'obviousness', and 'naughtiness'. The link between these qualities is that they are all seen as desirable, when nature is connected with them. So the precise *meaning* of nature as a symbol, i.e. of 'the natural', is less important than the significance of its being used as a symbol at all. There have been periods in the history of our society when 'artificial' was not a pejorative word as it is today; and when 'natural' did not have the bundle of positive connotations which characterise it now, and have done so since the eighteenth century and the 'Romantic' era. This change in society's view of 'the natural' no doubt stems from a change in material conditions—the importance of 'the natural' increases directly in proportion as society's distance from *nature* is increased, through technological development. A society which is in open contact with nature, whose boundaries are constantly being defended in a battle with natural forces, may well see nature as chaotic, if not hostile: it can bring famine, sickness and death. Man's relationship with nature is inevitably a dialectical one: it gives him his existence, and yet he must work on it and struggle with it to survive. The complexity of this relationship is present equally in 'primitive' societies and in technologically 'advanced' societies like our own. However in 'primitive' societies the fact that subsistence is drawn from nature and that nature may also destroy that subsistence is a far more immediate reality than it is to us in Western society—where death itself, the most 'natural' of facts, is our strongest taboo. But Romanticism has provided us with a solution to the complexity of our relationship with nature, in the form of a sort of *condensation*: the harshness of nature means that society is good and beneficial in overcoming it; but then, this goodness is found in nature itself, so that the area of contrast is lost. It reappears, in fact, in reverse because once nature is set up as a symbol of what is good, everything undesirable in society can be called 'unnatural'. The terminology of 'natural/unnatural' thus erects nature as an absolute symbol, and in isolation: what means is *it*, not our relationship with it. Here again, ideology replaces a recognition of relationships between things with an exchange of meanings between things. The way in which culture interacts with nature is entirely reduced to the level of a signifying process which actually *inverts* the real, material relationship.

In this way the tension of the dialectic is lost, or rather, disguised, because nature is set up as a *parallel* to society and the grid of cultural meanings is imprinted on it in a direct symmetry which makes nature merely society's mirror image,[1] they become congruent systems of meanings. If what is socially acceptable is called 'natural', and what is socially unacceptable, 'unnatural', it is clear that social values are simply being hammered into nature, as onto a carbon copy, which may then be produced separately as if to ratify the original. Nature and culture are thus completely elided, and this elision necessarily 'removes' the complex and contradictory area of their

[1]See Chapter 2, section e.

interaction. It has been the supreme achievement of Romanticism to create this one-to-one symmetry between the good and the natural, the bad and the unnatural—thereby investing nature with a moral value. It creates an *imaginary* unity between two meanings which are only able to exist as symbols at all because of their underlying difference: it is important to recognise that this unity or symmetry *is* imaginary because 'natural culture' is something we strive after constantly but can never attain.[1] Thus Romanticism involves the concept of perfectibility, it is in fact a sort of Platonism where the perfect forms, of which society sees merely the shadows, are found not in some 'ideal' area but in 'nature'—which of course then *becomes* an ideal area.

A75

'Why do the Cullens seem to get 70 minutes out of every hour?'

Some couples have the time and energy to enjoy things that other people never get around to. Wouldn't you love to get that much out of every hour? Think about your day and the way it begins. Are you sure you're getting all the vitamins and iron you need? The simplest way to make sure is to take one Sanatogen Selected Multivitamin, or Multivitamin Plus Iron, every day. As regularly as brushing your teeth.

Just one pleasant-tasting tablet each day provides you with the seven vitamins and minerals you need for the positive health that can seem to put more minutes in every hour.

sanatogen selected multivitamins plus IRON

sanatogen selected multivitamins

Sanatogen Multivitamins. One a day-for positive health.

A75: In this example the ideas of perfectibility and the ideal are expressed in 'getting 70 minutes out of every hour'. This extends a cultural unit, an hour, suggesting that a period of 70 minutes is actually natural. Of course, the hour *is* always an hour, but what is natural is the 70 minutes: culture takes into itself nature (i.e. unmeasured time) but gives it a measurement. This doubled time is analogous to another important element in the photograph. Although the couple are so packed with vitamins that he can catch all those fish, whose silvery corpses are scattered beneath the easel, and she can paint, their attention is fixed on what she has produced, the *image* of nature. We can only partially see this painting—just as the black and white photo (the original is black and white) robs us of the colourful multiplicity of nature. But it clearly points out towards nature which is, in a way, its 'reverse-field'. Nature here is doubly caught by these energetic representatives of culture. It is transformed into objects for consumption (his dead fish) and into a representation, her picture. The ad only half pretends that it is showing nature—its chief demonstration is that nature is *representable*. Here 'the natural' is itself perfect and can also be perfectly captured.

[1] ibid.

A76

Wright's
HERB
SOAP
Wright's Herb Soap cares for your ski
Naturally.

A76: Here, the 'naturalness' precedes the product's insertion among images of nature, because the soap actually *contains* herbs, indicated by its name, and the herbs placed around it in the picture are already on the packet. The contrast between the wrapped and unwrapped products, gives the *unwrapped* soap the status of 'the natural' like the herbs that both surround it and are contained in it. The simultaneous presence of both wrapped and unwrapped soap not only makes the unwrapped seem 'raw', but almost *more* 'raw' than the actual herbs: for these herbs are connected with the packet, where a representation of them parallels their representation in the advertisement; and the way the packet encloses the soap, and the herbs also wrap themselves around it, makes the soap like a sort of core, at the heart of all this natural goodness.

But in this ad 'the natural' has more than one meaning, and the word 'naturally' in the caption is a kind of pun; on one level the herbs make the soap 'natural' (although soap, the great cleaner-up, is a supremely cultural artifact) but the other sense of the word is 'obviously', or 'inevitably'. Thus we see the idea—which will be discussed further in the last part of this chapter—that what is natural is obvious; 'naturally' means 'of course', so there is an element of determinism attached to it, and it removes power from our own hands. The double connotation of 'naturally' in this context is more than a duality of meaning, as these meanings are very much bound up together, and are not alternatives as in some puns. *Because* the soap is '*natural*', it functions naturally, *of course*. The two meanings are inseparable.

A77: This ad shows some more of the magical properties of herbs—one of society's latest obsessions. It is ironic that this 'naturalness' should actually be seen as having unnatural or *magical* properties. The 'mysterious wild flowers and green herbs' are made almost *super-natural*, and the product indeed promises to transport you away from the real and natural world—'like you're somewhere far away beyond the ordinary world in a wild enchanted garden'. But notice that the *garden*—enclosed nature, *not* 'wild' nature as it claims—is again the place to which you can be transported: gardens and greenhouses crop up in advertisements claiming to be about 'nature' with surprising frequency. The exotic quality of nature suggested in this ad also gives it the aura of something alien, unusual, mystical. Thus the romantic interest in 'the natural' is the very opposite of materialist—nature is never physical, but becomes a dream, a paradisial fantasy. I am not saying that the advertisement really intends you to believe that the product will carry you away to paradise, or that anyone will believe it. But this is irrelevant: what is important is *the kind of nature referred to*, what 'the natural' is seen to be—even if it *is* blatantly unattainable. And the *image* of nature that this ad exploits is one of a fantasy, an ideal and exotic haven which is located *not* in the natural, the 'ordinary world', but far away beyond it. 'The natural' is thus situated *out of* nature.

The Clairol
For your hair, you
Experience the most
beautiful shampoo on earth.
Come. Discover Clairol® herbal essence
shampoo with natural protein,
fragrant with mysterious wild
flowers and green herbs.
Your clean, conditioned
hair will shine and
feel alive.
And you will
feel very, very free.
Like you're some-
where far away beyond
the ordinary world in
a wild enchanted
garden.
herbal
essence
shampoo
herbal
essence
CREME
RINSE
Then experience
herbal essence cre
Linger in the sa
enchanted garden wi
herbal essence creme
conditioners.
Your comb will gl
wind through your h
your hair will feel a
your fingers as ex
petals.

A77

A78

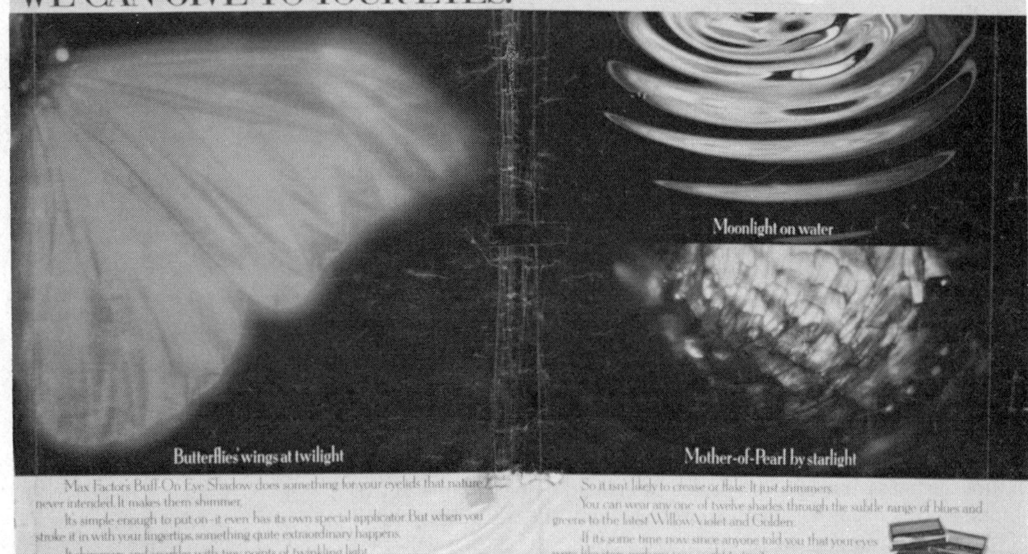

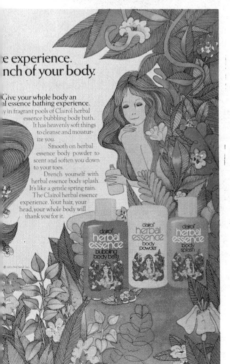

e experience.
nch of your body.

Give your whole body an
al essence bathing experience.
y in fragrant pools of Clairol herbal essence bubbling body bath.
It has heavenly soft things to cleanse and moisturize you.
Smooth on herbal essence body powder to scent and soften you down to your toes.
Drench yourself with herbal essence body splash.
It's like a gentle spring rain.
The Clairol herbal essence experience. Your hair, your head, your whole body will thank you for it.

clairol herbal essence bubbling body bath
clairol herbal essence body powder
clairol herbal essence body splash

A77

A78: Here the illustrations are of 'butterflies' wings at twilight', 'moonlight on water', and 'mother of pearl by starlight': all totally Romantic images of nature. And Max Factor is able to *imitate* nature—reproduce these natural shimmers to do the work of nature itself. Yet while creating the 'natural' look, Max Factor is also doing 'something for your eyes that nature never intended.'

This ad therefore works in two ways. Its basic assumption is that nature is primarily decorative. Nature cannot be seen as also cruel, destructive and terrifying: we are shown it as shimmering moonlight, butterflies' wings, stars. However on a much deeper level we are clearly shying away from nature with a deep-rooted fear, or why should we be painting our eyelids with Max Factor at all? The product here is *un*naturally imitating a romanticised and idealised aspect of nature, yet with the emphasis on manufacture: indeed, nature is seen as a vast subject (as Science is, cf last chapter). 'Nature' *gave* the shimmer to these things, it is a kind of artist or deity, but definitely a subject; imitated by Max Factor who thus becomes a sort of shadow-subject, copying, and yet tidying up after, 'the natural': transplanting a natural phenomenon, the shimmer, to a place where nature never meant it to be, the eyelid. When this transplant takes place, we are told, 'something quite extraordinary happens'. Thus nature again is seen to hold all these unnatural surprises: it has the capacity, apparently, to transcend itself. Nature becomes more and more *magical* (cf. next chapter) instead of *material*.

A79

A79: Here, 'Sudden Beauty' works so fast that we can actually see both the process and the result of the face pack simultaneously in the model's divided face: it brings an 'instant result', condensing nature's work both physically (getting Country Air in to a tube) and temporally—'the natural glow of fresh country air in just 5 minutes!' The product 'helps nature do its good work': again, nature is both copied and improved. But notice that the metaphor used is a highly cultural one: 'feel the tingle as it *revs up* your circulation . . .'—this is an idea drawn from motor mechanics and it is ironic that it is presumably car exhaust fumes etc., that have destroyed your skin's natural country glow in the first place. And the result of the mask is described in strange terms, leading up to a very 'unnatural' adjective: '. . . a texture that looks finer, silkier, . . . *polished*'. So we are polishing up nature, while helping it with its work.

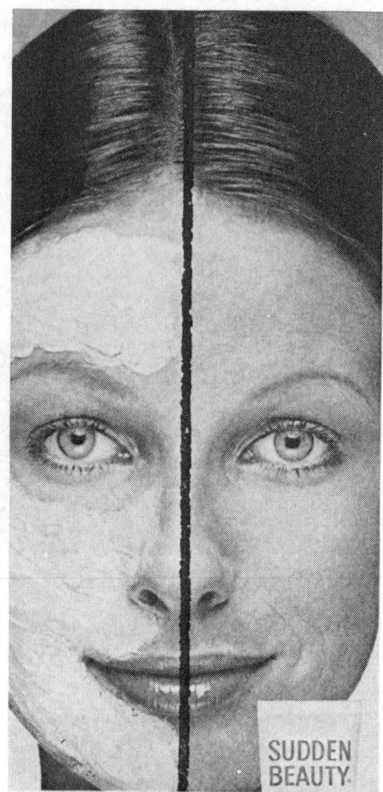

SUDDEN BEAUTY
Country Air Mask
Gives your skin the natural glow of fresh country air in just 5 minutes!

Your skin is constantly renewing itself and Sudden Beauty COUNTRY AIR Mask helps nature do its good work. COUNTRY AIR Mask sloughs off dead skin and removes the oily build-up that can plug pores, cause blackheads and other blemishes. Feel the tingle as it revs up your circulation, draws out deep-down dirt. In just 5 minutes...rinse away. Instant result: a country air rosiness, a texture that looks finer, silkier...polished.

A80: The contradictions which have been implicit but disguised in most of the preceding ads are very apparent here, where we are presented with burning and coolness simultaneously. This ad offers back-to-nature freshness through the health-destroying, air-polluting act of smoking. This promise is implied in the picture: the clean damp smell of the grass and stream are correlatives for coolness; but they will soon be destroyed by the cigarette in the girl's hand. The opposition of coolness/burning is so extreme yet so completely denied by the ad, that this is a good example to make the point yet again, that advertisements work on concealed, unconscious and irrational levels; juxtaposing things not only unconnected but in this case actually *opposed*, but giving these juxtapositions the status of a 'natural' order (cf. surrealism).

A80

The longer you smoke, the more you'll like KOOL Super Longs.
Long-size cigarettes can taste extra hot. But KOOL Super Longs, with the taste of extra coolness, are refreshing for all their length.
Lady be cool.
KOOL
Super Longs

81

Designed for the way you see yourself now
Seascapes
A new group by Catalina

82

A, THE SOUND YOU THOUGHT YOU'D NEVER HEAR AGAIN
It's like learning to listen all over again. Because AIWA (say Aye-ee-wah) are sound innovators in over 70 countries with exclusive ideas about audio equipment. Like better sound and more convenience refinements than comparable equipment.
The TPR-930 is incomparable. A portable stereo/radio cassette recorder with a unique MS stereo system embodying four variably angled speakers in the cabinet. Unique too, is the TP -770 cassette recorder/player. This high powered compact unit has advanced CrO_2 switching. And, brilliantly, pitch control. Or consider the *Dolby AD 1500 stereo cassette deck. A professional performance level with wow and flutter an astonishing 0.07%. Signal to Noise Ratio 60dB, plus oil damped elevation.
Sensational, all three from the range, and the cognoscenti are on to them.
AIWA®
It could be the sensation your life has been missing

A81: This ad needs little comment. The new 'real skin' look shows an attempt to *re*-create even our body and skin; and the attitude to nature is, 'so natural it's almost *naughty*'—the genuinely natural is seen as something rather scary. This shows how the 'natural' look is actually an attempt to cover up the 'naughtiness' of Nature, illustrating the point that 'the natural' is a cultural re-presentation of nature, and is *not* nature itself. The naturalness of the ad is 'designed for the way *you see yourself now*'—not the way you see nature, which is simply a mirror for the cultural self-image to reflect in.

A82: Here, technology literally reproduces 'the natural'. Despite the romantic image of the sea, the horizon, the shell, a sort of misty romantic myth in the background, the products in the foreground and the mystifying verbal section show an equal preoccupation with a technological myth, which blends with 'the natural' in the idea of perfectibility. The electrical equipment can *capture* the sound of nature, and also works with the mystical perfection of nature. Manufacture has taken on a romantic rather than a scientific image. The products have names like 'TPR-930, TP-770'—and the language is highly technical: 'advanced CrO_2 switching . . . wow and flutter an astonishing 0·07%. Signal to noise ratio 60 dB plus oil damper elevation. . . .' Few of the people reading this are likely to understand any of it; it is as incomprehensible, as inexplicable, as nature itself. It is a new, technological myth of *complexity* presenting nature as a simple, romantic, idealised myth of girls on seashores with shells. The creation of 'the natural' through manufacture, shown here very clearly, runs as a thread of contradiction, simplification and fear throughout these chapters. Nature is connected with perfection: yet this perfection can only be achieved mechanically. And in a way, technology is offering us here a key to nature, 'the sensation your life has been missing': it is the final point of perfection in your life, it fills the gap left by nature. The actual products also fill the gap between the romantic background, the picture, and the very technical verbal part of the ad, beneath: because the tapeplayers are placed as if on the surface of the paper on which the writing is situated, yet they spill over into the sea-scape picture, almost as though the girl was listening to them, and not to the shell. So *formally*, the products do precisely what they also do on the level of connotation: they partake both of the romantic, and of the technological, perfection.

This setting of machines in nature, to give them the quality of 'the natural', can give us a new angle on some of the ads showing machines in natural surroundings that were used in the last chapter to illustrate the image of *science*. A65 and 66 draw very heavily on Romantic imagery and this, as much as the more overt, scientific image, is what sells the products.

A65 (*b*) (*Please see page 112*): Although the Peugeot car is able to defy nature's threats, it enjoys a very romantic image in the midst of them: the little red car all alone in a vast expanse of snow and ice. The aura of danger is, besides being a way of proving the safety of the car, paradoxically attached to the car itself. The more 'civilised' and controlled our lives become, precisely *because* of such products—mechanical, accurate, labour-saving—the greater the need to compensate, by reintroducing danger and excitement in the surrogate form of advertising 'adventure stories'. Although the overt message of this ad is that the Peugeot will get you out of this situation, the implicit suggestion is that it will get you into it, and create this exciting adventure.

A66 (*b*) (*Please see page 113*): Although the product claims to be so practical and tough, the conditions of its use as described and illustrated here are completely irrelevant to most people. In this genre of ad, the spaceship/polar expedition/Mount Everest theme only removes the context of the product further from our ordinary lives. The images involved in this are, despite the scientific, gritty tone, very romanticised: as in A65, we are sold on the idea of adventure, exploration, excitement. Chris Bonington is the Romantic (almost Byronic) hero engaged on a lonely, challenging exploit: and the image of the mountain itself, its craggy peak shrouded in white mists, is romanticised by its setting in the frame, as it represents a sort of pinnacle of achievement; we just see it in the shape of an arrow, pointing upwards into the sky, and drawn into the page out of all scale or context.

This placing of a machine in a natural setting in order to give it the aura of 'the natural', can result in extraordinary juxtapositions, and the final example in this section will lead us straight into an examination of 'surrealism' and its relation to advertising.

A83: The Citroën is supposed to be 'very beautiful' and hence its place among flowers, symbols of natural beauty. There is a slight pun in the caption, providing the supposed reason for the car being in a greenhouse: the point is that the car gives you 'plenty to show' just as your prize flowers do. This is using nature as a referent to connote something owned and displayed. There are a hundred other ways to connote beauty besides flowers in a hot-house, and thus the real significance of their presence as 'natural' correlatives is that they have been appropriated from the outside world, subjectivised by being owned and tended and 'grown' by the owner, who then shows them as *his*—he as subject has taken over from nature as subject. The final phrase in the ad is 'More to show for your money': since the car can be

The Citroën GS gives you plenty to show for £1780.
Citroën GS
More to show for your money.
CITROËN GS

A83

bought, this suggests that nature can also be bought and owned—nature becomes *property* like the car. The car in the greenhouse (a most extraordinary place for it to be) provides a very condensed image that connotes beauty, property, and 'the natural' all in one. The connection underlying this strange placement of objects (it is impossible even to conceive how the car got *into* the greenhouse) depends on the existence of a *subject*—he who owns the car and the plants, who displays them both. Without this way of making sense the image would be completely inexplicable: it is the owner who links (by displaying) the two disparate things.

Placing a bar of soap in a nest of herbs, a tape recorder on a seashore, or a car in a hothouse full of flowers, shows how some very strange connections can be made in advertisements when 'cooked' objects are brought 'back to nature'—but we hardly notice just how strange these placements are, because we *assume* a sense behind them. We exchange the meanings from one part of the ad to another without questioning that such different or even contrasting things should be brought together at all. Surrealism is a form where the bizarre nature of certain juxtapositions is not concealed, but what *is* concealed is the reason underlying their placement. In the previous examples the connecting factor has been 'nature' and this has blurred the jarring of particular images—e.g. cigarettes and mountain streams. But in surrealism the images are allowed to jar: we simply have to look a little further for the 'underlying' sense, which may be an 'unconscious' one. In this aspect the idea of hermeneutics is again relevant (cf. Chapter 3). The short section on Surrealism which follows has a relevance outside the sphere of advertisements, since the real Surrealist movement followed on from the Romantic movement historically, and is based on many of the same ideas of subjectivity. This move from images of the subject in nature, to images ordered 'naturally' by the subject, is one which takes place in 'Art' only as a spin-off from a similar movement in the increasing complexity of the place of the subject in ideology, which is discussed in the final section below.

(*b*) *Surrealism*

In this section I am only concerned with the cultural image and myth of Surrealism, rather than with the movement itself. The question is—What use can this myth serve in advertising?

Surrealism can be traced back to Romanticism in its construction of 'sealed', subjective worlds from disparate objects. In Dali, the most mythic and public of all the surrealists, this is apparent in a painting like 'Apparition of a

Face and Fruit Dish on a Beach'. Here an object and a portrait are brought together in an incongruous location (not unlike Catherine Deneuve and Chanel). It is clearly to Dali that advertisers have looked: in some of the examples that follow you can see that glossy, photographic style of his most famous paintings. Surrealism has been described as 'the road to the absolute'[1] (perhaps in reference to Freud's 'royal road' to the unconscious). By using this absolute world, that can be bracketed off from the real, advertising again finds ways of placing objects in juxtaposition. The cultural image of Surrealism means that the spectator of the ads assumes a link between them. In these examples we *interpret* a puzzling juxtaposition but do not expect an answer—for the hermeneutic of the surreal has no key or solution as in the Double Diamond ads (see p. 88). It is precisely this absence of explicit relationships that makes us assume a link deeper than we can say—indeed the more the objects are disjunct the greater the unconscious link we expect. Our knowledge of Surrealism denies us knowledge of the actual relationship between things—that butter has been produced, for example (see A86 below). And in its assumed representation of subjective and unconscious states the spectator's own unconscious is reached out for and drawn into the ad.

A84: The Dulux series consciously makes use of the mythic structures of surrealism. One crucial factor in producing this 'openly' surrealistic effect is the blue sky: the 'natural' background used to make the objects of the picture seem like natural objects, the foreground surface meeting the sky at the 'horizon' and thus taking on the place of 'the ground', although it is a shiny surface. The 'vanishing point' of the perspective in this picture is located in or behind the paint tin. But besides the 'surrealist' blue sky, the effect of surrealism is achieved in the arrangement of the objects. We see the product, the tools for its use, and the effect of its use (the wall and door) and the two symbols (the dog, advertising symbol for Dulux, and the ICI symbol of the manufacturers). All these necessary ingredients for the ad (like the elements of a dream) are placed together in one picture. This is, however, how *all* ads function. It is simply that most of them pretend to be realistic; but in fact, they are all as bizarre as these, which have chosen to make use of 'surrealism' as a referent system. The collection of disparate objects into a mythic structure—always a pre-existing structure hollowed of meaning—or a dream-like structure, which can only be made sense of by a knowing subject, is the essence of all advertising. The associated objects are the product and its correlatives (as discussed in Chapter 1), and the structure is one which is part of

A84

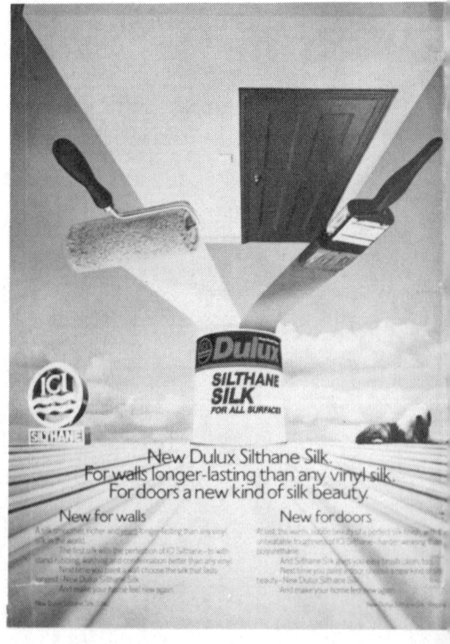

[1] André Breton.

85

A86

ideology. While two of the things in this ad are 'known' symbols, the 'Dulux dog' and the ICI symbol, everything in the picture actually becomes symbolic, because there is no other way to account for the strange structure. The picture cannot even pretend to be representational, so it must be symbolic, representing not an external reality but only its own internal reality—which we do not question. Everything here symbolises the product, which provides the only reason for the other objects to be there. There is no actual relationship between the things presented: they are only related *symbolically*, in other words, not by relationship but by representation, not materially but only conceptually. There is a closed circle of meaning here because the symbols are only justified by their place in the structure, and the structure is only justified by the symbols in it. You can only understand the picture in its own terms, or not at all.

A85: Here, the connection between surrealism and 'the natural' becomes apparent. While surrealism orders objects that have been displaced from their 'normal' (natural) surroundings, in sequences of association representing the sequence of a dream, advertising uses the associations of the cultural dream or myth—the primary example of which is 'nature'. This ad shows products, *symbols* of nature, juxtaposed with nature—an association that can only be brought about by our dream-like belief in the product's status as 'natural'. These are 'cows' in a field: the symbol replaces the reality—literally, here, but this only makes explicit what always happens in advertising (cf. Chapter 3).

A86: While the previous ad replaced cows, natural beings, with the product, we now have cows *and* the product together in a field. A85 was an example of the hollowing out of a place in a system and then inserting the product: the cows had been removed from their place in the field and the bottles had taken over their place and some of their significance (though there is no rational basis for this since the product did not come from cows).

However in this picture butter, the product *of* cows, is placed alongside them, apparently 'naturally'. Notice how the plants overflow the frame here: thus drawing attention to it *as* frame. No attempt is made to be realistic, 'natural', in the actual representation. But the 'natural' quality is only displaced, from the representational level to a deeper one, that of the connections which justify and explain precisely this lack of 'naturalism' in the picture as a whole. An association between processed butter and cows actually has attention drawn *to* it, by the apparently odd juxtaposition. We feel that the connection must lie on a deeper level than that of the visual.

Thus, although it looks strange, the butter, produce of cows, and cows themselves, are placed together in such a way as to give them an equal status, and a similar essential quality: the cows seem remarkably undisturbed by the presence of a huge block of butter in their field. This is confusing origin with result, and thus denying *process*: producer and produced are placed next to each other so as to negate the materiality of production. The butter just seems to be 'naturally' *there*: there is no hint of its being made, of the circuit of cultural 'cooking' which it runs through between the two stages shown, cow (potential butter) and packet (marketable butter). Surrealism and advertising leave out connections between things, as dreams leave out grammar, according to Freud, fixing on things as symbols and ignoring the relationships between them. The butter and the cows simply exist: they are related *symbolically* (the cows exchange their 'natural' status with the butter, transferring meaning) but not in any way that could involve *change*. The simultaneity of this kind of picture denies even the space of time in which transformation could take place, the finality of both cows and butter leaves no space at all for either to have any but an absolute form.

The replacement of real relationships by symbolic relationships, which are undialectical and require a *status quo* of symbols as a precondition, is one of the primary functions of ideology. The misrepresentation of relationships is not enough on its own to conceal the actual relations of production in society; this misrepresentation must have an 'order' and 'rightness' about it, so much so that it will never have to explain itself because it will never be questioned. In surrealistic pictures, we assume a logic of connection between things simply because they are presented as connected; with the Hereford 'cows' the connection carried no further than the product's name. But in the butter ad, a complexity is introduced in that the butter and the cows really *are* connected—only, not in *the way* the picture makes out. And in surrealism the distortion of relationships between things also involves a distortion of our relationship to that distorted connection; because we assume a subject to whom the connection *is* logical, and in trying to see the logic of it we try to place ourselves in the position of the 'initiating' subject. Thus this brief study of 'mythic surrealism' has simply brought into sharp focus many of the properties of advertising that have been seen already in the first part of the book. The use of surrealism itself *as a referent system* helps advertising to protect these properties from exposure, by appearing to expose them itself.

(*c*) *The Ideology of the Natural*

'Many of us . . . find the exploitation that takes place between men just as natural as that by which we master nature. . . .'[1]

We have seen that surrealism, as a 'referent system', has accustomed us to seeing an unstated link between things, a static

[1] Brecht, *The Messingkauf Dialogues*.

and not a dialectical link; we assume an 'order of things'. It has become clear, in examining the relationship between nature and science, culture and 'the natural', that not only does science order nature (cf. A67, the ICI greenhouse) but nature is taken up by culture as 'the natural' in a symbolic form that enables a transference of meaning from nature to culture to invest cultural objects and culture itself, with a 'natural' order. The meaning of the word 'naturally' in A76 provides an example of this transference: the system of nature has been drawn into social usage, to connote inevitability.

Having shown in almost all the examples of nature/culture relationships just how complex this relationship is, it may be helpful to re-run the circuit of 'cooking' → science → back to nature in the simplified form of a diagram:

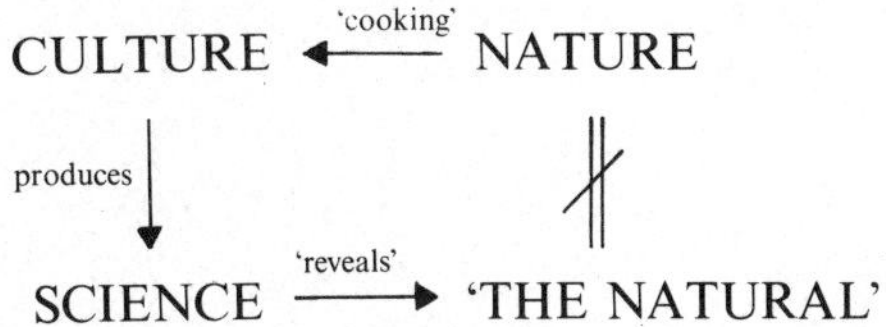

Advertisements, in their production of exchangeable images of nature, provide a 'currency' that may work round and round this circuit—which of course is never static—a currency which we use, and thus perpetuate certain ideas about the status of nature and culture. These ideas, as I have shown, involve culturally determined misrecognition of the real relationship between the two—in other words, an ideology. However, the above diagram is not purely a representation of this ideology and its perpetuating motion: the relationship between nature and culture is a real one, and the fact that science works on nature by experimenting and compiling results, does not necessarily deny the reality of nature. The point about the diagram is that it charts the production of *images*, the relations of symbols and not material things. Nature is cooked by culture, fed into it to provide fodder for 'Science', in the sense (described in Chapter 4) of a metaphysical organiser: *through* 'Science' we may see ordered nature; in the transparency of its own workings we see what is 'natural'. Beyond Science, behind its neatly framed window, is 'the natural': thus the genuinely two-way relationship is *apparently* completed. But it is never completed in fact, because 'the Natural' though ideologically located with 'nature' (they are together on the right hand side of the diagram) is absolutely irreconcilable with it, for the simple reason that the one is real, the other is symbolic. 'The natural' signifies nature, but sign and referent can never be conflated, however much advertisements try to convince us of the opposite. Thus culture never relates to nature directly, never looks at it 'raw': society draws on nature for physical materials, used for manufacturing the goods sold in advertisements, and nature is also the symbolic material for the images reunited with those products in advertisements. So the movement is all in one direction: society never looks back over its shoulder, as it were, to take an unshielded look at the nature that supplies its physical and ideal needs. It looks onwards, into the mirror which seems to reflect that background of nature, but only succeeds in bringing into focus the image of society itself.

To continue using my diagram: we may add one more arrow, that by which the 'false circuit' is completed:

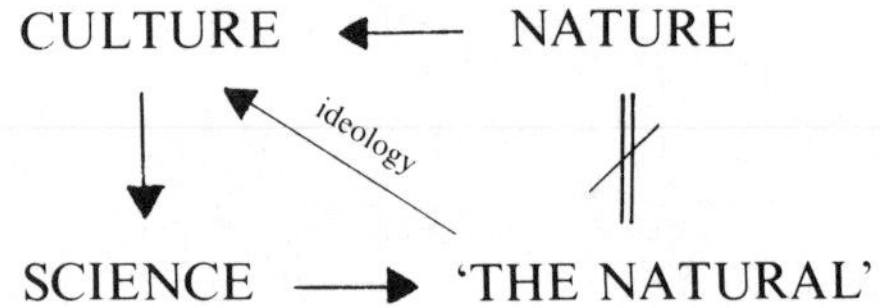

Our manufacturing society, once it has created images of 'the natural', then draws on them to validate its own workings, and the static, ordered and inevitable connotations of 'the natural' can thus be found in society's own view of itself. For all this juxtaposition of nature and machinery is not arbitrary. It indicates in symbolic form precisely the status of that machinery, and more importantly, our imagined relationship to it—'*natural*'. Ideology functions by misrepresenting our relationship to the means of production: and advertisements in their constant presentation of *availability*, show us our '*natural*' relationship to that revealed and revealing process of mechanical reproduction. We 'see through' technology to nature: it is entirely innocent in its transparency. Moreover, it invites us *as subjects* to look *through* it, so that we forget to look *at* it. The very use and current meaning of the word 'natural' in our society shows its value in ideology: what is natural is justified in being as it is, for it is unchangeable and obvious. And the setting up of 'natural' as a desirable way to be, of 'the natural' as the apex of all that is good and wholesome and beautiful, therefore means making this justified *status quo* the object of all our efforts and desires. Thus two connotations attached to 'nature' intersect at a point which is very ideologically charged. Science makes nature seem ordered, in a *synchronic* way, for all classificatory systems must have this quality. The natural system is thus timeless, almost metaphysical, but paradoxically always the '*real thing*'. This is one strand of connotation. The other is desirability. Who, today, wants to be 'unnatural', to look 'unnatural', to eat 'unnatural' food, to live in an 'unnatural' way? While we all *do* live thus, we simultaneously strive towards the lost paradise of herbal shampoos and whole wheat bread, wearing 'natural' make-up and 'invisible' girdles. Nobody will deny wanting to be natural, or actually say they prefer canned foods and false eyelashes. Now, while advertisements did not invent the first strand of meaning, they use it in their internal 'currency' (A76) and as for the second strand of meaning, they virtually *did* create it, in their insatiable need for referent systems which will suck in our desires. Advertisements cannot create or invent referent systems, but as I have shown, they can shake the meaning out of them and insert their own: so the system of 'the natural' comes to be filled with products that we are urged to buy, and this means that because the product has been made to *symbolise* nature, we are always trying to buy and attain 'the natural'.

When these two meanings are elided the result is the paradox of desiring the inevitable—or to put it more mildly, wanting things to be how they already are. In this way the whole confused but symbolically resonant area of 'nature' and 'the natural' is denied recognition of its material function in our lives by being made to perform an ideological one.

CHAPTER SIX
MAGIC

A87: This ad incorporates many of the strategies discussed in the first part of this book—'objective correlatives', absence, language, hermeneutics, narrative—but these are organised according to a referent system which is appealed to in two ways: firstly, in the brand name; secondly, in its transformation into adjectival status—'. . . the black, magic box'. It is the myth of magic that allows our knowledge to intersect with the transactions between the signs in the ad. Because we know what 'magic' does, the replacements in time and space which have been discussed in Part One are provided with a short cut in our assumption of a *magical* transformation.

The objects in the ad signify two presences—unseen, as in the kitchen example (A40). There is the woman whose letter is partially revealed; and the man who has sent the gifts and will receive the letter. The crucial phrases in this letter are: '. . . the last time we met . . .' and 'I would like to see you again soon'. Both of these narrative possibilities are left open for conjecture. The shadow of the box is cast over the details of their previous encounter, and the letter ends: 'perhaps we. . . .' I have already shown that the function of absence (here, of both people and language) is to form a place for the spectator of the ad—it is we who may complete the narrative, fill in the details of the preceding events, and construct the people who have experienced them. We may also purchase and consume the magic box of chocolates which contains the secret of its contents and whatever went on at the Christmas party. What is the man signifying in his magical present? Something sweet, magical and dark. The 'Black Magic' both connotes what has happened and holds the secret promise of what will happen: which is coded according to what we already know about the chocolates. The magic box allows the man to be present in the same space as the woman (since they are both signified through objective correlatives) and *magically* to obtain her favour—she doesn't 'know what to say' because the spell of the present has already determined her actions.

The 'Black Magic' suggests a yet to be experienced sweetness (an absent series of events for absent people) in the consumption of the box's contents and the development of a relationship; and this possibility is also seen in the relation between the unwrapped, but unopened box, and the still wrapped, smaller box beside it. In an obvious way, this is a point in favour of the 'Black Magic', since it has been opened first. She seems to have *magically* known what it contained, for there is no other explanation for this being the only unwrapped parcel. Magic gives a privileged access to information. The relationship between ourselves, we who actually construct the woman from the puzzle of the objects, and *what* we have formed, the woman herself, lies in that shadow cast across the letter. She knows what is written—while we do not. Where our knowledge intersects with the woman's is in magic. What we have in common with her is the knowledge of the magical powers of the box. It has brought the man into the room and promises the fulfilment of the Christmas encounter. Since we know these are magical objects we too can be promised the effects suggested in the ad. We can buy a box of 'Black Magic' and present it once again. It is this possibility that is as yet unrealised,

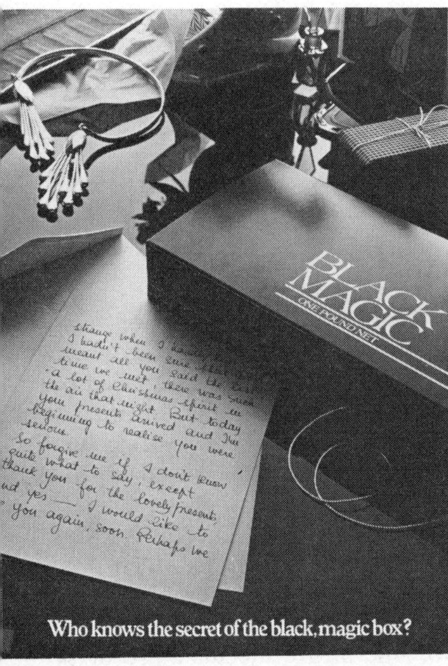

7

generated by our knowledge of the box's powers, that draws us into the ad as Sorcerer's Apprentices.

Not only has she opened the magic box first, but she has also written the letter before proceeding to the other present. Because it is unopened it guarantees her continuous presence—she must return to the space represented in the ad to discover the lesser secret of the other box. Presents/presence/present: of course, in the ad the box will never be opened, just as she will always be about to place the freshly written letter in the envelope that awaits it. This is another string in the chocolates' magical bow, for the 'Black Magic' box is forever unwrapped and about to be opened. It is the presence of the other, unwrapped box that produces a movement in the ad, between what is closed and what is open. Other details indicate this: the closed perfume bottle, that suggests a potion, and the open powder compact. This movement is enacted ad infinitum in the perpetual present of the ad.

The status of the other objects as objective correlatives, that stand for the woman, means that the *woman herself* is about to be unwrapped. She who unwraps will be unwrapped for she is trapped in the implications of that 'Perhaps we. . . .' This is already indicated in the discarded jewellery—which signifies her and her future conduct.

There is also the possibility that all the objects are presents. This means that what is used to signify her presence are presents. In the top left hand corner the purse is placed on top of wrapping paper. If all the objects are placed within the narrative of the man—*he who gives*—then her story is merely that she has been given presents/presence. In which case their presence in the room is all the more magical, for what signifies her has come from someone else, the man, and also signifies another place, from which they have been sent. Now *magic* produces effects in time and space: it transforms one thing into another, just as we can make the objects in the ad stand for the people who possess them; it can transport something to a different place, just as the magic box places the man in the room. And it produces results, just as the box will reveal its contents and fulfil the events preceding its presentation.

'Who knows the secret of the black, magic box?' It is this caption that binds together the transactions of the ad. The '*who*' that knows is, of course, the person who has written the letter and has experienced what it describes. She will also experience what it promises. But the guarantor of this 'who' is the spectator of the ad addressed in the question. We construct the characters of the narrative and fill in the gaps left in the story. This status of the spectator, in guaranteeing a content for the referents of the objective correlatives, means that the 'decipherer' and the 'deciphered' are merged in the hermeneutic of the black box. This merging is performed by magic, for it is we who potentially know the secret, since we may buy a box of 'Black Magic', and it is our magic wands that make the ad function. The question in the caption is tautologous—for the answer to the secret of 'black, magic' is 'Black Magic'.

The assumption of the ad is that we know magically and that what we know is magic. The box and the ad are both things that can be known—or rather things that imply knowledge. The box can be opened; the ad deciphered to reveal what is absent. And this absence is both spatial and temporal—there are the man and the woman, who are spatially absent, and the past and future events, which are merged in the box, since it refers back to past events (the Christmas party) and carries on to future events ('perhaps we . . .'). So we cut across time and space in finding out 'the secret of the black, magic box.'

The Uses of Magic

Magic is not a single unified referent system, as it is not a 'thing', like nature, but a process, a mythical means of *doing* things. Thus unlike 'nature' or 'time', it does not involve a particular area in relation to which we may be misplaced by ideology—it represents the misplacement itself, and is an area *of* transformation rather than an area of time or space *in* which our position may be transformed. Magic is therefore a kind of pivot around which misrepresentations may be produced—it is a transformational referent system, a short cut for moving between other systems. It is important to realise, then, that magic does not stand in this part of the book as on a level with 'nature' and 'time', but as a particular twisting of the relationship between the two. And far from being a prototype for one kind of transformation, it is simply the heading, the organising mythology, under and in which a multiplicity of transformations, productions, and actions can be short-circuited or misproportioned without explanation—since the explanation *is* that it's *magic*.

Magic always involves the misrepresentation of time in space, or space in time. Time is magically incorporated into space, in such things as the crystal ball—an object which *contains* the future—and space is magically produced out of time, in conjuring up objects out of nowhere, *instantly*, by means of spells or alchemy. In the centre of these magical processes, the axis of their performance, is the subject: you, the buyer or user of the product.

Consumer products and modern technology provide us with everything ready-made; we are always users, not creators; manufactured goods make up our world, removing the need for any action from us. In advertising it is essential to compensate for the inactivity forced on us; hence advertising's Romanticism, its emphasis on adventure and excitement (cf. A65b). But the only thing we can *do* in fact is to buy the product or incant its name—this is all the action possible as *our* part of the excitement offered. Such minimal action inevitably creates a 'magical spell' element: from a little action, we get 'great' results (or are promised them). That action is our buying, although in the advertisement it is usually transposed into something else. Thus, whatever aspect of magic is actually referred to *in* the ad, the primary piece of magic that is referred to *by* the ad, is our act of buying and consuming, which is misrepresented *not* as consumption but as *production*.

Magic is the production of results disproportionate to the effort put in (a transformation of power—or of impotence *into* power). In this sense, as I have suggested, all consumer products offer magic, and all advertisements are spells. But the ads in this section all go further than this in that they appeal specifically to our sense of magic, they assume a system of transformation where such disproportionate results appear, miraculously, but precisely *because* of this miraculous quality, we do not feel we need ask for an explanation, since this is the definition of a miracle. It is rather like the situation described in our interpretation of surrealism: the less sense it makes, the more sense it must 'really' make, and the deeper this sense must lie. The more amazing results advertisements offer us, the more these come within the non-explanatory system of 'magic', and the less amazing they thus seem, because it is *not* amazing for *magic* to be amazing.

Magic can therefore be used to misrepresent any system of production. The magical results of buying a product, have, as I said, the function of turning consuming into producing—the *end* of the ad (to make us buy) is turned into a *beginning*—it initiates all these miraculous events; in Chapter 3 we saw how a hermeneutic constitutes us as producers of meanings while limiting us to the role of consumers of solutions. The misrecognition of consumption and production is of crucial ideological importance, as has been discussed in Chapter 2. Magic allows us to feel that we may not only be producers of meaning, but of *material effects*—thereby even more efficiently than hermeneutics diverting our attention from the process of material production of goods. In the advertisements that follow, it will be clear that *products* themselves are seen as producers—of effects disproportionate to their size. But the process of *this* production is of course always an absence, since magic is instant, it just 'happens', metaphysically, and does not *work*, *materially*. It is one absence in ads that we need never fill in: since the reference to magic, the evocation of it implicitly even if not overtly, in itself fills the gap between action and result and makes it cease to be a gap at all. There is an elision in space and time which negates precisely the space and time of production. This is clearly analogous to the negation in ideology of the actual system of production in society. In emphasising the effects of the product, in other words its role as producer, the image of magic in advertisements denies the fact that the product is produced, removing it from its real place in the world and at the same time promising a product from the product. We are allowed to be producers only by being consumers. Thus we can produce by proxy, merely, since we buy the product, and it will then produce the magic result—beauty, love, safety, etc.

Our act of buying, and saying the product's name, is thus a spell which provides a short cut to a larger action, performed not by us but by the product. A similar kind of short cut is seen nowadays in the pressing of buttons, and in mechanical gadgets. In its promise of instant results with very little effort, magic as used in advertising reflects an indisputable element of modern everyday life. The passivity of the individual increases with the ability to plug into a vast source of external power, though like the magician of old (cf.Faustus) we never produce or control the forces we have learned to tune in to. Electricity and electrical media have made the 'instant' quality of magic come true: immediacy and fast results are no longer the province of witchcraft and sorcery. And as short cuts and passivity go together, the former creating the latter, so does passivity necessitate the promise of more short cuts, short cuts to wonderful activity which will compensate for that passivity. This creates a never ending exchange between passivity and action, a translation between technological action and magical action with our own *in*activity as the turning point. Technology deprives us of a control which we are given back in the surrogate form of spells and promises.

But of course, we are *not* in control of the results of these magic practices: the result is already determined by the product, the magical object, and by the words we are told to use, the spell. Magic is a kind of determinism: it consists of particular rites which have particular and predetermined results and effects. This is why you need a book of spells, the formulae for producing different things on different occasions. Every child who reads fairy stories knows this. Thus magic is closely related, in its process, to the idea of hermeneutics already discussed: it is the physical parallel to that conceptual determinism, and has the similar effect of making the subject feel active while in fact chanelling his action in one direction. The result of a 'spell' is as much 'already there' as the answer to a puzzle. Things will happen after a Badedas bath, but all we can do to spark them off is to have the bath, and we cannot *choose* what will happen: the picture shows us that what happens is that a young man arrives in a sports car. The nature of what happens after the bath is thus determined as being sexual: you do not, for example, get offered a new job or become able to play the violin.

Since the only element of chance in magic is whether or not you will tap in to these predetermined channels of power, and not what these channels will do (the two ends of the process are always fixed) it is clear that magic involves a very definite order—though not an order of *things* but of results. It is therefore very closely enmeshed in the idea of 'nature', as the magical forces, in their determinism, have some 'natural' status. In fact 'magic' constitutes a sort of pre-scientific ordering of nature, not by an actual organisation of the elements of nature but by an assumption that some organisation does exist, some inherent causality.

It is precisely because the invisible lines between things, the tracks along which magical forces run, are so 'natural' and inevitable, that they may be (apparently) completely arbitrary. The disproportion of their two ends, of cause and result, is the very measure of their magicality. And the determinism which links the two is what makes the idea of *process* superfluous: producer and produced, cause and effect, are collapsed together since one already implies the other. Therefore the result is always *contained* in the cause, just as a certain kind of question (what does 2 + 2 make) contains its answer.

This aspect of magic is again closely linked to modern technology, which in its production of transistor radios, pocket calculators, mini-cameras etc. places such an emphasis on miniaturisation. This could almost be described as one of the great myths of our time: the focus of the *microcosm*, the part that contains the whole—the great in the small and the many in one. The microcosm appears not only in real 'science' but in many current trends of ideas. The Subjectivist Idealist tradition in literary criticism has always been centred on the idea of the illuminating moment, the part which reveals the whole—in other words, the hermeneutic key. Thus, a little does not only produce a lot, but *contains* it. The condensed content only has to be released. This is true equally of the atom bomb and a can of condensed soup.

The technological image of the great-into-small, complex-into-simple idea is shown in the following advertisement for a bank's services:

.88

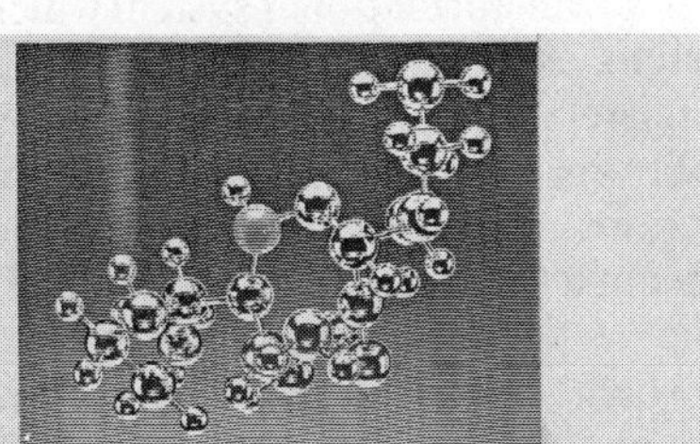

simpler way to tackle complex problems

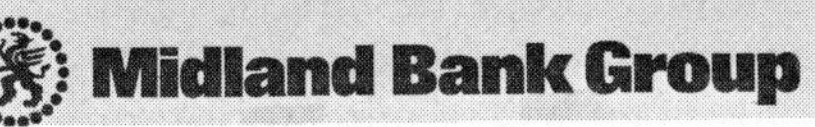

A88: The 'simpler way to tackle complex problems' is illustrated by an atomic structure: which represents simultaneously the complexity and the clarity of 'Science'. It is mystically complicated, but offers a magically simple entrance to such complication.

I have argued that, as always in advertisements, the images produced and organised around a particular referent are not random or complete in themselves, and do not actually signify that referent, but are fundamentally and inextricably related to the material basis of our society. Images of nature, as already seen, and of magic, do not 'represent' nature and magic but *use* these systems of reference to *mis*-represent *our* relation to the world around us and the society we live in. The organising referent system is not *signified* by the images drawn from it, but is made to signify something else, about a product and hence about production and consumption generally. Our very misplacement in relation to the *referent system*—as its signified, which we 'know', is snatched from under us and made to mean something different simply in *terms* of the system—this displacement in relation to our knowledge is the means of our imaginary misplacement in the relations of society. Magic is, however, different from nature and time, in that it *always* involves a mis-relation: we *do* exist in nature and time, and it is the creation of imaginary forces in nature and time which deny that existence, which constitutes magic. Magic is a sort of black hole in both nature and time—it is the creation of the *un*natural in no time at all. It is also like a black hole because by involving *us* in this creation and making us actually seem to be the initiators of it, we are sucked into this unnatural, non-temporal and non-spatial time and space. We are invited to spend summer in Haigland (see below) or become somebody else, invisible after using a blonde rinse ('Where's Jane?' she went blonde with Hiltone): in other words, to spend time in non-existent places, to become a non-existent person. This is an 'absence' which does not gape, for us to fill it up, but an 'absent' absence which denies us any position at all, draws us into its non-being.

It is thus clear that magic is a transformational system which can incorporate many different elements of ideology: it is a meta-system where all the misrelations and elisions of other systems take place, a point of translation and exchange. Since it has so many ideological functions—or rather, so many bits and pieces of ideology run together in it (hermeneutics, 'the natural', determinism, myth of the active subject, 'Science and Technology', etc.) all of which ultimately have the *same* function, to misrepresent to us our place in the productive system, it is not surprising that 'magic' itself is, within its own myth, comprised of many different properties. It is, again, common nursery knowledge that magic involves genies in lamps and bottles, rites and spells, sudden growth or miniaturisation, turning things to gold, magic wands and implements, and a vast number of other things from carpets to rings, all of which make up the *iconography* of magic. It is these things which will be found in the examples to follow: they have been organised in terms of different myths to be found 'within' the myth of magic itself, that is, by the 'magical' property, rather than the ideological function. Having outlined the relationship between magic, nature, time and ideology I shall simply proceed to show how the idea of magic is present in ads where it may not be immediately apparent, as it was in A87 with the 'Black Magic'.

(*a*) *Alchemy*

89

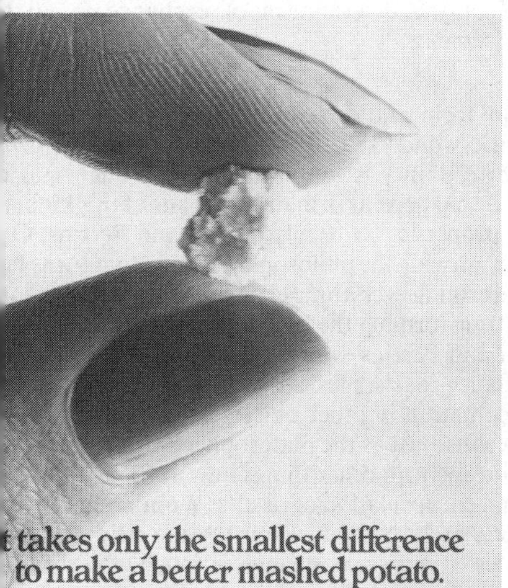

t takes only the smallest difference
to make a better mashed potato.
New Wondermash is real mashed potato pieces. But now it's even better. It's in smaller pieces. So it mixes more easily, makes smoother, tastier mash.
6 out of 10 women in independent tests said they preferred New Wondermash to the other leading brand of instant mashed potato.
Try it yourself. You'll see that it takes only the smallest difference to make a better mashed potato.
WonderMash
ndermash makes smoother mash.

A89: Here we are shown a potato microcosm—an atom: it is the *smallness* of the potato pieces which guarantees their magicality. After all, they produce '*Wonder*mash' which, even on the level of its name, claims to be more magical than ordinary potato powders. There is no logical reason why the smallness of the pieces should make the mashed potato better, other than that their being small enhances the 'wonder' of the transformation. 'It's even better. It's in smaller pieces.' The *scientific* magicality of the picture is shown by its magnification; you can see all the lines of the finger and thumb, every peak and cavity of the microcosm. This gives you the impression of looking through a microscope, and the enlargement of the potato atom only serves to show how small it must be when *not* seen under microscopic conditions. The idea of 'the smallest difference' also brings in the whole idea of differentiation, yet with a transformational imbalance: so that the smallest difference in the causal area, the magic potion, can create a great difference in effects, in the magic released. The little granule magnified in the picture encapsulates a vast amount of mashed potato. But note that we are shown the granule and not the result, the actual mashed potato—because the granule contains and represents the result. Thus the magic microcosm, the capsule, has a lot in common with the symbol.

This ad shows several magical elements, then: the word, 'Wondermash', the condensation and encapsulation which can release forces greater than themselves, the scientific miracle of breaking things down into minute particles, and yet being able to see these particles. And nature is transformed—'cooked', as in A61, to produce a short cut in time, 'instant' mashed potato instead of arduously peeled, boiled and mashed potato.

The sparkle in champagne.
The lift in loaves.
New life in your skin.
A LOT OF MAGIC COMES FROM A LITTLE YEAST.
Yeast Pac is the only face pack which contains nature's miracle worker, yeast. It's what makes Yeast Pac different.
Before your next night out give yourself a quick ten minute facial with Yeast Pac and feel the difference.
It deep cleanses the pores and draws out the impurities, freshening up your skin, leaving it delightfully clear.
There are two types of Yeast Pac, pink sachets for normal skins and blue for problem skins.
Also in 6-treatment economy tubes. Look out, too, for Yeast Pac Cleansing Lotion.
It's the yeast in Yeast Pac that makes it different.
Yeast Pac

A90

A91

With a little
Lea & Perrins,
casseroles taste a whole lot better
Chicken Casserole for 4
Once you've tried Lea & Perrins
you'll never cook without it

A90: This ad makes explicit the magical nature of producing a lot frc a little: 'A lot of *magic* comes from a little yeast'. The form of this ad very similar to that of A78, where Max Factor gave to your eyes t shimmer that nature gave to stars, butterflies, etc. Here, we are shov examples of 'natural' magic (rather different from the scientific ma that *re-created* nature in the previous example) where something *see* to come from nowhere, like the bubbles in champagne which strea from the bottom of the glass, or the 'lift' in bread, which is a magic growth. The blurb of the ad tells us that yeast is 'nature's mirac worker'—this assumes that nature is full of miracles, and that mirac are 'natural'; no contradiction between the miraculous and the natu interferes with the image of transformation. The point about the ye is that it transforms what is already there, it is able to work over natu *naturally*. So that the new life in your skin is created in a miraculo way, yet also, because of magic's determinism, it was already the potentially, the new skin is still 'natural' because the magic is natu magic and has fixed results. The combination of the natural and t miraculous is a paradoxical one but as with most of the paradoxes advertisements, it is carried off successfully because it seems inevitab The determinism of the rising loaves and the bubbling champag ensures this. The connection between specific causes and specific resu is shown by the colouring of 'pink sachets for normal skins and blue f problem skins'. There are formulae, spells, with given effects; magic the ultimate form of guaranteeing results. It involves transformati and *exchange*: but an exchange which is entirely within determin bounds, making explicit the determinism of exchange in all t signification of advertisements.

A91: Here again, the 'lot from a little' transformation is seen. One dr of the magic potion works wonders: it adds 'the final touch of *perfecti* to your casserole'. Perfectibility is only attainable through magi means. Another point is that here, as in many other ads of this kind, t product has *alchemic* properties. Not only do Lea and Perrins, Ox etc., go a long way, they provide the philosopher's stone that turns ba metals into gold, transforming everything else in the stew. It is the sa principle as the yeast transforming the bread, or champagne, or yo skin, by alchemy. Lea and Perrins 'brings out all the other succule flavours', and will 'enhance roasts, pies, stews' and so on. The catal which effects a transformation in other objects is part of the proc itself, only felt by its results; just as the philosopher's stone is not its made of gold, but can transform other things into it. So here we ha moved from the original encapsulation of results (Wondermash) to t encapsulation of process itself. Nobody wants to eat a stew that *tas* of Lea and Perrins sauce. It represents change, a 'touch of perfectio in other words an improvement: and stands for the improving proc rather than the result.

A92: This product does not claim to transform a whole stew, but whole life, turning one person into another. 'Where's Jane?' She too enclosed, framed, firmly encapsulated in the past, in the inset pictu

A92

That picture of her is the capsule that has exploded into the larger, unbounded picture: so each contains the other, although they are so different. In the 'microcosm' inset, 'Jane' seems to be dreaming of the future, of the new self shown below: she is the 'little' that gets turned into 'a lot': 'Bigger eyes, brighter smile—everything about me seemed different, more alive, much more exciting'. Notice that magic helps her to come alive, or 'more alive', just as yeast pack gave 'new life' to your skin. Magic compensates for lifelessness, inactivity. So the 'little' Jane becomes the 'cool, beautiful blonde', who is bigger; thus the small picture leads to the larger one. But it is spatially *contained* in the larger one: and the way it is placed directly over the head of the 'new' Jane (or non-Jane) makes it seem like merely an idea in her head—just as 'thoughts' in comic strips are always positioned above the thinker's head. So plain Jane's dream is made to come true and she herself, or her original self, becomes no more than a dream in the new world. The inset picture where she has brown hair, has an eyeline looking out of the frame *away from us*: we are not meant to identify with her, she is just dreaming. The blonde Jane looks straight at us, catches us like a glance in a mirror, turning the opposite way from the inset face.

This is the 'Cinderella' syndrome, the magic of personal transformation. However, I have so far only mentioned the two 'Janes' in the ad: but there is another face, the blueprint for the new Jane. This is the blonde face, or rather, half-face, on the Hiltone packet. The new Jane looks more like the packet face, than like her own face as shown before she dyed her hair. The magic potion, the stuff that works the transformation, draws you into it, giving you its own qualities. Thus the packet is what really encapsulates the new Jane: between the bottom left hand picture and the top right hand one, an exchange has taken place, to produce the main picture, bottom right, where the two axes of the insets meet.

The words of the ad are clearly relevant to the Lacanian idea of the 'mirror phase' as discussed in Chapter 2. 'Next time I looked in my mirror a cool, gentle blonde looked back. . . . And I thought, "Where's Jane". . . . "Is that cool, beautiful blonde really me?" And then I realised. . . .' This also has a magical element about it: 'Mirror, mirror on the wall, Who is the fairest one of all?' (I suppose in this context 'fairest' could be taken literally.) There is the *Through the Looking Glass* referent as well.

The final magical aspect of the ad is the importance of the *word*, the product's name. 'I chose Hiltone because I knew the name'. She knew the right thing to say, the spell that produced the results. She did not choose Hiltone because she *knew* anything about it: she just thought 'the creamy conditioners sounded nice'—enticed by the mystical *sound* of the words.

(*b*) Spells

Having seen how a commodity can be placed between an action and its effects, or rather, between desire and result, encapsulating in itself a transformation, we can go on to see how language can also be placed in this position: functioning so as to enclose process and eclipse production's temporal space.

A93

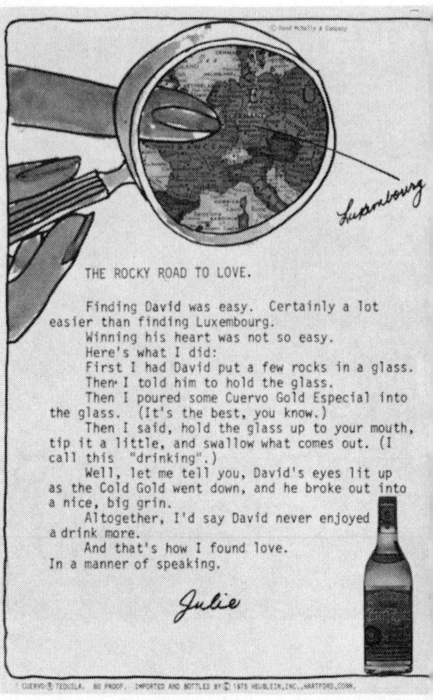

A93: This ad involves the classic formula for a spell: there is a special gold liquid, a prepared vessel, a series of ritualised gestures and an act of consumption—and all directed by an ordered sequence of words. The performance of these 'rites' as described, in a specified order, produces a miracle: love. The whole thing reads like a conjuring trick and a spell. Even ordinary words are given a magical quality: 'Then I said, "hold the glass up to your mouth, tip it a little and swallow what comes out." (I call this "drinking".)' So an everyday action and word are transformed, taken from our field of knowledge and into the structure of a mystical order, given a more than ordinary 'meaning' and power. Obviously the magical element here is not, on one level, meant to be taken seriously; but the idea of producing love, though not explicitly through magic but through a drink, is still a magical one—it offers dramatic results to a specific action and incantation.

A94: The magical emphasis on spells is a very convenient one for advertisers with brand names to project, since the idea of *incantation*, saying the spell, is made to coincide with the act of purchase and saying the product's name. Here, 'Dunlop Aquajets' become magically special words: they are the invocation, they provide safety in the face of danger. They are almost a prayer: but one with guaranteed results. The utterance of words is our only participation in the business of creating safety in the car: there is nothing else to do except be glad we said 'Dunlop Aquajets'. We have to rely on a power greater than us, beyond us, doing the work for us: the manufacturers, who thus gain almost a supernatural status. Yet *we* are made to feel like producers: we *say* 'Dunlop Aquajets', and thus create safety in the rain. This replaces the fact that somebody else actually made the tyres and *materially* created their safeness: we *re*produce the force of their production.

Here the referent of the words has become their *effect*: 'Dunlop Aquajets' signifies safety, and is made to *produce* safety: the process described in Chapter 1 under 'the product as generator'. Referent and sign become joined along the axis of action. The sign will produce or ensure the referent: together they *do* something. Activity is removed from us and transferred to *signs* and *symbols*.

Once again here we have the inset: the enlarged, encapsulated, representative microcosm, the *key* to the rest of the picture. It shows the secret of the whole spell and of the large illustration: it magnifies the unique Aquajet itself, that little detail from which such great results are produced.

And the important point is that they are produced, initiated, by you, by the words, the sign itself. There is even a sort of ritualistic exchange of words, as the forecast says 'rain' and then you will be glad you said 'Aquajets': the forecast *saying* 'rain' is substituted for actual *rain*. The ad does not say 'when it rains you'll be glad' . . . but involves a series of determined lines, a password—and events are apparently produced by words: the forecast saying rain produces the rain in the picture, and our words 'Dunlop Aquajets' produce safety in the rain.

A95

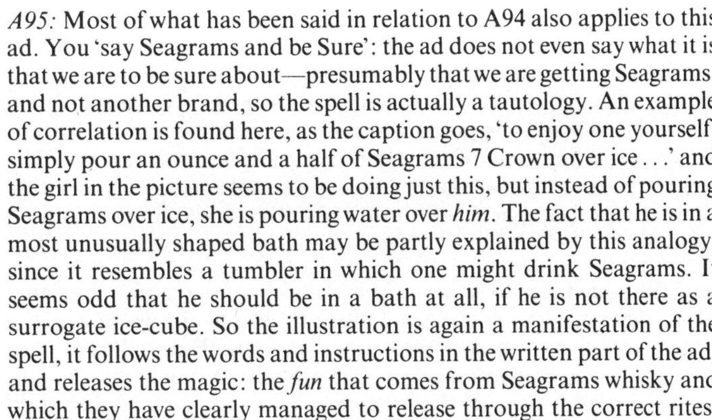

A95: Most of what has been said in relation to A94 also applies to this ad. You 'say Seagrams and be Sure': the ad does not even say what it is that we are to be sure about—presumably that we are getting Seagrams, and not another brand, so the spell is actually a tautology. An example of correlation is found here, as the caption goes, 'to enjoy one yourself, simply pour an ounce and a half of Seagrams 7 Crown over ice . . .' and the girl in the picture seems to be doing just this, but instead of pouring Seagrams over ice, she is pouring water over *him*. The fact that he is in a most unusually shaped bath may be partly explained by this analogy, since it resembles a tumbler in which one might drink Seagrams. It seems odd that he should be in a bath at all, if he is not there as a surrogate ice-cube. So the illustration is again a manifestation of the spell, it follows the words and instructions in the written part of the ad, and releases the magic: the *fun* that comes from Seagrams whisky and which they have clearly managed to release through the correct rites.

This merging of referent, effect and sign is seen in an ad already looked at in an earlier chapter, A53, where words magically appear on the gold packet. The referent becomes the result of the sign, they appear together. In the A53 picture there is a smoking lamp, precisely like Aladdin's, and the orient jewels give a further 'Arabian Nights' effect. This introduces another feature of magic:

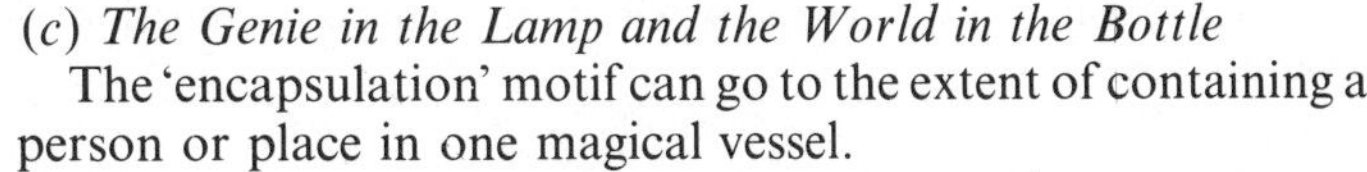

(*c*) *The Genie in the Lamp and the World in the Bottle*

The 'encapsulation' motif can go to the extent of containing a person or place in one magical vessel.

6

A96: The brandy glass here contains someone, in a variation on the genie in the magic lamp idea. The glass really is a perfect microcosm for the world around it, as the figure in the glass holds up *another* glass; thus the brandy encapsulates and is a microcosm of its own reality, just as all products are seen to represent the realities or myths shown in their advertisements. Notice how the glass gives us a privileged access not only to a world, a figure from the past, but it actually seems to magnify some barrels on which are inscribed mysterious hieroglyphics. Thus a mystical writing is revealed, full of magic symbols and strange carvings, a spell *inside* the product, revealed to us by it, rather than being our invocation of the product. This strange writing is also present outside the glass, however, since the bottle and glass, and cork, and some papers (more secret messages, since we cannot read them) are all lying *on* a barrel with scratched symbols on it, like the ones in the glass-picture. The 'explanation' for the man and barrels 'in' the glass is that they are *reflected* in it: but this must mean that the man is standing just where the spectator must be, and *he* does not belong in the eighteenth century. So either the spectator is magically transformed into this eighteenth century connoisseur, with his (probably smuggled) barrels

A97

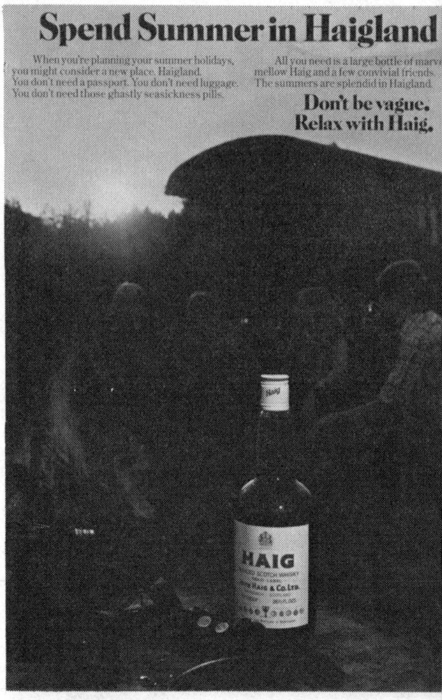

of brandy, and thus the reflection is perfectly normal, *or*, the spectator is perfectly normal in which case the reflection is magical since it shows someone who is not there, and who is from a different historical era. Again, this aspect of the ad involves ideas discussed in various different parts of this book: the product's ability to reflect/create, the mirror-image, the capturing of time (cf. next chapter) and so on. The importance of magic is that it provides a blanket referent for any kind of unusual or inexplicable transformation or production.

Spend Summer in Haigland
When you're planning your summer holidays, you might consider a new place. Haigland.
You don't need a passport. You don't need luggage.
You don't need those ghastly seasickness pills.
All you need is a large bottle of
mellow Haig and a few convivial friends.
The summers are splendid in Haigland.
Don't be vague.
Relax with Haig.
HAIG

A97: We are invited to spend our holidays in 'a new place'—Haigland. Here, the bottle has not only a containing effect—the world is in the bottle—but a magic carpet effect as well, because Haig will take us to this new place. 'All you need is a large bottle of marvellous mellow Haig...' and 'You don't need a passport... You don't need luggage... You don't need those ghastly seasickness pills'. So not only can Haig produce this place, Haigland, it can take you there in no time with no trouble. The people in the picture are hardly visible in the obscurity of the night, but there is a fire and they are arranged in a semi-circle around the Haig bottle; although it is in the foreground and they are in the background, not *literally* sitting around it but apparently so in the spatiality of the ad. This is like a magic group, a rite: drinking Haig round the fire like witches round a cauldron. As in many magical myths, fairy tales and legends, an object is the means of reaching a mystical place, one which is not in this world. This aspect of magic thus relates to the fetishism of products, their supposed ability to create auras and effects—the projection of which idea is the main function of advertisements.

Ideas, feelings, time past (Martell, A96) and time future (Embassy, A99), worlds and people can all be miraculously contained in objects. This makes objects seem very important: society overemphasises and clings to them as the material representations of otherwise ungraspable things. Life and meaning are attached to objects that might seem worthless in themselves. In all societies but our own we call this fetishism. To return to the 'Black Magic' ad at the beginning of this chapter: the 'black, magic box' (the comma cleverly turns the *name* of the product into two meaningful adjectives) is a fetishistic object, it holds a secret, has a mystical aura quite out of proportion to its actual contents. It is endowed with a power that, for a simple object like a box of chocolates, can only be magical. Thus boxes can hold not only products but can *produce* in themselves.

A98: It would not be an exaggeration to see the 'World of Lambert and Butler' as a kind of sect, separated from us by an altar-like table, enclosed by it and set apart by being behind it, just as in all religions

A98

A99

A100

only the priest and the initiated may be behind the altar. (Of course, they are also set apart by smoking the Lambert and Butler cigarettes, which are themselves endowed with a 'quality and style that *sets them apart* from other cigarettes'.) Thus, as in Lévi-Strauss' analysis of totemism, a thing, a product, which is differentiated, is used to differentiate people. This ad (though with a different picture) has been referred to before. However, this picture shows most clearly the magical elements of the ads. Not only does the altar/table cut the Lambert and Butler sect off from us, but certain magical objects of no apparent use (all made of either gold or glass, magical substances) are placed on the 'altar'. Certain drinks are being passed round and drunk, and cigarettes of a certain kind are burning, like incense, in this inner chamber of the élite. This room and its arrangement and the cigarettes themselves strike me as extremely fetishistic and if the people were not of our own culture we would no doubt see it as such.

One of the magical objects on the Lambert and Butler altar was a round, shiny globe, with obscure reflections and images in it. This object has a particular place and name in the mythical bricolage of magic:

(*d*) *The Crystal Ball/Magic Circle*

A99: There is a whole series of Embassy ads like this one. It illustrates the microcosm idea, the enclosure of a world; however, the global image here involves more than just encapsulation, a world in a world. *Time* is involved: the architecture in each of these ads is ultra-modern and *futuristic*. The crystal ball is used to indicate the future: it is a microcosm of space and time, encircling time in space. It is ironic that the caption is '*Today's* outstanding value', because the picture suggests that today is already tomorrow, that the Embassy is pointing into the future, as the cigarettes lean up into the centre of the ball, the muffled globe of light.

A100: Here we have another spatial way of expressing and enclosing time: the magic circle. Again, there is the 'just a few drops' line, the magic fluid that has such power. There is also something like a rite (cf. A97 round the bottle) in the very picture, the bodies and the circular vessel with its slightly strange markings (Roman numerals are less familiar than Arabic ones)—which, in making a phrase 'round the clock', *physically* real, have a calligraphic function (see Chapter 3). I have already shown the way in which calligraphy conflates sign and referent. This is part of the idea of the spell, where words conjure up the very thing which they represent. Someone is shown in this ad *literally* round a clock; and this uses the circle and physical image to enclose and capture (through representation) a non-physical reality, time.

CHAPTER SEVEN
TIME: NARRATIVE AND HISTORY

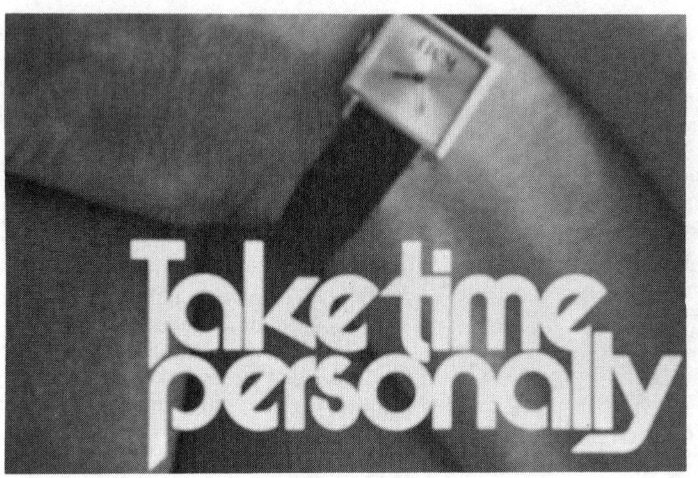

We have seen the spatial construction of the subject in advertising, in the way he/she is required to read between signs across the surface of the ad. In this chapter I intend to show the temporal location of the subject, whether this is a synchronic, a-temporal location, or alternatively, a misplacement of the subject in terms of his own past and the shared past of 'History'.

A picture can represent not only an event, but a series of events, and I shall be looking at ads which evoke the past, promise the future, or tell a story which encompasses both past *and* future. But it is important to realise that, in a very real way, *everything* in the ad is already past, since the picture is finished and the future events are never open, but specifically *directed* (as with 'hermeneutics' and the results of 'magic', cf. above). So the spectator is put in possession of a *closure*, a narrative sequence which is inevitably pre-determined. This is, of course, an obvious contrast to the spectator's real situation, which is one of unordered, alterable events, and a completely open future. The open future belongs to a present which may be changed, while the closed future belongs to a deterministic and unalterable present. Thus the closed narrative has an obvious ideological function: as in the nineteenth century novel, for example.

Since closure *contains* the events which lead to it (a temporal reverse of the situation where in magic, an object contains the events which will issue *from* it, i.e. inverted closure) it must have a synchronic status, it draws events *out* of time and into a sort of eternal moment. Perhaps this is the kind of thing that Eliot had in mind as the 'still point of the turning world'. But too much emphasis on this (imaginary) 'still point' can obscure the fact

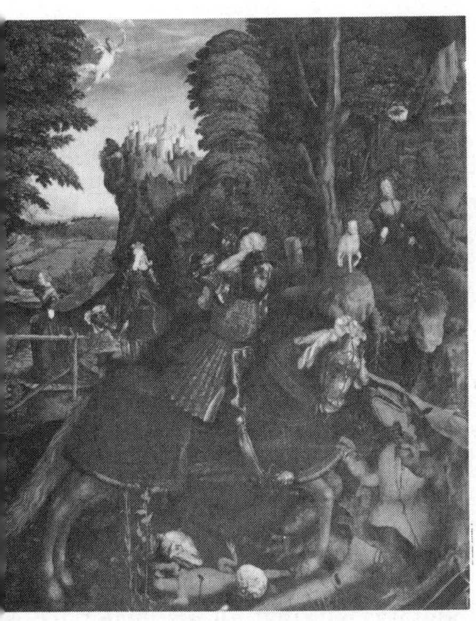

that the world is indeed turning, and with it turn a multitude of events that change and can be changed.

That this 'timeless' moment can be seen as a *point*, shows that it is given a position in *space*, while being denied its temporal materiality. The discussion of advertisements to follow deals almost entirely with the incorporation of time into space, since pictorial representations must be spatial in their structure. As a preliminary to the examination of this phenomenon in advertisements, I am taking a painting which shows the same features as those that will be found in examples below, only more blatantly than in most ads; which aim at an illusion of 'reproducing reality', which is absent from early art.

This illustration is an example of an old mythopoeic painting—St George and the Dragon.

The picture seems to be full of disconnected objects. There is a definite split between the foreground and background, since the same figures appear in both: St George on his horse, and the lady in the red dress. Strange objects and animals are distributed around the foreground.

These things only make sense if you know the story: they are connected by a sequence of events in time and to understand them, you must have access to this invisible structure, in other words, the *myth*. (Every picture tells a story—but it helps if you know it already.) Objects are extracted from the myth and located in such a way as to retell its story. The picture gives us a narrative, of St George slaying the dragon in the foreground; he has already slain several monsters (extreme foreground)—these objects signify *past* events, for example, his lance is fallen upon the ground and part of it has already pierced the dragon. This is the past of the story. Now the lady is being saved.

In the background a patch of light falls upon distant fields and a remote castle. This signifies the future; a technique that will be seen in very many advertisements. In this area we see St George riding off towards the future (cf. sunsets at end of Westerns)—the lady rescued and freed, an angel above signifying heavenly approval.

Thus the picture links past and future in the structure of a myth, and so is synchronic. I have suggested that there is an ideology of the synchronic—a category that is used to misrepresent history, since it can represent history as a story (full of mythologies) which has an end, and thus might just as well have happened all at once, from the vantage view-point of the present (which is somehow separated from 'history'; the story ends before the present day—just as school history always 'ends' around the turn of the century). Story-pictures like this one rely on linking what has happened to the future, in an unbroken chain of events, a total sequence of time; the dragon *has been* pierced with the lance, St George *will* ride off into the distance and the castle. It is impossible to take any one point on the line between these two events, and say 'this is the present of the picture; this is the moment shown'. The time of the picture is a continuum, and because the events are inseparable they come to have the status of one, 'permanent' event. There is an inevitability of events because they are all *present* at once; this reflects the inevitability of myth, where given beginnings have given endings (as with magic). Things are always happening and always *ending* (the dragon killed, the lady saved) in the same picture, so there is no possibility of change. The closure is incorporated into the depth of space in the picture, since we are led 'in time' *into* the back of the picture, though of course the picture has no real temporality but that of its material construction, and the duration of its observation by the spectator.

In advertisements the 'continuum' of time made synchronic, as in this painting, can be apparently broken by a prolonged emphasis on one moment, the moment before consumption, halfway between past and future. But this position in time is not a real 'present', since it is a time represented by the advert, and precisely because it is poised between a given past and a given future, it is not 'open' like the present in which we live. There is a 'closure' of possibility.

It is important to study carefully the way in which the St George picture works, as its basic structure is repeated in many advertisements. We no longer have the naïveté to show the same figure twice; the human figure is frequently absent altogether, for we are meant to supply ourselves in his place. However, note the objects in the foreground, signifying events which will lead to the Elysian field-like background of the future, and note the special light that marks out this area. In this painting it is indisputably clear that the foreground represents the present, and the distant fields, the future—since we see St George riding off towards them. In advertisements this signal is missing but the basic use of spatial structure to perform a temporal structuring is the same.

The subject is constructed outside history by advertising in three ways: synchronically, as will be seen in A101, in the past, and in the future. There is no real present in advertising. You are either pushed back into the past, or urged forward into the future. No present pleasure exists because in the actual present you are looking at the ad, anticipating but not enjoying. A strange corollary of this is that sometimes you can be led to feel that 'consumption can perfectly well be accomplished simply by looking';[1] we are so far alienated from our present state that *looking* is equated with the sensual pleasure of the product. Thus our own present—the only time we really have—is taken from us. It is sometimes substituted by the false present of the advertisement, which may indeed become our *real* future; i.e. 'I am just about to eat/drink X' (instead of 'I am looking at an advertisement for X'). This false situation into which we are invited to project ourselves refers also, unless we do actually buy the product, to a false future (in reality a double step away, through *a* anticipation of X to *b* enjoyment of X) of pleasure resulting from the product's consumption. In advertisements there is an illusory perfect balance between the time of desire and the time of consumption; they are as inevitably linked as the elements of the St George story.

Where advertisements tell a 'story' (this applies to many of the ads in previous sections) we are forced to decipher this synchronically, to comprehend a series of events all at once. Thus time is given a 'being' rather than a material existence: the synchronicity must be outside real time, since all time is available to us at once as we stand in real time, in front of the ad. We move out of this reality into the metaphysical time of the ad. Of course, many forms of art involve the representation of a time other than our own, but in advertisements the difference is that *we* are constituted in this false time, it is substituted for ours. A real historicity is denied as history is either condensed to a synchronicity, or appropriated in the notion of memory or projection. Memory and anticipation become our only access to time outside our own, and they are emptied of any real content and completely absorbed by the constitution of the subject: the past and future are deliberately represented as vaguely as possible so that we may insert *ourselves* there. Paradoxically, our real past, history, is appropriated by the advertisement to be filled by the *product*, or to become represented by a single subject—as will be seen in the last part of the chapter. The first part will show how the subject is captured in time, and time in the subject.

[1] Barthes, *Mythologies*, Paladin, 1973, p. 79.

The desire to capture time is a very basic one. Advertisements can make a lot of mileage out of this because material goods have always been seen as a barricade against the passing of time and the insecurities of change. They provide a spatial continuity which cannot be found in such activities as doing or hearing. Seeing, and owning things that can be seen, is a comparatively more stable affair.

Time, of course, is not something that can be owned; it is common to us all, and cannot be divided. It is the extreme *spatiality* of our consciousness that leads us to assume that we *can* partition time and make it our own, through material objects.

A101: This room is like a museum. It is crammed with objects and at a closer look it appears that they represent an extraordinary variety of eras. There are: Art Deco wall lamps and a strange Art Deco clock placed very high above the Regency mirror. The mantelpiece and fireplace and the shape of the room are all Regency. There are Art Nouveau lamps on the two tables and an Art Nouveau standing lamp. There is a Classical bust which indicates very early Western civilisation, possibly Roman. There is an Oriental carpet and plant pot, suggesting even earlier Eastern cultures. The tall vase of lilies is Pre-Raphaelite. Behind a strange tree lurks an old, indefinably masterpiece-ish painting. The music at the piano dates from the 'Naughty Nineties', and the candy striped awning on the Regency windows reinforces this element. The piano itself being painted blue is a phenomenon of sixties style, and the glass-topped table is also sixties or seventies, the most modern thing in the room.

A101

These things drawn together remind me of Eliot's eclecticism in *The Wasteland*—'These fragments have I shored against my ruins'. Into one room, symbols of almost every past era are collected—very jarringly—as if against some terrible destruction. This destruction is, of course, time. But all the objects are linked by the product: because they are all painted with Vymura: 'We painted everything in the photograph with Vymura gloss—the walls, ceiling, floor, radiator, even the piano'. The product provides the synchronicity, the connecting 'story' for the disparate representatives of time: the 'story' is, 'we painted everything . . .' and this implies a *subject*, one who does the painting. You too could cover everything with 'All Over Gloss': and this suggests that the events and eras in which the objects have or had a material place, are 'all over', finished, as the objects themselves are coloured with a gloss 'finish'. Cracks in time—changes, disruption, even simple historicity itself (i.e. one era coming after another) are plastered over, and all the historically *different* times of the different things in the room are made the same through the same paint. The synchrony thus produced is inevitably an imaginary one: the things themselves have been used precisely because they have a symbolic function, representing a variety of historical periods. But once the past has been symbolised by these things, they are merged into an imaginary a-temporality, which both unites them, and also provides a place for the subject since he can be active in painting and joining these objects through the product.

This example shows how the subject is given a synchronic time in the product, and *through* the construction of himself; because a subject is implied/created in the advertisement, in the 'we' who painted—a pronoun which is left open for our inclusion. The construction of a 'self' is also achieved through memory, and anticipation, both of which exclude the subject from history: while in the previous example he was invited to exclude history from himself and his room by denying its differences through paint. Memory is the main vehicle used by ads to create a subjectivity, as it presupposes a remembering subject, while the notion of history does not. A similar misplacement occurs in the kind of ads (some of which have already been examined in Chapter 3, since they involve absence) which lead spatially to an internalised 'future' where a subject is necessary for the achievement of events yet to come. We will see how the spectator is absorbed into the past of memory and the future of desire.

(*a*) *Time Past: Memory*

'... I had only the most rudimentary sense of existence, such as may lurk and flicker in the depths of an animal's consciousness; I was more destitute of human qualities than the cave-dweller; but then the memory, not yet of the place in which I was, but of various other places where I had lived, and might now very possibly be, would come like a rope let down from heaven to draw me up out of the abyss of not-being, from which I could never have escaped by myself: in a flash I would traverse and surmount centuries of civilisation, and out of a half-visualised succession of oil lamps, followed by shirts with turned-down collars, would put together by degrees the component parts of my ego.'[1]

'... "I can remember summers in the past. The quiet days that gave way to calm evenings. And picnics on the green. There were always sounds of children, in the distance, echoing over the tall trees then falling silent on the blue waters." Reflections in summer. Recapture them with great moments from Kraft.'[2]

[1]Proust, A la Recherche du Temps Perdu.
[2]Kraft Peanut Butter.

Proust describes how memory creates consciousness, putting together a 'consistent self' out of surrounding chaos, from the symbolic components of the past. Advertisements rely to a great extent on this property of memory; and since it is impossible for them to invoke the actual, individual past of each of their spectators—the past that does go to make up personality—they invoke either an *aura* of the past, or a common undefined past. The past can be seen materially as leading to the present, creating the present, and therefore interesting; it is not in itself a 'misplacing' concept. However, in advertising, the *present*—use of a product like drink or perfume—is seen as a way of getting back to the past. There is an *imaginary* collapsing of past and present in memory: in Chapter 2 the 'imaginary' was described as the realm in which actually separate things are united. There is another 'imaginary' merging of differences in 'memory' ads in that *our* past and memory of the past, are confused with someone else's (or nobody's, since the 'past' in the picture is a total construct). We are shown a hazy, nostalgic picture and asked to 'remember' it as *our* past, and simultaneously, to construct it through buying/consuming the product.

In advertising the nostalgia is often created in the photographic style. There are numerous ads, of which the following is just one example, where the past is implied in the blurred misty quality of the photography—this can be seen in many television advertisements as well. This misty, unclear quality is crucial in drawing *us* into the ad, since it must be *vague* enough for us to identify with it, to allow us a place in that very *undefined* place suggested by the photo.

A102

Remember with Mateus Rosé
The light refreshing wine from the people of Portugal

A102: The 'Mateus Rose' series consists of photographic ads which are all either blurred, like this one, or bleached, as in their current series—but the bleaching has the same effect of vagueness as in this one. (The new series also include a green lawn in the distance—see the discussion below.) In all the ads the people are wearing old-fashioned clothes. So two techniques are used to evoke the past—the haze of memory, and the physical dress of past eras (though again, this 'era' is left deliberately vague, impossible to locate in real history).

However, *what* are we supposed to remember? The past shown in this picture is not *our* past. It would seem that what you remember *is* the romanticised, blurry 'past' scene in the ad—the picture represents a memory. But they are drinking the product in the picture; thus *they* are in the process of 'remembering with Mateus Rose'. The words here, the caption exhorting us to 'Remember with Mateus Rose', does not make any sense in terms of the picture: who is remembering what? If *we* remember them, what are *they* remembering? Of course, the point of the ad is simply to invoke a general aura of nostalgia and it is only on examination that it proves to be nonsensical.

This 'nonsense' comes from the fact that the subject who is observing the ad is not temporally differentiated from the people in the ad. There is an elision of time; it is constructed as one *moment* in the imaginary realm of unity; *we* are joined with *them* (the people drinking in the picture) along the axis of memory, theirs and ours, the picture drawing together the past (the blurred image) and the present (drinking Mateus Rose and remembering). The word 'remember' refers to someone as undefined as the 'who' who knew the secret of the black, magic box. Its subject is both in the picture, and out of it (cf. the Mirror Phase).

Also contributing to the idea of a single, imaginarily unified time, comprehending both past and present, is the frozen action, the crystallised moment caught forever as the movement of the girl on the swing is arrested. This shows that time has been effectively stopped, for the picture to signify a 'time' not actually *in* time.

The same gap between the aura, the mythical time of the ad, and its literal, verbal meaning, can be seen in all ads of this genre. The Kraft ad quoted above invites us to recapture the days of 'summers in the past'—'Recapture them with great moments from Kraft'. Yet it is the nostalgic characters themselves, in the picture (not shown here) who are eating the Kraft peanut butter cake (for it is Kraft peanut butter that is being advertised). Moreover, the ad incorporates a recipe *for* the Kraft peanut butter cake, thus suggesting that by a *future* action, making the cake, we can be transported into the past (represented by the figures in old-fashioned clothes who are *eating* the Kraft peanut butter cake *in* the ad) and thus the ad is eternally poised between 'our' past and 'our' future, but bypassing our actual present. There is no guarantee that we *will* make the cake, and it is obviously untrue that the hazy scene in the photograph is *our* past summer day: so we are given a false place in an imaginary time by the movement between past and future, or rather, *from* a future event back *to* the past. Notice also that the past is 'recaptured' with 'great *moments* from Kraft': Time consists of 'moments', which will reveal all the rest of time, the 'illuminating moments' which I mentioned in the last chapter. The material existence of time is collapsed into an existential 'moment' that has a being *outside* time, since it encapsulates different parts of time.

103

The fragrant mist of love.
Suddenly it's another world, another time,
and a love more beautiful than you ever imagined.
Remember each perfect moment,
with "In Love" by Hartnell.
in Love by Hartnell

A103: This perfume ad shows the same confusion of past and future, since the future use of the product will *create* the past which is to be remembered. The perfume claims to help you remember: 'Remember each *perfect moment* (note—the *moment* again!) with "in Love" by Hartnell'. But these perfect moments that we are to remember have, it is implied, been created by the same product: 'suddenly it's another world, *another time*'. The perfume transports you to this magical time, which consists only of moments—which are by definition static, frozen crystals from the great flow of real time. So we see that advertisements invite us to remember a past that they have themselves created; Mateus Rose and Kraft create beautiful nostalgic worlds which we may then remember by using that same product, and 'in Love' creates its own memories in just the same way. But memory is always subjective: it always *belongs* to somebody. These products are connected by a magical (q.v.) route to a 'past' which becomes equally a commodity, something which we can own too, through the product. However, once we own it, it in fact owns, or rather, creates *us*; since the past leads to the present, and to give us subjective memories is to give us a 'bought' subjective existence. Time is elided as 'in Love' creates an affair and remembers it in one and the same instant. And we are elided with the 'subject' of the memory which performs this collapse, since our projected use of the product will make that memory ours, in the present.

A104

Memories are made of this.
Kodak pocket 'Instamatic' cameras.

A104: Here is another way of capturing the past in the present. 'Quick enough to catch the moment, as it happens. The *little moment* that makes a *magical memory*'. It must certainly be a magical memory, since it is one that can be given to us, through a product. The 'memory' is still seen as a *moment*, *static* time rather than changing time. 'Memories are made of this': of the product, the mechanism for arresting time.

All the preceding ads have a slightly frantic note about them. They are all for products which *create* a past, and this is particularly clear with the camera; one click and a 'moment' has become a 'memory'. This is an attempt to create a past out of the present in order to capture it; the past is secure; the present is not. It must be stopped; caught and processed into something that can no longer slip away—in other words, it is made into a product. Time is a commodity, bought and sold. This camera advertisement is at the extreme end of the scale, but its insistence on processing and destroying the present characterises all advertisements. For the present is not only real, but it can really be changed. Advertisements deny this.

When the present is changed, it becomes the future. But advertisements must represent the future as already determined by the present, leading from it so clearly (like St George riding off in the background towards the castle) that we need do nothing to help bring it about. We are drawn into the future, dragged into it, as though it were already there; and not something which we ourselves must create.

(*b*) *Time Future: Desire*

'Is there no change of death in paradise?
Does ripe fruit never fall? Or do the boughs
Hang always heavy in that perfect sky,
Unchanging. . . .'

Wallace Stevens

In advertisements the products are always unconsumed, waiting. The eating or drinking of advertised products is never, in the advertisement, fulfilled; even when the ad involves people, they are like characters on a Grecian urn, trapped in their expectation of enjoyment. We are led to desire an imaginary unity with the subject who *will enjoy*, and this also creates an imaginary unity between our time and the projected future time of the ad.

105

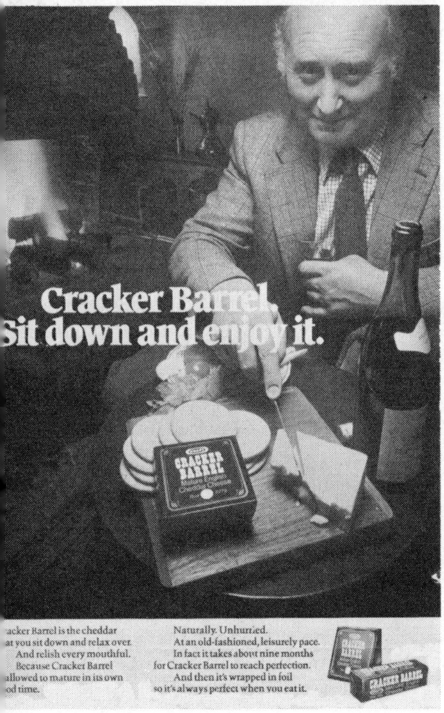

A105: This man is caught forever on the verge of enjoying his snack. 'At an *old-fashioned*, leisurely pace' uses the idea of the past as a referent, to show how his action is predetermined—if it is connected with the past it must be already decided upon. But the pace is in fact so leisurely that his movement has stopped altogether: 'Naturally (q.v.). Unhurried'. The past is evoked as some sort of natural, *slowed-down* time, and this quality *drawn* from the past is then projected into the future, since the caption refers to a *future* action: 'Sit down and enjoy it'.

But here, as in the 'nostalgia' ads, we are in a state of confused identity, because *he* is sitting down to enjoy it, yet the writing applies to us. Real, sensual consumption is not shown but the ad hovers on the brink of it, so that in our anticipation shared with the man in the picture, we may indeed share his action and go off and eat Cracker Barrel cheese.

All the enjoyment we can really have from advertisements is the anticipation of consumption, since this is all the advertisement can materially bring us. We are continually presented with close-ups of food and drink *as though* we were about to consume it—as in the poster advert for a beer, which shows simply a huge beer mug tilted towards the observer, as though he/she were about to drink it—but we cannot reach into the advert and take it. So a false future is dangled before our noses, denying our real position as spectators, drawing us into the mythic time of advertising.

With the idea of myth I would like to return to the St George and the Dragon painting and its method of indicating the future. The same structure of foreground objects or events leading to a distant, differently lit, Eden-like area of the future, is seen in countless ads. The hint of the repeated figure (i.e. St George in two places) is lost, but is replaced with symbols such as open windows or steps. The following advertisements all display a similar pattern.

A1

A106: Here the open window links the present of the foreground to the future; it signifies promise, and the distant light in the sky bears this out. The objects in the foreground are part of the structure of the myth, the story of the picture. The cricket ball and wicket show what *has been* happening: they were playing cricket, when it rained and spoilt the game. The pictures inside and the old church provide a basis in The Past (this hovers on the boundary of 'history' since it represents a cultural, common 'past'). All these things give clues as to the type of person this is (and we are invited to *be* the person—cf.Chapter 3). It is quite clear how in one static shot, the story of the situation may be told. However there is a less clear dimension involving projection: the advertisement links a mythical present (the 'story' already described) to a mythical future, via the product; drink/smoke this and you will be led out of the window (or up the steps—in other ads) in the direction of the future; but a future constructed, as in the St George picture, out of a mythically structured past (the old church, the tankard, etc.).

The perspective of the picture helps this transporting to the mythical future: the edge of the picture frame and the frame of the open window form a bounded perspective pointing inwards to the church at the other side of the cricket pitch. The movement is then carried up and out of the picture, via the church spire. So in fact our vision skims over the present, the abandoned cricket pitch, the rainy window, and already lodges (imaginarily) in a brighter future. As the caption says: 'Every cloud has a golden lining'. This implies a deterministic 'happy ending' to present events—also that time is as uncontrollable as the weather; you must simply *wait* for the sun to come out again, or for things to improve.

There are two ads which should be included in this chapter that have been used before.

A13 (see p. 33): Here, the steps perform the function of the window: they lead upwards to the (slightly blurry) green lawn, the far-off mythic paradise to which you will be transported by Belair.

A39 (see p. 78): Here the same product as in A106 is part of a different story. This traveller, with a French postcard, a distinguished hat and glasses, 'The Times', and a stiff drink, is different from the country-style, beer-drinking aristocracy of the village green. The setting for this story is Istanbul—with echoes of the 'Orient Express': again, a shared 'historical' referent. Although the key objects here—like words in a sentence—tell a different story from A106, the structure is the same; the objects in the foreground (present) and the window lead back into the picture and into a brighter area, the future. The train is located in this area, waiting to transport you still further away from the present, just as the spire in A106 also led *out* of the picture altogether.

Thus the spectator is drawn *through* the picture. His own present position in front of it is implicitly incorporated into the ad by the positioning of foreground objects so that he feels he could actually reach out and touch them; in other words, *his* present is exchanged for that of the ad's story. But then within the ad, this mythic present is thrown back (paradoxically—since the temporal movement indicated is meant to be *forwards*), towards the *back* of the picture, in a movement of perspective that dives into the heart of the page. Then, in the 'future' area thus positioned, there is the spire or the train, leading out of the ad and thus completing your journey through it to a metaphysical, unreal 'time' which is not just *in* the ad, but *beyond* it. This is obviously similar to the 'hermeneutic' idea discussed in Chapter 3. It is always the product, however, that is supposed to be the magic carpet that takes you out of your own time: the light from the sky falls on the Benson and Hedges packet in both A106 and A39, giving it the gloss of the 'brighter future', and performing a similar function to the Vymura gloss.

A107

A107: In this example the open hamper has the effect of the open window or the steps. There is an opening, a promise, a future; there has been a row up the river to this landing stage and now the picnic is about to begin. The elegance of the objects tells us what class these people are. The lighting, the small boat, the two glasses and plates, tell us that it has been a romantic occasion. The open hamper is a correlative for the cigarette box, one open box leading to another. The hamper is open, and the meal laid out, for *consumption*; notice how in all these ads there has always been another kind of oral consumption taking place (or about to)—a drink, and in this case, a drink *and* a meal. So we weave into the story the idea that the cigarettes, the product, will be consumed. This is the central point of the myth, the story of the future that *we supply*.

But there is a confusing twist about this future, because *we* are told, '*Next time* out, pack some gold with the silver'—but the people in the picture have *already* packed some 'gold' with the silver: thus the picture is in fact representing *our* future, the 'next time' (not 'this time') when we *will* take along Benson and Hedges. This is rather like the advertisement for the duty-free shop at London Airport: it says 'You forgot, didn't you' (i.e. to buy your duty-free liquor) but between the 'you' and the 'forgot' there is an omission mark and above, the word 'almost'. So the past time, when you probably *did* forget (not having seen the ad then) is transformed into or merged with the imaginary *future* time, when you will *not* have forgotten (although you almost did). The ad may be read in two ways simultaneously—in terms of a past and also of a future *improvement* on that past, which are elided in the subtle working of the sentence.

The pictures in this section have captured time in a different way from—for example—the camera ad, A104. That offered a means to 'stop' time; but these perform the same *narrative* function as the old St George painting, creating a synthesis of time through telling a temporal story. The same is true to an extent of the 'nostalgia' ads; they tell us a story of time gone by. The 'unconsumed' ads tell us a story of events to come. The more sophisticated ads just shown, however, link a series of events incorporating both past and future. As with St George's story, the spectator has to partake of the myth, to understand the signs and their structure, in order to put together the story. We have to know about cricket, and Istanbul, and what kind of person it is that reads 'The Times'. The story does not *give* information, so much as *use* information.

These narratives are all collapsed in time, so that their closure is elided with the point of consumption, even though theoretically the consumption must precede the events it is supposed to produce. However, these ads also represent a culmination point of a story which precedes the ad itself. There is a completeness about the objects assembled; they have already been determined by the story, and do not create it themselves. All these narratives imply closure, both in the straightforward sense of the already-happened, and in producing an ontology of the about-to-happen, which makes time static and draws the present into an eternal closure, forever in the future, but forever as closed and determined as the past. And *we* are implicated in the narrative that we have, deterministically, deciphered and constructed, so that we are drawn in both as narrator and as actor.

(*c*) *History*

The Benson and Hedges ads that we have just seen are teetering on the brink of historical representation, since they do refer to a time outside that of the subject's. Yet this iconographic past (Orient Express, Old Church) is still totally subjectivised—only given meaning through the idea of an individual's story. Real events, or objects connected with real events, are hollowed out, as with other referent systems, leaving only the interiority of the subject, an inside without an outside, denying 'objective' historicity. In the following advertisements we will see history itself appropriated by advertisements and denied its actual content. The 'memory' ads gave us an imaginary relation to past *personal* time; these give the subject an imaginary relationship to history (athough this misplacement in history is already achieved in all the ads so far seen, in that they give us a time other than our own, which *is* a historical

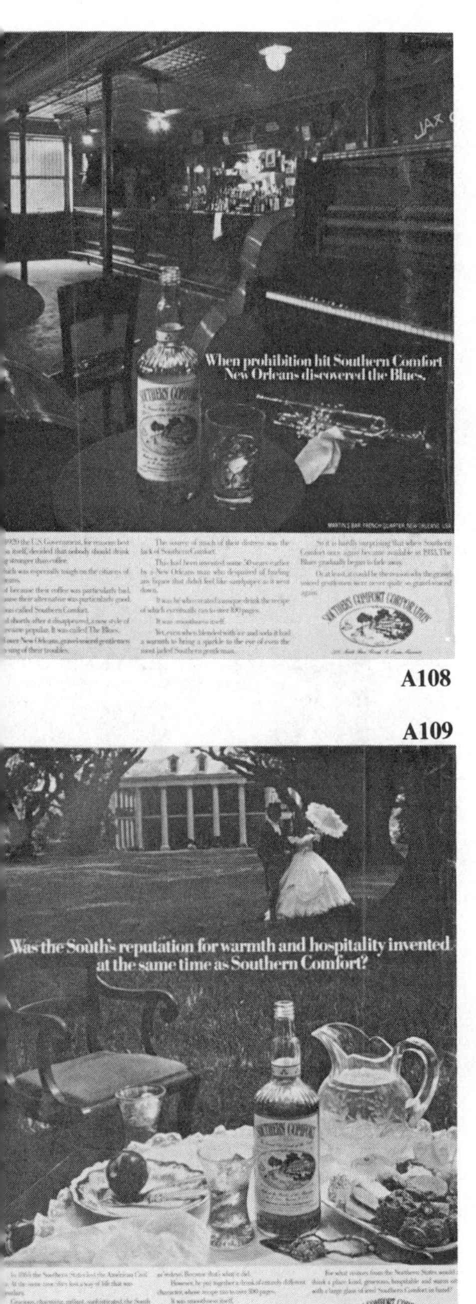

A108

A109

time, the present) and replace historical information with mythical information about the product. This shows how very capable ideology is of incorporating the *real* into itself; it does not invent total lies, but uses reality as its material and simply misrepresents our relationship to it.

A108 and A109: Here, we start off with 'facts'—'In 1865 the Southern States lost the American civil war . . .'; we know that it is 'real history' that is being referred to. But this is quickly absorbed into a myth, as the product is inserted in the hollow shell of historical events and fills the space of the '*in*'—the hollow referent. Thus a cultural phenomenon in history, 'the South's reputation for warmth and hospitality', becomes accounted for by the product: 'For what visitors from the Northern States would not think a place kind, generous and hospitable with a glass of iced Southern Comfort in hand?' A piece of social mythology is thus ascribed to the advertised commodity, which takes on a mythology ready-made, absorbing the idea of 'the South' and its past.

In A109 the misrepresentation of history is even clearer, for what is only suggested by the Civil War ad, is explicitly spoken in this. Again, there is the date at the beginning, establishing 'authenticity'. 'In 1920 the U.S. government . . . decided that nobody should drink anything stronger than coffee.' Then, we are told, the Blues originated. This is supposedly caused by the lack of Southern Comfort: 'The source of much of their distress was the lack of Southern Comfort.' (This is presumably meant to be a joke, however, since the very 'facts' are incorrect; the blues originated long before 1920 in any case.) Thus a cultural movement is emptied of its real meaning (which in the case of Blues, is one deliberately hostile to an oppressive society) and totally taken over by the product. This is precisely the process I have described as being the essential function of all ideological misrepresentation: reality is not described or explained, but *referred to* in such a way as to make it mean something exterior to itself; it signals away from itself (in advertising, to the product) and has therefore been scooped out to form an empty shell of relations without content. In these Southern Comfort ads a whole historical system, complete with (questionable) dates and facts, is at the disposal of the advertisement—its relations (drink banned/Blues begin) (war ends/hospitality begins) are appropriated, but its own *meaning* is replaced by the meaning relating to Southern Comfort whisky; the product becomes the *content* of a system whose material content has been excluded.

That advertisements can do this with history itself, shows how great their recuperative capacity is—they can use *any* material at all, however hostile its content may appear to be to their own method and aims. This will be discussed further in the final chapter. Yet it is important to remember that the spectator is never detached from the process described above: he/she is in fact the culminating point of misrepresentation, the person whose place in history is denied at the same time as his/her constitution as a subject is made to seem the point at which history fulfils itself. History used as a referent, must refer to something's (Southern Comfort's) or someone's (see A110) place in it, since something/someone must replace the real content of history. The next example shows the subjectivisation of history, and its fulfilment represented in a single individual.

A11

A110: Here a historical past is shown in the picture, a scene from the era of the early motor car. It is used to represent a historical (cultural) cliché: 'Women are lousy drivers.' But the past is evoked only to be discarded—'we've come a long, long way'—and the whole historical development from the invention of the car, to aviation (the woman is wearing a flying outfit) is contracted into the idea of the product—cigarettes for women—and epitomised in the woman herself; whose clothes are the same colours as are used in the 'historical' picture, which are also the colours of the cigarette packet. The historical scene is drawn into a closure, in the single woman, the *subject* who is made to represent social and technological change. But this change has been robbed of its real historicity; it is only meant to signify that women have changed into 'Virginia Slims' smokers as they have become more 'dominant'. The caption, 'At last, a cigarette we can call our own' is very appropriate in terms of the subjectivisation and the *appropriation* of the past—it is a *past* we can '*call our own*', along with the cigarette, bought like the cigarette. The colour correlation shows, as in Chapter 1, that the one thing/person is made to stand for something else linked to it by this visual means. Here it is the woman aviator who is made to stand for the *passing* of a past era, she is its closure.

Thus 'history' can be made into a referent, just like 'nature' and 'magic' and countless other social phenomena; used as a language in advertisements. There is a poster advertisement for the 'Sunday Times' which shows a deliberately 'dated' looking, '50s style picture of a boy and girl with their father, saying, 'What did *you* do in the Sunday Times, daddy?' This *refers* to the 'What did you do in the war, daddy' cliché, and the stylistic dating of the picture to make it represent the post-war era heightens the 'historical' effect. But of course, the advertisement is not about the war at all, nor about the '50s; it is simply using these as a form that is filled with the 'Sunday Times'. There have also been a series of beer advertisements on television recently, evoking the past with scenes of jolly pub life—again referring to a communal past, but one that is only significant in that it gives a meaning and aura to the beer. Far from creating ideas or meanings, advertisements actually *remove* all meaning from objects and events in terms of material *context* and *content*, thus leaving gaps which can be filled by the product.

CHAPTER EIGHT CONCLUSIONS

'Capitalism has the power to turn into a drug, immediately and continually, the poison that is thrown in its face and then to enjoy it.'

Brecht, *Brecht On Theatre*

Advertisements (ideologies) can incorporate anything, even re-absorb criticism of themselves, because they refer to it, devoid of content. The whole system of advertising is a great recuperator: it will work on any material at all, it will bounce back uninjured from both advertising restriction laws and criticisms of its basic function (such as this one) precisely because of the way it works in hollowing historical meaning from structures: the process I have described in the second half of this book. No matter how much you try to talk about what is 'in' the ad, you always end up back at the signifier, the structure of signs in an advertisement, because what the signs should or did refer to has been totally effaced and they have been made to point inwards, to the ad itself and the product it is selling. In Part One I outlined the theory of how ads work, by an exchange of signs, and an enmeshing of the subject in that exchange; a process concealed by the participation of the 'active subject'. If the first half of the book was about *how* ads get messages across, it might seem that the second half has been an attempt to find out what these messages are, what the 'content' is, the location of the *signified* of the signs shown in Chapter 1. But an examination of 'real' areas of life (nature, history) as the 'content' of ads has shown that, far from being 'in' the ad in the sense of being its meaning, these areas are simply re-used without their material content or historical context, so that mushrooms are made of, and 'mean', cans of soup; Stonehenge is propped up by a packet of Benson and Hedges, literally inserted into a historical structure; and the 'Blues' was caused by a lack of, and 'means', 'Southern Comfort'. The nonsensical nature of this appropriation of forms, of signifieds as signifiers, is shown by this very example: the Southern Comfort ad. For although the story goes that 'historically' it was the *absence* of Southern Comfort that caused the Blues, and therefore the two have a negative relationship where logically, Blues means '*no* or *not* Southern Comfort', the result is a connection of the Blues (now a very fashionable kind of music) and Southern Comfort in a positive sense; so that the 'style' and aura surrounding New Orleans Blues music rubs off on the whisky. This shows that the *structure only* of the ad is of any significance, and that it functions so that there is a potential reversibility of content, as with Blues/no Southern Comfort—Blues/Southern Comfort. It is the structure of connection which provides the significance: the actual relationship between the elements may be reversed without destroying the basic significance which is simply the connection of two things. This has also been seen in A44, with the smart people not watching TV. The point there was just the connection between the people (smart) and the TV (hence smart)—even though it was the TV they *didn't* watch. These examples prove that it is structure which signifies in ads: not genuinely 'significant' things, but things arranged so as to *transfer* significance from themselves to something else. This is how the idea of exchange in ads, elaborated in Part One, carries into the idea of 'referent systems', hollowed-out systems of meaning: because an exchange of meaning inevitably means that an object (or person) must lose its own meaning in the process. This is what I call 'turning signifieds into signifiers'.

A final example of this is A111, which, because of the particular referent system it is using, belongs in Chapter 7, but in its method provides a very clear demonstration of all that has been said about appropriation and emptying of 'real' systems:

A11

A111: On every bottle of Holsten we will see a picture of the Black Knight, we are told. And this advertisement actually makes explicit the total lack of substance in its signification: 'Nobody knows for certain who he is but he's long been a symbol of the Holsten brewery in Hamburg'. *Nobody knows for certain who he is*—we don't actually *know* anything about this 'historical' character at all, despite the fact that it is his substantial 'historicity' which is meant to transfer this quality to the beer, and make it 'The *historic* beer of Germany'. So history becomes identified with a total mystification: there is a 'symbol' about which we know nothing, except that it signifies this beer, and our only access to the beer is by 'looking for the Black Knight on the label'. Action is located around the symbol, while history is somehow suggested as being both unknowable, and yet 'obvious': 'the rest is history' implies that it need not be told, it stands so objectively and solidly on its own. So a completely hollow symbol is used to signify both history and the beer: and in connecting the two the beer becomes the '*historic beer*'. Clearly the material substance which has been knocked out of history has become transferred to the beer: the referent system may be empty, but the beer has a '*full*, distinctive taste'. What history has lost, the taste of the beer has gained. This shows precisely that the loss to the referent system is always replenished by the product: history may have been relegated to the level of 'tradition' ('*tradition* says the Black Knight is Duke Adolph III and it's a happy explanation'), i.e. not 'true' necessarily, but 'happy' (since it coincides with the mythical origins of the product)—but this loss of real content is sustained by the grafting on of a whole mythology attached to the product; so that in the 'wood-engraving-style' picture of *beer* being made, the caption is '*History* in the making'. History and beer have become totally confused because they are both subject to the same mythological structuring. Once a reality like history has been made into a 'symbol' about which 'nobody knows for certain' and a 'tradition' which may offer at the most a 'happy explanation' (in other words, a myth), its elements have become, not significant of *themselves*, but signs; which like counters in a game may be exchanged with signs from any other system, including the product's own mythology. These signs are exchanged in the meta-structure of the advertisement. This process is at its most obvious when we see beer in the making and read that it is history in the making. All that we know about the Black Knight is that he is a symbol of the Holsten brewery—he has no other meaning. Signification can mean that things *and people* are used to create mythic structures which are really nothing to do with them, and so we can never see what anything means in its own system as it is always pointing to another. The 'historical' bit of the ad here tells us absolutely nothing about Duke Adolph or Germany but nevertheless implies that there is a whole body of knowledge (but *unknown* knowledge) which suggests a 'body' to the beer.

There is nothing 'wrong' about symbols as such—obviously systems of signification are necessary and inevitable. But besides the function of symbols in ideological systems, which, as I have suggested, is to deprive us of knowledge and create a mystification about history, nature and society, there is also a danger in having *people* involved as part of the currency in these systems. When people become symbols they need not be treated as human beings. This is an obvious point but it is probably little noticed how much of the human symbolism of advertisements carries over into 'real life'. Women are especially liable to this phenomenon. But in all areas of life it is clearly very dangerous to see only what people '*mean*' (e.g. a threat, a status symbol) rather than what they are. And ideology is the system whereby society gives itself a 'meaning' other than what it really is. If meaning is abstracted from something, from what 'means' it, this is nearly always a danger signal because it is only in material circumstances that it is possible to 'know' anything, and looking away from people or social phenomena to their supposed abstract 'significance' can be at worst an excuse for human and social atrocities, at best, a turning of reality into apparent unreality, almost unlivable while social dreams and myths seem so real. We wipe a great deal of our actual experience in life from our minds—our lives become the lives we don't lead: like the TV that wasn't watched. Smart people/modern people/magazine people/people in *our* society—don't do half the things *we do*: they don't sweat, neither do they go to work and produce. Most of our lives are the 'unlived' lives of advertisements, the underside of their world picture. So this reality becomes almost literally unreal—sublimated, unconscious. As a teenager, for example, it is really possible to live almost totally in a sort of dream world of magazine stories and images, and this *seems more real than reality*—though few people will admit it. The reason for this 'reality' is that the social dream—dream though it is—is a *shared* one: what is *commonly* perceived (in the sense of a shared—though also a frequent—perception) has a more 'objective' status than something particular to ourselves. People's real experience may be very similar but it remains isolated while what *is* a universal experience is the impact of media and social images. So it is in fact a positive instinct, the desire to share in a social reality, which deprives us of a true knowledge of social realities. Advertising may appropriate, not only real areas of time and space, and give them a false content, but real needs and desires in people, which are given a false fulfilment (see Chapter 2). We need a way of looking at ourselves: which ads give us falsely (cf. advertising and the mirror phase); we need to make sense of the world: which ads make us feel we are doing in making sense of *them* (hermeneutics).

Thus the idea of the 'referent system' is, I think, a very important one because it is the point at which ideology and symbolic or signifying structures combine to form an almost Platonic system where everything means something else, and nothing is what it is. I have stressed how reference replaces knowledge and content, in advertising's use of 'history' with ads like Southern Comfort, Virginia Slims, and the Holsten ad above. But it can also do exactly the same with ideas, systems, phenomena in society whose actual content and body of thought is hostile to advertising and might seem completely alien to it. But the more hostile, the better use advertising can make of it, for its recuperation from criticism then seems all the more miraculous *and* inevitable. To take just one example, the movement of 'Women's Lib' has provided advertisements, one of the most sexist fields of communication there is, with a vast amount of material which actually enhances their sexist stance. There is a television ad for an aftershave 'Censored' where a woman is beating a man at chess. But then he puts on the aftershave and she is so wildly attracted to him that she leaps up, knocking over the chess board where she had him check-mated, and jumps on him like a wild animal. Now, far from the effect being to make us realise how inadequate the man is if he cannot stand being beaten at chess by a woman, her 'cool' and intelligence and obviously 'liberated' image are in fact made to devalue themselves: because the point is that *even* a cool, 'dominating' woman, an intellectual threat to a man, even she will become little more than an animal, and a captivated one, on smelling 'Censored' cologne for men. It is obviously more of an achievement to win over a 'liberated' woman than one who was submissive all along. Many ads are based on this sort of line: 'she's liberated *but*. . . .'

Advertisements also incorporate structures which belong to truly *revolutionary* standpoints. There is the Watney's Red Revolution, and there are the imitation—Che Guevaras on cigarette ad billboards in America. And a London underground advertisement for a department store uses slogans usually used in a revolutionary context—we are told that at this shop, 'You'll want everything and you'll want it now'. This is usually chanted at demonstrations.

But advertisements do not only use other systems as signifiers, without content. Advertising itself may be the referent system, and can be referred to by advertisements which will use the structure of one ad to signify something about the product in their own.

A112

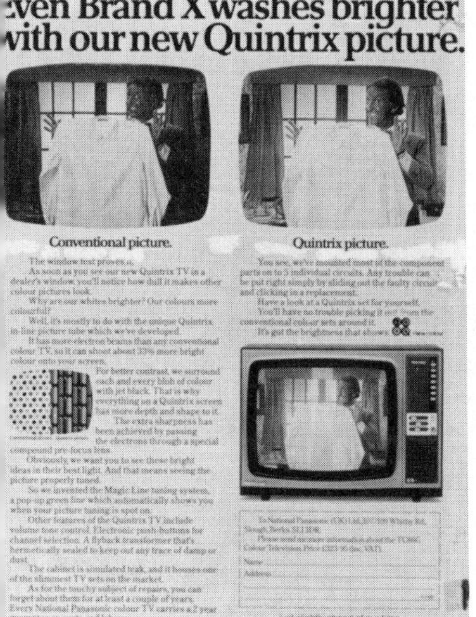
ven Brand X washes brighter
vith our new Quintrix picture.
Conventional picture.
Quintrix picture.
just slightly ahead of our time
National Panasonic

A112: This ad for a television exploits the famous genre of washing powder ads, making a clever play on the 'Whiter shirt' image; the whiter shirt is due to better colour TV. Even the *un*whitening brand, Brand X, produces whiter results on Panasonic. So this turns the original ad upside down: it is brand X which is used to signify whiteness and better colour—i.e. what previously signified 'unwhiteness' now shows *brightness*. But this ad uses precisely the same *structure* as the one it refers to, although it uses the content differently. It is structured on the 'brand X versus *our* brand' model, and instead of showing two shirts, one inferior and the other brighter, it shows two TVs in exactly the same way, while transforming the original substance of the soap ad by *not* using the brighter shirt. Thus again, a structure, a set of formal relations is stolen, and simultaneously the elements of these relations are transformed: here, literally transformed by the TV, which makes the dirty shirt white, reversing the soap-powder-ad significance of the shirt while using the form of that ad.

This joke depends on our knowledge of the original ad (even to the extent of understanding what 'brand X' means—a sort of code)—the one where housewives vow to exchange their packet of brand X for the wonder powder—and manipulates this knowledge in two different ways. This shows advertising using its own form as a referent system; and it relies on our recognising that form.

A113: Here we have exactly the same thing as in the previous example. Again, the structure of another ad (the one where housewives—those magical arbiters—try to tell the difference between Stork and butter) is used: but the content and context are different. And again, a joke comes out of our knowledge of the thing referred to: this ad only catches our attention because of the obvious reference to the margarine ad. Its basic message is that these paints are different—in price.

However, here the inclusion of material from another, very well-known ad, has a further function beyond simple humour. The 'can you tell Stork from butter' ad has become a classic, almost a parody of an advertisement, and representing a basic idea in people's minds about advertisements—namely, that they (ads) are rather silly. So by quoting the 'classic' ad, in such a way that it seems to *join in* the joke with us, and to be *aware* that advertising can be very silly, this ad seems almost not to be one at all, it is excluded from the criticism it implies about other ads. It admits that most products are the same. We are disarmed by this self-referential capacity of advertising. For the reference to the other ad fits precisely, in tone, with the main point of this one; Woolworth's is offering a down-to-earth, square deal—we are being practical and nitty gritty, and paying sensible prices for products which are the same as others of higher prices—and we are realising that ads are silly and false *with the exception of this one*. Its honesty is guaranteed by that quote from the Stork ad.

A113

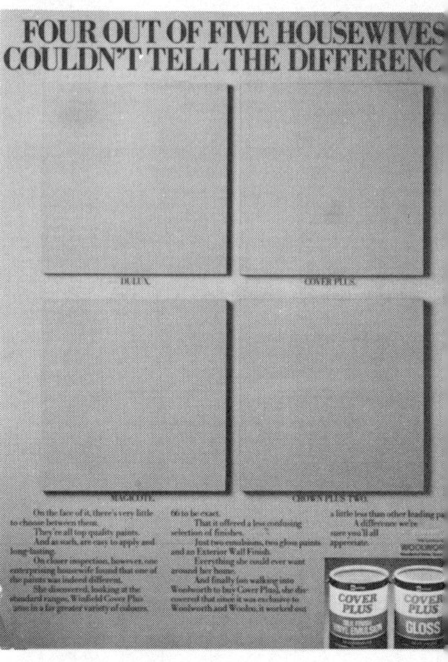

This shows that self-reference, or use of other structures within the same ideological system, is not a 'neutral' process or just a good joke, but has an essential self-validating function. We will give the Woolworth's paint ad more credibility because it mentions another advertisement in a 'conscious' way. Self reference can take place visually, though, as well as verbally as in A112 and A113.

A114: This advertisement *shows* itself: the woman is reading the Sunday colour supplement which is open at the page of this same ad. The self-referential quality works in a paradoxical way. Originally it helps break through the 'illusion' of the ad, by presenting itself *as* an ad in a magazine. However, this very self-consciousness makes the ad convincing; at the point where it refers to itself as an ad, our scepticism is satisfied and with our guards down, as it were, we are *more* susceptible to the 'reality' of the ad. While appearing to incorporate some kind of external 'reality' (one in which it, the ad, may be shown as an element) by representing itself apparently from the outside, the ad in fact leads endlessly back into itself. For the 'reality' outside and around the ad—the people reading, their living room, the 'nature' outside the window—are all inside the ad in the first place and although external to the small ad *in* the big one, are obviously inside the latter.

Thus *self-reference* is a type of reference where it is impossible to have any bearings at all: the referent system that is 'hollowed out' is that

A114

of the advertisement itself and thereby its own lack of context is revealed.

By placing the advertisement within an 'ordinary' world which is not, on the face of it, the world of the advertisement since the advertisement is 'in' it, we can more easily feel that this represented world in which the advertisement is being read, merges with our own—where the advertisement is being read too. This is in many ways one of the most effective of 'mirror' type advertisements. We are actually shown 'ourselves' looking at the ad. But as I have said, the advertisement, in its picture of someone looking at the picture in which someone is looking at the picture, etc., leads nowhere but to itself and is a completely closed off, sealed ontological plane. So while seeming to 'place' itself in a world adjacent to ours, implying a continuum of reality between us and the people in the picture, it ensures not only that the ad is well sealed off from the actual context in which it is being seen but that we are sucked into this self-referential void as well. This is a typical 'mirror-phase' ploy: we are both like and unlike the people depicted. We are reading the same newspaper; but it is not our living room that is shown.

A similar kind of self-reference is used in a TV ad for Hepworth's clothes. After a long chase from one place to another for incomprehensible reasons, someone says 'What is this, a runaround?' and someone else says, 'No, it's an ad for Hepworth's.' Again, we are given a position within the ad that offers the same view-point as our own as spectators; thus although the man who says 'It's an ad for Hepworth's' seems to 'get outside' the ad myth, in fact conversely we are taken inside it since there is a space there analogous to our own.

Another example of advertising referring to itself as a genre (i.e. ads about other ads, like A112 and A113)—a different kind of self-reference from A114—is the sausage ad on posters which says, 'I'm meaty, fry me'. This is a take-off of the airline ads where girls say 'I'm Jo/Susie/etc.—fly me'. As with the 'four out of five housewives' example, this serves to *validate* the ad which makes the reference.

To find out why this should be so we must take advertising as a referent system and apply to its use of its own forms, the theory which emerged from conclusions drawn about other referent systems. This case is, however, clearly going to be rather different since advertising itself seems to consist of a 'bricolage' of other social myths. But if we are to explain why Woolworth's should be using the Stork margarine advertisement to give *Woolworth's* the status of honesty, it will be necessary to recognise that advertising does have a mythic structure of its own, to which, as in this case and the colour TV ad (A112), it can refer, while (as with all referent systems) denying its content.

The advertising myth in our society is not a naïve one, nor is it an ideological brain-washing forced upon us from above. Ads are generally regarded as lies and 'rip-offs'. Whatever *effect* advertising has on people, it is true that their 'conscious' attitude to it will usually be sceptical. The fact that some advertisements, like the Stork one, have virtually become *jokes*, shows that they are not always taken too seriously as far as their overt content goes. 'It's a pack of lies', 'Just after your money'—these are the sentiments most often heard about advertising by people who are actually asked what they *think* about it (as on various recent TV programmes). So the basic structure of ideas surrounding advertising is, in fact, that of dishonesty and exploitation. When the Woolworth's paint ad refers to the Stork ad, it is precisely this structure, this mythic framework that it is referring to. As in the use of other referent systems, where our knowledge is appropriated, so here our knowledge of the falseness of advertising is called upon—the paint ad draws on our *critical knowledge of advertising*. It thus sets itself up as honest, down-to-earth, *aware*.

But in doing so, it is inevitably denying precisely the content of the myth that has been referred to—namely, that advertising is untrustworthy. This idea is appealed to in us purely formally, for any real application of it in practice is immediately precluded by the illusion of the Woolworth's ad's *honesty*. It replaces the content of the social mythology of advertising with a suggestion about itself—and a suggestion which directly contradicts the reference-structure. This bears out the 'referent-system' theory, that emptied structures of real knowledge are used as the frame for 'ideological castles'. The use of our belief in advertising's *dishonesty* in order to give an aura of *honesty* to an ad is a supreme example of the denial of the actual content of any structure of thought—of reference replacing knowledge.

So advertising can incorporate its mythic status (as a lie) into itself with very little trouble. Advertisements will always recuperate by using criticisms of themselves as frames of reference which will finally *enhance*, rather than destroy, their 'real' status. It is like their use of the 'liberated woman', already mentioned; '*even* she' will go crazy about aftershave lotions. This is all the better for aftershave lotion adverts. Similarly ads which can incorporate criticisms of themselves have a much higher credibility than those which don't.

However, while one way of dealing with this critical material is for ads to incorporate it, the major corollary of the fact that advertising's social image is one of dishonesty, is that advertisements must function *not* at the overt level of 'what is said' ('Persil washes whiter' etc.)—because this is not believed—they function on the level of the signifier (cf. A1). The advertising myth ('a lie') makes it necessary for the selling to be located in the mythology *of* the signifier, directing attention to other myth systems, and away from the system of the ad. This can be made clearer in relation to particular examples. In washing powder ads—the type referred to by A112—there is usually a 'Persil washes whiter' slogan of some sort which is not really taken very seriously by most adults. However, a knowledge of the exchange of signs in the ad must make us look at whatever is being used as a *signifier* of the 'image' of the powder. This will usually be a mother/child relationship (who is the kid with the grey T-shirt?): and in fact it is maternal 'love' and care, within a framework of family loyalty and competition with other families, that provides the main structure for the ad (cf. the father-daughter/mother-son inter-family competition of 'The Generation Game'). A mother may not 'believe' that brand X really washes whiter than brand Y but she may unconsciously absorb the message of the signifier, which offers a 'mirror relationship' with herself and *her* children. In television ads, *everything* is sold at the level of the signifier-people, the kind of people who are shown using any product. Again, you may not really believe that some minor ingredient is going to transform your casserole into a cordon-bleu dish, but the *images* of the grateful, hungry, appreciative husband and son tucking into a hearty meal provided by the woman, stay long after the actual claims made on behalf of the product have been forgotten. It is the images we see in ads which give them significance, which transfer their significance to the product. This is why advertising is so uncontrollable, because whatever restrictions are made in terms of their verbal content or 'false claims', there is no way of getting at their use of images and symbols. And it is precisely these which do the work of the ad anyway—as was shown by, for example, A54, where the different words had no effect on the image put across by the same pictures. Therefore advertisements will always escape any criticism of them which bases its argument on their deceitfulness or even their harm in being 'capitalist', 'sexist' etc. Not that these criticisms are invalid: but they by-pass the ideology of the *way* in which ads work. The exchange between images has *not* been banned by any law, and cannot be; that is why the Smirnoff ads are still successful. The following set of examples provides, firstly, another example of an ad's use of a different ad's structure (the Vymura ad)—which here is a structure of magical transformation achieved by the product—and secondly, an illustration of the above point, that it is images and not words which ultimately provide the currency in ads.

A115: In A115b we can see another straightforward instance of what has been discussed above—an advertisement validating itself by its reference to another well-known ad. The Smirnoff ads of the 115a type (i.e. where they made excessive claims, before they were legally banned) were, in fact, never taken completely seriously. They have provided the basis for many jokes outside advertising, as well as within it. Nobody really thought they would stop being Mr Holmes of Household Linens overnight: but perhaps because they were never made to feel that they *were* Mr Holmes in the first place. You were not meant to identify with the original character, only with the result. This is made quite clear by the fact that the pictures always showed the resulting trendy person and never the old, pre-Smirnoff one. Nobody 'believed' in the transformation—that Smirnoff actually could make you completely different. What we were really given to identify with was simply the image of 'after' the transformation—an image of trendy, outlandish people who were drinking Smirnoff. This is no different from all drink advertisements—Bacardi Shorts (A49) for example. The 'transformation' was always so extreme that it *started off* as a joke. Because it was not credible, it was valuable as a reference for the Vymura series, one of which is shown in A115b. The 'I was . . . before I discovered . . .' formula had become synonymous with *in*credible advertising and so when Vymura selfconsciously uses this formula it is in fact, not imitating but drawing an implicit *comparison* with, the Smirnoff claims. It draws attention both to the change and to the absence of change. 'Until we moved to Vymura' is clearly a *joke*, not to be taken seriously (this is unlike the Thomson holiday ad A31, where the suggestion of transportation to mythic regions is *serious*)—because the whole point is that they didn't have to move, their *own home* was transformed. So the point being made is that unlike Mr Holmes, who appears to have moved from some suburban housing estate to a sort of Mediterranean fishing village overnight, these people did not and do not need to move. Vymura will work enough changes for them in their own sitting-room. This ad relies on a partial joke to suggest that *it* offers a more realistic transformation (as indeed it is—painting a house is easier than becoming a fisherman) than the Smirnoff ad does. So, as with the Woolworth's ad and the 'brand X' colour TV ad, a structure is used 'critically' but is filled with a meaning which conflicts with its original premise. In A115b fun is made of the Smirnoff idea of extreme change, while the ad also advocates and promises change on behalf of *its* product.

What A115c and d show is that images in advertisements are the essential signifiers and can function in the same way even after a particular verbal implication has been banned. For the people in the new Smirnoff ads (since the overt connection between alcohol and social/sexual success was made illegal) are *signifiers* of exactly the same things as the people after transformation in the old series. Here, the criticism is actually referred to—'They say Smirnoff *won't* . . .' is the formula—but the ads have simply moved onwards one level in trendiness because now they show people who don't *need* to be transformed. (The woman in 115c is already sexy—she doesn't want

A115a

A115b

The most dramatic thing in our house was the Wednesday Play. Until we moved to Vymura.
Make the move to Vymura.
Paints & wallcoverings that go together

A115c

115d

hairs on her chest in any case: the man in 115d is *already* the boss. The couple in the 'They say Smirnoff won't make us the perfect couple' are already a perfect, though unconventional couple.) But—this is precisely what they *showed* before. The old images were always of what people had *become* through drinking Smirnoff, and thus, although involving a *narrative* difference (before/after), precisely match the new Smirnoff images. The image of the *new* Mr Holmes is what we connect with Smirnoff, just as the images of the man and woman in A115d and c respectively are connected with it. It is also interesting that the eye-line matching has been much more carefully done in the new series: the sexy woman and the boss look at us from an angle, as though sharing some hidden, subversive secret. The secret is, presumably, what it is they have that has pre-empted the image previously shown as purchasable with Smirnoff. But the shift is simply to the 'alreadyness' described as an advertising strategy in Chapter 2, of using the image of 'already' trendy and *therefore* drinking Smirnoff, instead of the same *image*, but one that comes with, and not before, Smirnoff. The idea of transformation is really a side issue to the same basic exchange in A115a, c and d. And in any case, transformation is implied by all the ads because once an image is transferable it is transferable to us—via the product. The only major change in Smirnoff ads from 117a to d is that the later ones refer to the very restriction imposed on them and therefore seem all the more daring in the image they offer.

In other words, you clearly do *not* 'drink it for what it is': you drink it in order to become like the signifier in the advertisement, the distorted mirror-image that confronts you in the person or people shown in the ad. We, like them, can also become signifiers of sexual success/chic etc.; for, once meanings are allowed to come loose and are exchanged out of context, they become the currency for a sort of pass-the-parcel where an abstract 'significance' can be endlessly passed on from people to things and back again. This is why only when meaning has a material context can it really be grasped and become the substance of knowledge, rather than inference. But it is because advertisements use 'meanings' as a currency and signification as a market, that they can always exchange them, take anything out of its context and replace it: *re*-presentation. It is a reliance on empty structures that keeps ideologies going, and an understanding of those structures, even when a critical understanding, does no more than provide a platform on which ideology can *seem to know itself* while still being absolutely devoid of knowledge. It is easy to analyse endlessly the structures of ideology without noticing the vacuum at its heart. The ability of advertisements to incorporate criticism should remove any possibility of complacency in having laid bare some of their formal strategies. Indeed, an advertiser who read this book might well find material which could be very *helpful* to him. It would be stupid not to be aware of this. We can never *finally* dismantle ideologies because one of their basic qualities is that of adaptability. Their tenacity and elasticity arise precisely from their lack of real content: a framework can be filled with anything, and structures of social myths are re-used and re-used. Similarly, *real* things are rearranged in false positions while their reality seems to validate those positions.

Thus, ideologies cannot be known and undone, so much as engaged with—in a sort of running battle, almost a race since the rate at which all their forms, especially advertising, reabsorb all critical material, is alarmingly fast. This incorporation is also, however, increasingly subtle. That is why the tools of structural criticism are valuable within certain limits. The only reason for the complexity of parts of this book is the complexity of advertising itself. All the same, there is clearly a danger involved in this kind of analysis—it can lead back into itself just like A114, and can also become mystifying instead of clarifying. There is an advertisement which to me epitomises the danger of allowing analysis, an understanding of relations, to become a *value in itself*—in some way making perception more important than *what* is perceived.

This advertisement always makes me think: 'Decoding Advertisements. If your friends know a sign from a referent'. Ultimately it is *not* this knowledge in itself that is valuable, but its potential to change the system which is its object. And having described the difficulty in criticising or even keeping abreast with, advertising's ideological system, because of its powers of absorption, and the danger in structural analysis, because of its introversion and lack of context—I will finish with an example which shows most clearly of all what ads are about and why they *must* be criticised and their values fought. This is an ad for ads: it is a magazine speaking to advertisers, and therefore shows more blatantly than in examples intended for *us*, what is going on.

Deinhard Green Label.
If your friends know a sprat from a mackerel.
Gently chilled,
this fresh, delicate moselle
brings the tastes of good food
into clear focus.
Deinhard
GREEN LABEL
Green Label

A116: These are advertisements about advertisements—but not in the way that other examples in this chapter have been. They are for advertising space, advertising *for* advertising. The point is, they are selling the image created by advertisements back to advertisers: the people who have allowed their lives to be built up of certain choices of consumption have now become currency, objects of consumption themselves—*they* are the product in this advertisement. They are the product offered for sale by the 'Sunday Times' magazine. The price is the cost of advertising space. These ads are a precise parallel to all the other ads seen in this book, except that they work on a different level: other ads offer these 'Sunday Times' readers products which they can buy; these ads offer advertisers the 'Sunday Times' readers themselves,

A116

The clothes she wears,
the perfume she prefers,
the jewellery she cherishes;
the drink she lingers over,
the holiday she chooses;
the furnishings in her home,
the luxury in her bathroom,
the timepiece on her wrist . . .
Almost certainly
her choice is influenced by
The Sunday Times.
She's the woman you want
to reach. And your
advertisement in
The Sunday Times finds her . . .
just as ours has found *you.*

THE SUNDAY TIMES IS HER

whose buying power is also buyable. This shows conclusively that our place in the exchange of signs in advertisements, our involvement in their value system, is not one on the sidelines, detached; we also become exchangeable objects, with a price on us—our buying of images makes *us* buyable. When I have said that we become caught up as currency in an exchange, this is not an abstract conclusion but one arising from the very way in which advertising buys and sells itself.

These people are seen as the *creations* of advertising: 'the holidays they enjoy, the camera they take along, the home they furnish, the nursery they planned together. . . . Almost certainly their choice is influenced by the "Sunday Times".' They are seen as the product of a whole range of advertisements: which have been carefully selected to fit one 'image'. In advertising, elements of 'real life' are transformed into a structure that gives them a mythical status. Here, one step further, we have the advertisers' myth as the transformation of the 'real' elements of the original advertisements. 'The holidays they enjoy, the books they read . . . etc.' are the components of advertising; and this picture consciously welds them together into one image, that of the couple who *are* these things. However, this image, a 'meta-structure' of the elements of advertising, is doubly removed from the reality which provided the material for the original structure of advertising.

Of course, the original selection of 'real life' used to signify the product in the ordinary ad, is conditioned by the nature of the product and the mythology it is trying to project. At this second stage a selection takes place again, as the new myth depends on the kind of magazine the space is in. So this final image is doubly unreal, using people as the signifiers of an image which previously signified *them*.

But now, they signify the 'Sunday Times': their choice of chocolates may 'say something' about them, but here it is they who 'say something' about the magazine, which is the advertiser. In fact, they become totally identified with their buying capacity (as represented by the 'Sunday Times' image): 'The "Sunday Times" is *them*.' They buy the 'Sunday Times', therefore they are the 'Sunday Times'. Similarly 'The "Sunday Times" is *her*'. This is an articulation of the basic equation in all advertising: it establishes an identity between two social 'products' which originally belonged to different orders of social life but have become *exchangeable through their co-partnership in signification*—people and things. People become signified by, and then summarised by, things—'the chocolates they buy, the time-piece she wears' etc.: and hence equatable with other things—money (their spending power) and ideological images (the 'Sunday Times'). They provide the connection between the two: images are bought. This should make clear the very real material basis and substructure of the images that are valued and exchanged in society: they, the images, 'life-styles', meanings, may not be real: but the money that buys them is, and so are the people who earn it. As long as the structure of these realities remains, so will the structure which I have tried to analyse, that of the images which mediate material exchanges, and conceal them, while also suggesting that we create ourselves through them. These people '*are*' the sum of their consumer goods. We re-create ourselves every day, in accordance with an ideology based on property—where we are defined by our relationship to things, possessions, rather than to each other.

SELECT BIBLIOGRAPHY

Louis Althusser, *Lenin and Philosophy and Other Essays*, New Left Books, 1970.

Louis Althusser and Etienne Balibar, *Reading Capital*, New Left Books, 1970.

Roland Barthes, *Mythologies*, Paladin, 1973.
Elements of Semiology, Jonathan Cape, 1967.

Walter Benjamin, *Understanding Brecht*, New Left Books, 1973.

John Berger, *Ways of Seeing, BBC and Penguin, 1972.*

Bertolt Brecht, *Brecht On Theatre*, Translated and edited by John Willett, Hill and Wang, 1964.
The Messingkauf Dialogues, Eyre Methuen, 1965.

Michel Foucault, *The Order of Things*, Tavistock, 1970.

Freud, *Introductory Lectures on Psychoanalysis.*
The Interpretation of Dreams.
Jokes and Their Relation to the Unconscious.

Antonio Gramsci, *The Prison Notebooks*, Lawrence and Wishart, 1971.

Jacques Lacan, *The Language of the Self*, tr. Wilden, Delta, 1968.
'The Mirror Phase' in *New Left Review* No. 51.

Claude Lévi-Strauss, *The Raw and The Cooked*, Jonathan Cape, 1970.
The Savage Mind, Weidenfeld and Nicolson, 1966.

Marx, *Economic and Philosophical Manuscripts.*
The German Ideology.
A Contribution to a Critique of Political Economy.

Saussure, Jonathan Culler on *Saussure*, Fontana 1976.

ACKNOWLEDGEMENTS

The author wishes to thank the companies for permission to reproduce the advertisements published in this volume.

Two verses from '*I can't get no Satisfaction*' printed by permission of Mick Jagger and Keith Richard and Essex Music International Ltd.